How They Said It

HOW They Said It

WISE AND WITTY LETTERS FROM THE FAMOUS AND INFAMOUS

ROSALIE MAGGIO

PRENTICE HALL PRESS

Library of Congress Cataloging-in-Publication Data

How they said it : wise and witty letters from the famous and infamous
/ by Rosalie Maggio.
     p.   cm.
    Includes index.
    ISBN 0-7352-0132-3 (paper)
     1. Letters.   2. Wit and humor.   I. Maggio, Rosalie.
PN6130.H68   1999
808.86—dc21   99–42540
                                               CIP

© 2000 by Rosalie Maggio

Printed in the United States of America

10 9 8 7 6 5 4 3 2 1

ISBN 0-7352-0132-3

Copyright acknowledgments appear on pages 301–317.

PRENTICE HALL PRESS
Paramus, NJ 07652

On the World Wide Web at http://www.phdirect.com

To David

Liz, Katie, Matt

Contents

Introduction

How They Said It combines an original approach to the model-letters book with a collection of some of the wittiest, pithiest, most memorable letters ever written. Gathered into chapters on letters of apology, letters of complaint, thank-you letters, sympathy letters, and the other classic letter themes, this anthology of real-life successful letters brings you intriguing glimpses of other people's lives while inspiring you to write your own letters with renewed enthusiasm and skill.

The death—or at least the failing health—of letterwriting is periodically announced. But this has been going on for a long time, and it is probably not ever going to be true.

In 1909, Ada M. Ingpen introduced her anthology of letters by saying that letterwriting "seems to have fallen into disuse with the quill-pen." Twenty years later, Dorothy Van Doren published a collection of letters called *The Lost Art*. Today the excuse is e-mail. Despite the recurring death-knell, in the United States we are writing more personal letters to each other than ever before.

The 500 letters in this collection were carefully chosen from more than 100,000 letters on the basis of how lively, dramatic, humorous, poignant, provocative, or memorable they were. In his 1912 book, *Letters of Great Writers*, the Reverend Hedley V. Taylor says, "All really good letters have some of the fine gold of honest autobiography, for they sparkle with that priceless element, unmistakable yet indescribable, which we term personality." In addition to having "personality," the letters in this collection have all the qualities of effective letters; they are, in fact, model "model letters."

The 280 letterwriters in the book are people you know. The index reads like a "who's who" of cultural literacy: Queen Victoria, Zora

Neale Hurston, Napoleon, Groucho Marx, Gertrude Stein, P.T. Barnum, Ogden Nash, Ernest Hemingway, Isaac Asimov, Zelda Fitzgerald, Federico Garcia Lorca, Helen Keller, W.E.B. DuBois, Clementine Churchill, Mark Twain, the Reverend Martin Luther King, Jr., Frederic Chopin, Catherine the Great, Georgia O'Keeffe, P.G. Wodehouse.

Many of the letterwriters are writers and poets, which makes sense—they could count on finding pen and paper when they needed them. But there are also letters written by presidents, heads of states, politicians, musicians, saints, scientists, explorers, artists, philosophers, soldiers, dancers, architects, inventors, humanitarians, political prisoners, naturalists, singers, social activists, and others.

The letters themselves are generally very short—most are excerpts of much longer letters—in order to give you the broadest sampling of letter types and to focus narrowly on the letter theme. It also means you don't have to read the "boring" parts of people's letters. (Unfortunately, you and I may have different definitions of "boring." However, the complete bibliography at the end of the book will allow you to track down your favorite letterwriters and read their letters in their entirety.)

Infrequently some very small changes in distracting punctuation, capitalization, or spelling have been made. Some chapters are longer than others—for example, people report that sympathy letters are the most difficult letters to write, so there are more examples of them. Letters to family and friends are also well represented because we tend to get into old, stale patterns with people to whom we write frequently, and these letters can provide you with new perspectives.

In addition to chapters on the twenty-seven classic types of letters, two odd chapters are included. The last chapter features letters written on the subject of letters—a topic dear to the collective heart of letterwriters. The outspoken letters in the chapter of the same name have one thing in common: their writers are irritated or angry or impatient—and it shows! (Other particularly "lively" letters are found in the chapters on refusals, complaints, apologies, and responses.)

For those who believe, with M. Lincoln Schuster, that "Letters make the most interesting reading in the world—especially other people's," this book provides hours of reading pleasure, a bountiful assemblage of some of the most entertaining and delightful letters ever found in one place. If you have half as much fun as I have had, you will enjoy this collection very much indeed.

*A*dvice is seldom welcome; and those who want it the most always like it the least.

EARL OF CHESTERFIELD, LETTER TO HIS SON, 1748

No one can be a truly competent lawyer unless he is a cultivated man. If I were you, I would forget all about any technical preparation for the law. The best way to prepare for the law is to come to the study of the law as a well-read person. Thus alone can one acquire the capacity to use the Eng-

Letters of Advice

Hannah Whitall Smith, whose letter of advice appears in this chapter, said elsewhere, "The true secret of giving advice is, after you have honestly given it, to be perfectly indifferent whether it is taken or not, and never persist in trying to set people right." Too often, the person to whom you are giving the advice is like the one Erica Jong was thinking of when she wrote, "Advice is what we ask for when we already know the answer but wish we didn't."

lish language on paper and in speech and with the habits of clear thinking which only a truly liberal education can give. No less important for a lawyer is the cultivation of the imaginative faculties by reading poetry, seeing great paintings, in the original or in easily available reproductions, and listening to great music. Stock your mind with the deposit of much good reading, and widen and deepen

S.J. Perelman to Perry Howze, January 1975:

Dear Perry,

      Judging from your progressive-school handwriting, the content of your previous note, and the imperious tone of the message below, you seem to be a willful infant who is accustomed to getting her own way. Accordingly, you may profit from a word of advice and I'll give it to you for free.

      The next time you issue a demand for anything . . . whether it's a spoonful of farina or a Christmas card . . . examine the name of the person you're asking and spell it correctly.

      Now wipe the egg off your face and have a happy New Year.

Marshall McLuhan to Pierre Elliott Trudeau, November 13, 1968:

Dear Mr. Prime Minister:

      Just a note about media strategy. In your discussion with students from the floor, shown on "The Way It Is" last Sunday, November 10th you could not have been in a more dangerous position media-wise.

      An auditorium violates the very nature of TV, hence the disaster of the political conventions in the U.S.A. Television demands close, casual, intimate discussions. Also no notes, no script, and no debating. . . .

Mary Granville Pendares Delany to Mrs. Dewes, March 1, 1743:

      . . . I am very much concerned for my dear godson, but hope before this reaches you his ague will have left him. Two *infallible receipts* I must insert before I proceed further. 1st, Pounded ginger, made into a paste with brandy, spread on sheep's leather, and a plaster of it laid over the stomach. 2ndly. A spider put into a goose-quill, well sealed and secured, and hung about the child's neck as low as the pit of his stomach. Either of these, I am assured, will ease. . . . Adieu.

                                  M.D.

*N*apoleon to his son, Prince Eugène, April 14, 1806:

My Son,

You are working too hard; your life is too monotonous. It is all right for yourself, because you ought to regard work as a form of recreation. But you have a young wife, and she is expecting a baby. I think you ought to manage to spend the evening with her, and to ask a few people in. Why don't you use the royal box at the theater once a week? I think you should also keep a small stable, and go hunting at least once a week. I will gladly earmark a sum in the budget for this purpose. There ought to be more gaiety in your home; it is needed for your wife's happiness, and for your own health. . . .

*H*annah Whitall Smith to Mrs. Anna Shipley, August 14, 1873:

. . . I cannot help feeling a deep interest in dear Anna, and this is why I presume to offer my advice unasked. . . . Girls have a *right* to a college education. They ought to be *made* to get it, even if it had to be done at the point of the bayonet. But since the world is not yet sufficiently advanced for that, the least parents can do is to open the door very wide to every girl who feels the least desire for it herself. I regret my own loss in this respect every day of my life, and the world has cause to regret it too; for as I *will* be a rather public character, and will *insist* on undertaking to teach, it is a monstrous pity that I have this great lack of want of education. . . .

*T*heodore Roosevelt to Elihu Root, October 2, 1902:

Dear Mr. Secretary:

Is it not possible to give the Cavalry a smaller spur, by preference one fitting into the heel? At any rate one which will interfere as little as possible with their walking.

Anonymous woman to the Duchess of Hamilton and Argyll about the latter's son, 1779:

Madam,

  As my husband and myself passed through Brussels for Holland we asked for curiosity who and who of the English were together . . . as a sincere friend of your Grace I learnt what I must communicate to you, that Lord L-r-e and his traveling tutor are here and flattered to the eyes by Lady T— our minister's wife; she has a beautiful daughter about 16 years old—poor L—d L-r-e is smitten. I hope it won't be too late, but order him from here immediately. Lady T— is cunning itself, and thereby snapt up Lord J. Russell on his road for one of her daughters. If I am too busy, forgive me, but I have the honor of knowing your Grace, and shall when I return to England disclose myself to your Grace—therefore at present reveal not any correspondence on this head, but order L—d L-r-e *from this town*, lest your family pays Lady T—'s debts here, which I am told are very heavy ones.

  Adieu—and God prosper you.

Oscar Wilde to James McNeill Whistler, February 23, 1885:

Dear Butterfly,

  By the aid of a biographical dictionary I discovered that there were once two painters, called Benjamin West and Paul Delaroche, who recklessly took to lecturing on Art.

  As of their works nothing at all remains, I conclude that they explained themselves away. Be warned in time, James; and remain, as I do, incomprehensible: to be great is to be misunderstood. Tout à vous. . .

             Oscar

Felix Frankfurter to M. Paul Claussen, Jr., age 12, who had asked how to prepare for a career in law, May 1954:

My dear Paul:

　　No one can be a truly competent lawyer unless he is a cultivated man. If I were you, I would forget all about any technical preparation for the law. The best way to prepare for the law is to come to the study of the law as a well-read person. Thus alone can one acquire the capacity to use the English language on paper and in speech and with the habits of clear thinking which only a truly liberal education can give. No less important for a lawyer is the cultivation of the imaginative faculties by reading poetry, seeing great paintings, in the original or in easily available reproductions, and listening to great music. Stock your mind with the deposit of much good reading, and widen and deepen your feelings by experiencing vicariously as much as possible the wonderful mysteries of the universe, and forget all about your future career.

Washington Irving to his nephew Pierre Paris Irving, age 18, December 8, 1824:

My dear Pierre,

　　. . . I have been much gratified by the good accounts I hear of you from various quarters, and have been pleased with the little periodical work which you sent me, which gave proof of very promising talent. I am sorry, however, to find you venturing into print at so early an age, as I consider it extremely disadvantageous. . . . I speak from observation and experience as to the pernicious effects of early publishing. It begets an eagerness to reap before one has sown. It produces too often an indisposition to further study, and a restless craving after popular applause. There is nothing that a very young man can write that will not be full of faults and errors, and when once printed they remain to cause him chagrin and self-reproach in his after years. . . .

　　　　　　　　　　　　　　　　Your affectionate uncle,

*G*eorge Eliot to Eliza Eborall, October 21, 1859:

My dear Miss Eborall,

     The only plan I can recommend to your friend Mrs. Boyd is to forward her translations to the editor of "Blackwood," taking care to retain a copy, as the editor's box for rejected contributions is an abyss from which no manuscript returns. . . . I must warn your friend that she must not be surprised if, supposing the conclusion a negative one, she should receive no communication informing her of the fact. The editor is in the habit of letting silence do the work of refusal. . . .

                         Marian Evans Lewes

*A*nton Chekhov to A.S. Suvorin, February 21, 1886:

     . . . Thank you for the flattering things you say about my work and for having published my story so soon. You can judge yourself how refreshing, even inspiring, the kind attention of an experienced and gifted writer like yourself has been to me.

     I agree with what you say about the end of my story which you have cut out; thank you for the helpful advice. I have been writing for the last six years, but you are the first person who has taken the trouble to advise and explain.

     . . . I do not write very much—not more than two or three short stories weekly.

Mother Frances Cabrini to the members of her religious community in Italy, from the ocean liner en route from Genoa to New York, September 13, 1894:

My dear Daughters,

. . . Speak often of Heaven to those who approach you, make them love it as well as the virtues which are required before we can be admitted to our beloved country. For if you know how to draw souls there by your zeal, your good example and your exemplary religious conduct, you may be assured the gates will be opened for you also.

I wanted to go to Heaven, but what with one thing and another we have entered the New York Bay. . . . In the meantime I commend myself to your good prayers, as well as my intentions and new enterprises for the good of souls and the glory of God. I'll work hard and you'll pray, I'm sure. . . .

Lady Mary Wortley Montagu to her daughter, Lady Bute, January 28, 1753:

Dear Child,

You have given me a great deal of satisfaction by your account of your eldest daughter. I am particularly pleased to hear she is a good arithmetician; it is the best proof of understanding: the knowledge of numbers is one of the chief distinctions between us and brutes. . . . Learning, if she has a real taste for it, will not only make her contented, but happy in it. No entertainment is so cheap as reading, nor any pleasure so lasting. . . .

The second caution to be given her (and which is most absolutely necessary) is to conceal whatever learning she attains, with as much solicitude as she would hide crookedness or lameness: the parade of it can only serve to draw on her the envy, and consequently the most inveterate hatred, of all he and she fools, which will certainly be at least three parts in four of her acquaintance. . . .

I carried off Mr. Coe's sponge, but I seem to have left a set of my underwear in place of it. I'll trade back if he will. He mustn't think ill of me. I give you my word I didn't intend to take the sponge; I did it while thinking of something else; I was only intending to take his dressing gown.

MARK TWAIN, LETTER TO H.H. ROGERS, 1901

I am, by accident, not by nature, so abominably rude and unreliable that I have to spend the best part of the first week after my regular short visits to town in writing frantic letters of apology. Before these regular short visits, I work out my plans in the most pleasant detail; almost every day is arranged so that something nice happens in it. And then, when I do come to town, bang go my plans in a horrid alcoholic explosion that scatters all my good intentions like bits of limbs and clothes over the doorsteps and into the saloon bars of the tawdriest pubs in London. I was looking forward to meeting you and being taken to hear music; but minor nastiness followed rudeness (ringing you up for example, and

Letters of Apology

"Apology is a lovely perfume," wrote Margaret Lee Runbeck. "It can transform the clumsiest moment into a gracious gift." The famous and infamous do not generally apologize often or well—and sometimes their apologies don't even sound very apologetic, but a few of them do it handsomely (see Lincoln's letter, for example).

Lewis Carroll to a young friend, Annie Rogers, 1867:

My dear Annie,

This is indeed dreadful. You have no idea of the grief I am in while I write, I am obliged to use an umbrella to keep the tears from running down on to the paper. Did you come yesterday to be photographed? and were you very angry? why wasn't I there? Well the fact was this—I went out for a walk with Bibkins, my dear friend Bibkins— we went many miles from Oxford—fifty—a hundred, say. As we were crossing a field full of sheep, a thought crossed my mind, and I said solemnly, "Dobkins, what o'clock is it?" "Three," said Fipkins, surprised at my manner. Tears ran down my cheeks. "It is the HOUR," I said. "Tell me, tell me, Hopkins, what day is it?" "Why, Monday, of course," said Lupkins. "Then it is the DAY!" I groaned. I wept. I screamed. The sheep crowded round me, and rubbed their affectionate noses against mine. "Mopkins!" I said, "you are my oldest friend. Do not deceive me, Nupkins! What year is this?" "Well, I *think* it's 1867," said Pipkins. "Then it's the YEAR!" I screamed, so loud that Tapkins fainted. It was all over: I was brought home, in a cart, attended by the faithful Wopkins, in several pieces.

When I have recovered a little from the shock, and have been to the seaside for a few months, I will call and arrange another day for photographing. I am too weak to write this myself, so Zupkins is writing it for me.

Your miserable friend,
Lewis Carroll

Abraham Lincoln to Ulysses S. Grant, July 13, 1863:

My dear General:

I do not remember that you and I ever met personally. I write this now as a grateful acknowledgment for the almost inestimable service you have done the country. I wish to say a word further. When you first reached the vicinity of Vicksburg, I thought you should do what you finally did—march the troops across the neck, run the batteries with the transports, and thus go below. . . . When you got below, and took Port Gibson, Grand Gulf, and vicinity, I thought you should go down the river and join General Banks, and when you turned northward, east of the Big Black, I feared it was a mistake. I now wish to make the personal acknowledgment that you were right and I was wrong.

George Washington to his secretary, Tobias Lear, November 16, 1796:

My dear Sir,

I hardly know what apology to make for the positive manner in which I declared the Certificate for the hundred Shares in the Bank of Columbia had never been in my hands. The fact is otherwise, and I delay no time to correct any error.

I found it last night and account for it thus. Given to me, I suppose (for I have not the most obscure recollection of the circumstance) at a time when my mind was occupied on, or immediately called to, some other subject, I put it *loose* in my traveling Chaise-box. . . . It might have remained there till doomsday undiscovered if I had not, for another purpose, examined every paper therein, *separately* and by that means found the Certificate which has puzzled both you and me to know what had become of it. . . .

Margaret Cavendish to a friend, 1664:

Madam,

I was so surprised with the Lady A.N.'s letter . . . it being such a bitter and angry letter. But she had reason to be angry, because I had committed a very great fault by a mistake. I, one day sitting and musing with my own thoughts, was considering and pondering upon the nature of mankind, and wondering with my self, why nature should make all men some ways or other defective, either in body, or mind, or both. For a proof I chose one whom I thought the freest from imperfections, either in mind or body, which was the Lady A.N. and I took pen and paper and writ down all the defects I could think or had observed in her, and upon another all the excellencies she was endued with, by nature, heaven and education, which last pleased me so well I resolved to send her a copy in a letter. But when I was to send her the letter, both the papers lying upon my table together, I mistook the right paper that was in her praise, and sent that which was in her dispraise, never reading it when I sent it, and when she did receive it, it seemed she was in as much amaze as I was at her answer. But afterwards she fell into a very angry passion, and in that passion writ me an answer, which I opened with great joy, thinking she had been very well pleased with my former letter. But when I did read it, and found out the mistake in sending the wrong letter, I was as if I had been thunder-stricken. . . wherefore, pray Madam, make my peace if you can, go to her and speak for me, and let her know how it was (for I dare not write to her again) and so in my stead beg my pardon, for I dare swear by heaven . . . I was free from malice or envy, or any evil design, when I writ it, and not only from any evil to her, but I was full of love and admiration of her, and I hope she will pardon me, since I only writ it as a philosopher, and not as an enemy, and since there is none that lives but hath some faults or defects, though she hath the least and fewer than any other of Nature's creatures . . . pray her to pardon my mistake, and philosophical contemplation of her, and so hoping a good success of your petition in my behalf, I rest, Madam,

Your faithful Friend and Servant

Edna St. Vincent Millay to Arthur Davison Ficke, 1920:

Arthur, dear,

Please don't think me negligent or rude. I am both, in effect, of course, but please don't think me either. . . .

Hart Crane to Katherine Anne Porter, June 22, 1931:

Dear Katherine Anne:

My apologies are becoming so mechanical as (through repetition) to savor of the most negligible insincerity. So I have to leave most of this to your judgment of the potency and malfeasance of an overdose of tequila. . . .

I spent the night in jail—as Theodora has probably told you. That was, in its way, sufficient punishment. Besides having made a fool of myself in town. . . . However I was arrested for nothing more than challenging the taxi driver for an excessive rate. But if it hadn't been for waiting for you—hour on hour, and trying to keep food warm, cream sweet, and my damnable disposition—don't suppose I'd have yelled out at you so horribly en route to doom!

I don't ask you to forgive. Because that's probably past hope. But since Peggy C. will be here in a few days—I'd rather, for her sake as well as mine, that she didn't step into a truly Greenwich Village scene. . . .

I must send a line to tell you how deeply excited I am over your sonata. It came today; of course I at once played it through, and at the end I could not help bursting into tears of joy over it.

I've just finished your book, which I have been slowly imbibing over a period of weeks. Of course I am what my grandfather used to call the Igpub (Ignorant Pub-lic) so I cannot criticize but only admire and I do admire most heartily. It seems to me better than a good book, a really useful

Letters of Appreciation

The letter of appreciation is one of the most pleasant to receive because we do not expect it, and one of the most satisfying to write because we are not obliged to send it. Mary Kay Ash says, "Everyone wants to be appreciated, so if you appreciate someone, don't keep it a secret."

To write a letter of appreciation all you need is a generous heart, a person who has done something you admire, and a little notepaper. The hallmarks of a memorable letter—which can be seen in the examples in this chapter—are being specific about what you like and telling exactly how you felt about what you liked. A little humor is sometimes the sugar that helps the medicine go down—many people are uncomfortable with unleavened praise.

Isaac Asimov to Carl Sagan, December 15, 1973:

I have just finished *The Cosmic Connection* and loved every word of it. You are my idea of a good writer because you have an unmannered style, and when I read what you write, I hear you talking.

One thing about the book made me nervous. It was entirely too obvious that you are smarter than I am. I hate that.

Yehudi Menuhin to Joan Sutherland, June 27, 1963:

Dear Miss Sutherland,

You transported me last night: I have never heard such beautiful singing—your voice would be the dream of any string player, as in addition to the most wonderful articulation each note seemed to carry a warm weight as it were, as if your bow arm was drawing the sound out of the vocal chords in a way which makes me feel both inspired and discouraged at the same time. . . .

Groucho Marx to Elaine Dundy (married to Kenneth Tynan), September 30, 1959:

Dear Mrs. Tynan:

I don't make a practice of writing to married women, especially if the husband is a dramatic critic, but I had to tell someone (and it might as well be you since you're the author) how much I enjoyed "The Dud Avocado." It made me laugh, scream and guffaw (which, incidentally, is a great name for a law firm). . . .

Franklin K. Lane to Woodrow Wilson, January 9, 1915:

My dear Mr. President,

That was a bully speech, a corker! You may have made a better speech in your life but I have never heard of it. Other Presidents may have made better speeches, but I have never heard of them. It was simply great because it was the proper blend of philosophy and practicality. It had punch in every paragraph. The country will respond to it splendidly. It was jubilant, did not contain a single minor note of apology and the country will visualize you at the head of the column. You know this country, and every country, wants a man to lead it of whom it is proud, not because of his talent but because of his personality . . . and I want to see your personality known to the American people, just as well as we know it who sit around the Cabinet table. Your speech glows with it, and that is why it gives me such joy that I can't help writing you as enthusiastically as I do.

Theodore Roosevelt to Jane Addams, January 24, 1906:

My dear Miss Addams:

. . . Will you let me say a word of very sincere thanks to you for the eminent sanity, good humor and judgment you always display in pushing matters you have at heart? I have such awful times with reformers of the hysterical and sensational stamp, and yet I so thoroughly believe in reform, that I fairly revel in dealing with anyone like you.

Claude Debussy to Alfred Bruneau, October 17, 1895:

Mon cher ami,

Many thanks for your kind article about the *Prélude à l'après-midi d'un faune* and also for the example you provide of artistic solidarity! It's something pretty rare among composers! Especially with the "successes," who immediately turn into dogs guarding a hard-won bone! All praise then to those like you who admit the existence of another art than their own; they're really the ones who matter. . . .

Harry S. Truman to Ira R.T. Smith, 1948:

Dear Mr. Smith,

A man who has served his government faithfully and well through more than fifty-one years has indeed earned honorable retirement. I cannot allow you to leave our White House staff without this word of appreciation for the efficient manner in which you have discharged the exacting duties which have fallen to you as Chief of Mails.

We have all benefited from your expert handling of the distribution of the enormous volume of mail which is the daily quota at the White House. May I express my particular thanks for the uncanny way in which you have been able to segregate my personal and family letters from the great mass of correspondence which has gone through your hands day after day.

Hope you enjoy life to the fullest where the fishing is good.

May Sarton to Arthur Schlesinger, August 14, 1946:

Dear Arthur,

I've just finished your book, which I have been slowly imbibing over a period of weeks. Of course I am what my grandfather used to call the Igpub (Ignorant Public) so I cannot criticize but only admire and I do admire most heartily. It seems to me better than a good book, a really *useful* book. It has given me, in a time of great depression about this country, a sense of proportion again, a sort of over-all understanding which makes it possible to go on and to continue the fight. . . . What frightens me about America today is that in the large majority there is no active sense of the value of the individual: few citizens feel that they are the Republic, responsible for what happens. And when the individual in a democracy ceases to feel his importance, *then* there is grave danger that he will give over his freedom, if not to a Fascist State, then to the advertising men or Publicity Agents or to the newspaper he happens to read.

Your book is fine, wise, deep-going. As a job of synthesis it seems to me masterly. . . .

Charles Darwin to Johann Friedrich Theodor Müller, March 4, 1879:

I thank you cordially for your letter. Your facts and discussion on the loss of the hairs on the legs of the caddis-flies seem to me the most important and interesting thing which I have read for a very long time. I hope that you will not disapprove, but I have sent your letter to *Nature*, with a few prefatory remarks, pointing out to the general reader the importance of your view, and stating that I have been puzzled for many years on this very point. If, as I am inclined to believe, your view can be widely extended, it will be a capital gain to the doctrine of evolution. I see by your various papers that you are working away energetically, and, wherever you look, you seem to discover something quite new and extremely interesting. . . .

Charles Dickens to George Eliot, January 18, 1858:

Dear Sir,

I have been so strongly affected by the two first tales in the book you have had the kindness to send me through Messrs. Blackwood, that I hope you will excuse my writing to you to express my admiration of their extraordinary merit. The exquisite truth and delicacy, both of the humor and the pathos of those stories, I have never seen the like of; and they have impressed me in a manner that I should find it very difficult to describe to you, if I had the impertinence to try.

In addressing these few words of thankfulness to the creator of the sad fortunes of Mr. Amos Barton, and the sad love-story of Mr. Gilfil, I am (I presume) bound to adopt the name that it pleases that excellent writer to assume. I can suggest no better one; but I should have been strongly disposed, if I had been left to my own devices, to address the said writer as a woman. I have observed what seem to me to be such womanly touches, in those moving fictions, that the assurance on the title-page is insufficient to satisfy me, even now. If they originated with no woman, I believe that no man ever before had the art of making himself, mentally, so like a woman, since the world began. . . .

*P*aul Laurence Dunbar to W.D. Howells, who favorably reviewed Dunbar's first collection of poetry, July 13, 1896:

Dear Mr. Howells:

I have seen your article in Harper's and felt its effect. That I have not written you sooner is neither the result of willful neglect nor lack of gratitude. It has taken time for me to recover from the shock of delightful surprise. My emotions have been too much for me. I could not thank you without "gushing" and I did not want to "gush.". . . The kindly praise that you have accorded me will be an incentive to more careful work. My greatest fear is that you may have been more kind to me than just. . . . Again, thanking you, Mr. Howells, for your more than kindness.

> I am,
> Sincerely yours,
> Paul Laurence Dunbar

*A*lexander Woollcott to Margaret Mitchell, August 7, 1936:

My dear Miss Mitchell,

I have just finished reading *Gone With the Wind* and found it completely absorbing. Its narrative has the directness and gusto of Dumas. I enjoyed it enormously. I was almost through it when I said to myself: "God's nightgown! This must be the Peg Mitchell who wrote me once about the little girl who swallowed a water moccasin and the tall man in the wrinkled nurse's uniform who thronged the road from Atlanta to Miami." Is it?

If your royalties have begun to come in, kindly send a large share of them as per the enclosed instructions and oblige

> A. Woollcott

Lewis Mumford to Van Wyck Brooks, March 23, 1932:

Dear Van Wyck:

Your *Emerson* has been fizzing like champagne in my veins: it is so warm and humorous and poignant and complete that a draft of it would give a dying man a new lease on life. It is not merely your best work, but the best biography an American has written, and you make me proud of you and proud of my country all over again. . . .

Helen Hunt Jackson to Grover Cleveland, August 8, 1885:

Dear Sir,

From my death bed I send you a message of heartfelt thanks for what you have already done for the Indians.

I ask you to read my *Century of Dishonor*.

I am dying happier for the belief I have that it is your hand that is destined to strike the first steady blow towards lifting this burden of infamy from our country, and righting the wrongs of the Indian race.

W. B. Yeats to Beatrice Stella Campbell, c. 1915:

Dear Mrs. Patrick Campbell,

. . . Will you permit me to thank you by letter for the performance? Your acting seemed to me to have the perfect precision and delicacy and simplicity of every art at its best. It made me feel the unity of the arts in a new way. I said to myself, that is exactly what I am trying to do in writing, to express myself without waste, without emphasis. To be impassioned and yet to have a perfect self-possession, to have a precision so absolute that the slightest inflection of voice, the slightest rhythm of sound or emotion plucks the heart-strings. . . .

*T*his letter to you is about a year late. I always have so many things I want to tell you that instead of dashing off a note to you now and then, I wait, in my incurable optimism, for some quiet time. There is none.

ALEXANDER WOOLLCOTT, LETTER TO REBECCA WEST, 1938

You may perhaps believe, or opine, that I am dead!— that I am defunct!—or insane!—but no, I beg you will think no such thing, for to think is one thing and to do another! How could I write so beautifully if I were dead? Tell me now, would it be possible? I will not offer a word of apology

Belated Letters

Nobody knows if it is possible to be human and not eventually owe someone a letter. Napoleon was supposed to have instructed his secretary to leave all his letters unopened for three weeks, and then to have pointed out with satisfaction how much of the correspondence no longer required a response.

Groucho Marx once said, "Excuse me for not answering your letter sooner, but I've been so busy not answering letters that I couldn't get around to not answering yours in time." We understand that.

for my long silence, for you would never believe me; though what is true is true! I have had so much to do that I have had time to think of my little cousin but not to write to her, consequently I have had to leave it undone. Now, however, I do myself the honor of inquiring how you are and how you do?

Adieu little coz. I am, I was, I should be, I have been, I had been, I should

*W*illiam Faulkner to Malcolm Cowley, May 7, 1944:

Dear Mr. Cowley:

I just found your letter of last Feb. by idle chance today. Please excuse this. During the last several years my correspondence has assumed a tone of divination of which your letter implies. My mail consists of two sorts: from people who don't write, asking me for something, usually money, which being a serious writer trying to be an artist, I naturally don't have; and from people who do write telling me I can't. So, since I have already agreed to answer No to the first and All right to the second, I open the envelopes to get the return postage stamps (if any) and dump the letters into a desk drawer, to be read when (usually twice a year) the drawer overflows. . . .

Thank you again for your letter, and again excuse the time lapse.

William Faulkner

*L*illian Smith to Edwin R. Embree, February 5, 1948:

Dear Dr. Embree:

Sometimes I can scarcely understand how I can postpone the writing of certain letters. Strangely enough they are always the letters I want most to write, and herein lies the little seed of my big sin! It is because I am not willing to write a routine letter to certain persons whom I love and esteem, that I fail to write any at all. I keep believing there will come a quiet day . . . when I can quietly say what is in my heart: important things to me simply because I believe them or am troubled by them or want to tell some one who will understand what I am saying. Well, the quiet days are stuff of which only dreams are made. . . .

Mari Sandoz to Lynn and Rose Van Vleet, May 2, 1943:

Dear Boss and our Rose:

I'm sorry I'm such a dud about letters. I'll answer any crack brain from, say, California, who's sure he's a reincarnation of Chief Flying Bull but I never seem to get around to the people I like. . . .

Archibald MacLeish to Amy Lowell, March 1, 1925:

Dear Miss Lowell:

You must, if you've thought about it at all, have decided that I was either dead or indifferent. Which would come to the same thing because I will be when I am. The truth is however that I didn't dare write you until I had read J.K. [her biography of John Keats] which you so generously ordered sent us. And the further truth is that I am writing you now—although J.K. has not as yet arrived—because I don't dare permit you to continue in the assumption that I am an ungrateful wretch. In other words I write you as much out of fright as affection no matter which end you take it by. . . .

Affectionately yours,
Archie

Ambrose Bierce to a friend, February 3, 1906:

Dear George,

I don't know why I've not written to you—that is, I don't know why God made me what I have the misfortune to be: a sufferer from procrastination. . . .

I've done three little stories for the March number (they may be postponed) that are ghastly enough to make a pig squeal. . . .

Leslie Land to Roger Phillips, December 1, 1989:

Dear Roger,

Do forgive me for being so long in writing and no excuse really except a severe attack of Life.

Plus the weather has been inconvenient in the extreme—giant snowstorm on November 21, the earliest in my experience here. . . . At least the snow is beautiful. It's always such a relief to see the landscape smoothed out, simplified, made whole. . . . Spiders evidently as surprised by the weather as the rest of us: their webs were still everywhere—little silken laundry lines with perfect snowflakes hung out in rows to dry. . . .

Sylvia Townsend Warner to Harold Raymond, March 18, 1933:

Dear Chatto,

I have been shamelessly belated in writing to thank you for *The Chazzey Tragedy*. Local tragedies have rather taken up my mind, for all Beth Car has been ill, Violet seriously, and what with towing about reviving broths in covered jugs, fetching nurses at dead of night, holding hands and taking temperatures, let alone putting in the seeds and the spring vegetables, and inquiring after the postmistress who has also been at D.'s door, considerably to the derangement of the general level of village intelligence, since lately even postcards have been going about unhonored and unsung, anything like writing letters has seemed to be as indefinitely deferred as the end of this sentence. . . .

Oliver Goldsmith to the Rev. Thomas Contarine, April 1754:

My dear Sir,

I suppose by this time I am accused of either neglect or ingratitude, and my silence imputed to my usual slowness of writing. But believe me, sir, when I say that till now I had not an opportunity of sitting down with that ease of mind which writing required. . . .

Albert Schweitzer to Jawaharlal Nehru, August 5, 1951:

Dear Mr. Nehru,

I was very moved by your friendliness and your good wishes for 1951. Please forgive me for responding so late with my good wishes. Neither of us really has an easy life; we each carry a heavy burden of worries and responsibilities. I often think of all the difficulties that you have to brave as head of the Indian government—difficulties that are significantly increased by the fearful state of the world. How much energy you must have to muster to take the path that you have mapped out for yourself. . . .

I do not believe, dear Mr. Nehru, that we will ever meet again, but we think about each other and we understand each other, for we each have to carry out a task that absorbs us and that constitutes our destiny. . . .

Ignatius Sancho to Mr. Stevenson, November 16, 1779:

You have missed the truth by a mile—aye and more—it was not neglect—I am too proud for that—it was not forgetfulness, Sir—I am not so ungrateful;—it was not idleness—the excuse of fools—nor hurry of business—the refuge of knaves;—it is time to say what it was.—Why, Mrs. D. was in town from Tuesday till Monday following—and then—and not till then—gave me your letter—and most graciously did I receive it—considering that both my feet were in flannels—and are so to this luckless minute.—Well, Sir, and what have you to say to that? . . .

How doth Squire G—? odso—and his pretty daughter?—kiss the father for me—and drink a bottle with the fair lady.—I mean as I have wrote—so tell them—and do what's best in thy own and their eyes. . . .

Yours, etc., etc.,

I. Sancho

Louise Imogen Guiney to Mrs. F.H. Briggs, February 7, 1903:

My very dear Ada,

For your two long enchanting letters, I have been your debtor
for a very long while. I fear I have not even thanked you for your
Christmas gift. But you know that where I once stood towards a friend,
there I stand, and that no affectionate thought like yours is ever lost
upon me. Besides, I have meant to write, these many weeks, and could
not get up the necessary energy. You will have heard what has happened: that my darling old Aunty has gone away. . . .

> Yours always, Ada *mia*,
> L.I.G.

Wolfgang Amadeus Mozart to his cousin, 1778:

Mademoiselle, my very dear Cousin,

You may perhaps believe, or opine, that I am dead!—that I am
defunct!—or insane!—but no, I beg you will think no such thing, for
to think is one thing and to do another! How could I write so beautifully if I were dead? Tell me now, would it be possible? I will not offer
a word of apology for my long silence, for you would never believe me;
though what is true *is* true! I have had so much to do that I have had
time to *think* of my little cousin but not to *write* to her, consequently I
have had to leave it undone. Now, however, I do myself the honor of
inquiring how you are and how you do?. . .

Adieu little coz. I am, I was, I should be, I have been, I had
been, I should have been, oh, if I only were, oh, that I were, would God
I were; I could be, I shall be, if I were to be, oh, that I might be, I would
have been, oh, had I been, oh, that I had been, would God I had
been—what? A dried cod! *Adieu ma chère Cousine*, whither away? I am
your faithful cousin,

> Wolfgang Amadé Mozart

Katherine Anne Porter to Eudora Welty, November 8, 1951:

Dear Eudora:

    Scratting through my baskets of paper, your gay letter of just eleven months and four days ago, today, came up with a little tag pinned to it: "To Be Answered At Once."

    A good deal of history, general and particular, has bustled by since then, but your letter is as fresh as this morning. . . .

Samuel Johnson to John Levett, 1743:

Sir,

    I have been hindered from writing to you by an imagination that it was necessary to write more than I had time for. . . .

John O'Hara to Edmund Wilson, editor of The New Republic, about F. Scott Fitzgerald, January 20, 1940:

Dear Mr. Wilson:

    Please forgive my delay in answering yours of Jan. 7. The trouble is I read my mail in the morning, then go back to sleep, and when awake think I must have dreamt the letters.

    I would be very glad to reply in kind or in any other way to the disgusting hostility of some of Scott's obits. If you will tell me more about the kind of thing you want, I'll do my best. This, however, is only an armistice between The NR and me. I'm still annoyed about the Luce piece that you wouldn't print.

Ayn Rand to Gerald Loeb, April 23, 1944:

Dear Mr. Loeb:

I hope you will forgive me for my long silence—the length of this letter will serve as explanation and, I hope, as apology. You said in one of your letters that you have no ability for small talk. My trouble is that I have no ability for small letters—that is, I cannot answer casually and carelessly, particularly when there is a serious subject such as writing to discuss. I must always make a thorough job of it. So I delayed answering you until I could do it right. Please forgive me if I took too long. . . .

Ralph Waldo Emerson to his son-in-law William Hathaway Forbes, September 6, 1871:

Dear Will,

There are great advantages in a feeble condition of health, or in the reputation of it, chiefly in the neglect of all your duties unblamed. I hope you think I have been very ill, since I failed to make any reply to your heart-rejoicing telegrams on & after the 27th August & your good letters to Concord since; & your note of the 2nd Sept. to me shows your mercy to me unabated. Be it known then to you & Edith, that I have read & heard with joy every word of household news that has come to us from Naushon—that the young child is almost as well known & dear to its grandparents here as to you both, or to those small members of your family who treat him so well: that we wait with interested curiosity to learn his name. . . . Dear love to Edith,

R.W. Emerson

Edgar Allan Poe to Frederick W. Thomas, February 3, 1842:

My dear Friend:

I am sure you will pardon me for my seeming neglect in not replying to your last when you learn what has been the cause of the delay. My dear little wife has been dangerously ill. About a fortnight since, in singing, she ruptured a blood-vessel, and it was only on yesterday that the physicians gave me any hope of her recovery. You might imagine the agony I have suffered, for you know how devotedly I love her. But today the prospect brightens, and I trust that this bitter cup of misery will not be my portion. I seize the first moment of hope and relief to reply to your kind words. . . .

John Muir to General John Bidwell, December 3, 1877:

My dear General,

I arrived in my old winter quarters here a week ago, my season's field work done, and I was just sitting down to write to Mrs. Bidwell when your letter of November 29th came in. The tardiness of my Kings River postal is easily explained. I committed it to the care of a mountaineer who was about to descend to the lowlands, and he probably carried it for a month or so in his breeches' pocket in accordance with the well-known business habits of that class of men. . . .

It is lovely, when I forget all birthdays, including my own, to find that somebody remembers me.

ELLEN GLASGOW, LETTER TO J. DONALD ADAMS, 1936

Though I don't give birthday presents, still I may write a birthday letter. I came to your door to wish you many happy returns of the day, but the cat met me, and took me for a mouse, and hunted me up and down till I could hardly stand. However somehow I got into the house, and there a

Birthday and Anniversary Letters

Five of the birthday letters in this chapter use the expression "Many happy returns." Until the nineteenth century, this phrase (hoping the happy day would come again many times) was also used for New Year's and April Fool's Day greetings. However, as Olivia Goldsmith notes, it is "considered very bad form to wish authors on their birthdays 'many happy returns'" since authors fear and loathe above all things books that have been returned unsold to the publisher.

Harry Truman's letters to Bess are typical of the many warm and loving letters he wrote to her during their nearly fifty years together. And the last two letters remind us to honor the sad as well as the happy anniversaries.

Queen Victoria to her granddaughter, April 2, 1873:

Darling Victoria,

On this your *10th* Birthday Grandmama writes to wish you many many happy returns. May you grow daily in goodness and strive more and more to be a comfort to dear Papa and Mama. . . .

My presents are two pearls and a workbox which I hope you will like. Give my kindest love to dear Ella, Irène and Ernie and a kiss to Fritzie and Baby. . . .

Ever your devoted Grandmama,
V.R.I.

Vincent van Gogh to Theodore van Gogh, April 28, 1876:

Dear Theo,

Many happy returns, my best wishes for this day, may our mutual love increase with the years.

I am so glad that we have so many things in common, not only memories of childhood but also that you are working in the same business in which I was till now and know so many people and places which I know also, and that you have so much love for nature and art. . . .

Have a pleasant day today and give my love to all who may ask about me and believe me,

Your loving brother,

Louisa May Alcott to her mother, October 8, 1870:

Dearest Marmee,

A happy birthday, and many of 'em!

Lewis Carroll to young friend Georgina Watson, October 5, 1869:

My dear Ina,

 Though I don't give birthday *presents*, still I may write a birthday letter. I came to your door to wish you many happy returns of the day, but the cat met me, and took me for a mouse, and hunted me up and down till I could hardly stand. However *some*how I got into the house, and there a mouse met me, and took me for a cat, and pelted me with fire-irons, crockery, and bottles. Of course I ran into the street again, and a horse met me and took me for a cart, and dragged me all the way to the Guildhall, but the worst of all was when a cart met me and took me for a horse. I was harnessed to it, and had to draw it miles and miles, all the way to Merrow. . . .

 However I was glad to hear you were hard at work learning the multiplication tables for a birthday treat. . . .

         Your affectionate friend,
         C.L.D.

Empress Frederick to her mother Queen Victoria, May 22, 1899:

 As, alas, I cannot be with you on your dear birthday, these lines must convey at least a little of all I should like to say. . . .

 Eighty years of grace and honors—of usefulness and goodness—of trials and sorrows—with much happiness and many joys such as are given to few, though mingled with troubles and anxieties inseparable from a unique position as a sovereign and mother. Truly a reason for us to praise and thank God for so many mercies, and to pray that bright and peaceful years may crown the rest! . . . I join my sisters in the gift of candelabra for the Indian room and venture to send a tiny locket, which I hope you will put on a bracelet or watch chain.

 May the day be very fine and dear Windsor not too tiring for you. I must not write a longer letter today, as I know the flood of letters which will come in and how many will have to help to send answers! . . .

George Eliot to Charles Bray, January 30, 1852:

> Many happy returns of the day to you, dear friend. May every 31st of January in reserve for you find you richer in pleasant thoughts, in friends and in worldly goods.
>
> Your affectionate
Marian

Helen Keller to her mother Kate Keller, October 11, 1912:

> A happy birthday to you, dearest Mother, and many, many returns of the day! . . . With a heartful of love for you all, and with a bookful of news yet to come, I am,
>
> Your affectionate child,

Gustav Mahler to his wife Alma, September 30, 1907:

> My dearest Almscherl,
>
> . . . All the shops are shut and even if they weren't I shouldn't know what to buy you for your birthday. I can only hope that my love and good wishes for tomorrow will be accepted instead of a costly birthday present. And what else really is there to give when one has given oneself? When you are here and we take one of our happy strolls along the Kärntnerstrasse, we'll find something nice for you. How's that? I look forward to it eagerly. . . . A thousand greetings and kisses, my darling Luxi, and let me hear from you.

James L. Watson to James S. Watson, May 25, 1944:

My dear Father,

    . . . I just want to wish you the happiest birthday that a son could wish his father. I know that you will have many more. I only hope and pray that when your birthday rolls around again that I will be there to celebrate it with you. Dad, I could go on and write volumes about just what having you as a father has meant to me, but I don't think it necessary. All I have to say is that you're all that a fellow, any fellow, could hope for. Your kindness, unselfishness, love, and devotion to not only me but the rest of the family leaves nothing else to be desired in a man and a father.

    Many times before I've realized how fortunate I was to have a father like you and now that I'm in the Army I realize more than ever what a lucky fellow I am to have you as my Dad. Now, I'm not referring to your position in society as Justice James S. Watson. I'm just talking about Jimmy Watson the man and Dad the father. . . . I cherish and hold dear to me the wisdom and advice which you have handed down to me and only hope that I can be half the man that you are. . . .

Your devoted and loving son,
"Skiz"

P.S. Say, Dad, I have saved fifty dollars. Now if you need it for anything, don't hesitate to call on me. I know how things are. And remember I'm a man now and I am a member of the Watson Family (share, share, share alike). Well, I'd like to share in some of the responsibility, too.

E.B. White to Caroline B. Sergeant, April 26, 1952:

Dearest Aunt Crully:

Congratulations on this momentous occasion—your 90th birthday! I wish I could be there to see you and greet you, but that is not to be, and the best I can do is to send you my love and a small gift by mail. . . . If you could hear Katharine speak of you, as I so often do, with such grateful affection, I am sure you would be proud and happy, at 90, to look back on a life so useful and so rich in the unselfish gifts you have made to those around you. My own feeling and admiration is of comparatively recent vintage, but even to me—a rank newcomer in your circle of influence—you have given the kind of sober happiness that comes from knowing and loving a Lady of Quality. And you cannot imagine what fun it has been for me to see how young you are in everything but years. You are my dream girl in that respect. . . .

With deep affection, as ever,
Andy

Mark Twain to his wife on her thirtieth birthday, November 27, 1875:

Livy darling,

Six years have gone by since I made my first great success in life and won you, and thirty years have passed since Providence made preparation for that happy success by sending you into the world. . . . You are dearer to me today . . . than you were upon the last anniversary of this birthday; you were dearer then than you were a year before—you have grown more and more dear from the first of those anniversaries, and I do not doubt that this precious progression will continue on to the end.

Let us look forward to the coming anniversaries, with their age and their gray hairs without fear and without depression, trusting and believing that the love we bear each other will be sufficient to make them blessed.

So, with abounding affection for you and our babies, I hail this day that brings you the matronly grace and dignity of three decades!

Harry Truman to Bess Truman, for her birthday, February 12, 1931:

Dear Bess:

I hope this reaches you the morning of the thirteenth, because while I'm not there I'll be thinking constantly all day that this is *her* birthday and I'm not there. . . . I hope we see sixty more birthdays *together*.

Harry

Harry Truman to Bess Truman, on her birthday, February 13, 1957:

Dear Bess:

Here is a non-forgetter. . . . Now you are as old as I am but as young and as beautiful as sixty years ago.

You're the nicest sweetheart a man could have.

Harry

Harry Truman to Bess Truman, on their anniversary, June 28, 1948:

Dear Bess:

Twenty-nine years! It seems like twenty-nine days.

Detroit, Port Huron, a farm sale, the Blackstone Hotel, a shirt store, County Judge, a defeat, Margie, Automobile Club membership drive, Presiding Judge, Senator, V.P., now!

You still are on the pedestal where I placed you that day in Sunday school 1890. What an old fool I am.

H.S.T.

Abigail Adams to John Adams, on their anniversary, October 25, 1782:

My Dearest Friend,

    . . . Look (is there a dearer name than *friend*? Think of it for me), look to the date of this letter, and tell me what are the thoughts which arise in your mind. Do you not recollect that eighteen years have run their circuit since we pledged our mutual faith to each other, and the hymeneal torch was lighted at the altar of Love? Yet, yet it burns with unabating fervor. Old Ocean has not quenched it, nor old Time smothered it in his bosom. . . . I recollect the untitled man to whom I gave my heart, and in the agony of recollection, when time and distance present themselves together, wish he had never been any other. Who shall give me back time? Who shall compensate to me those years I cannot recall? How dearly have I paid for a titled husband! Should I wish you less wise, that I might enjoy more happiness? I cannot find that in my heart. . . .

          Adieu, my dear friend. Ever, ever, yours,
          Portia

Princess Alice to Queen Victoria, on the fifth anniversary of the death of Prince Albert, December 11, 1866:

Beloved, precious Mama,

    On awaking this morning, my first thoughts were of you and of dear darling Papa! Oh, how it reopens the wounds scarcely healed, when this day of pain and anguish returns! This season of the year, the leafless trees, the cold light, everything reminds me of that time!. . . Happily married as I am, and with such a good, excellent and loving husband, how far more can I understand now the depth of that grief, which tore our lives asunder!

Mary Todd Lincoln to Mary Jane Welles, who had written her on the first anniversary of Willie Lincoln's death, February 21, 1863:

My dear Mrs. Welles:

Allow me to thank you for your sympathizing and kindly remembrance of *yesterday*, when I felt so broken hearted. Only those who have passed through such bereavements can realize how the heart bleeds at the return of these anniversaries. I have never been able to express to you how I grieved over your troubles. Our precious lambs, if we could only realize how far happier they *now* are than when on earth! Heaven help the sorrowing, and how full the land is of such! Any morning you may have leisure I should like to see you. I would enjoy a little conversation with you.

Ever sincerely,
Mary Lincoln

*T*o be reasonable one should never
complain but when one hopes redress.

LADY MARY WORTLEY MONTAGU, LETTER TO HER HUSBAND, 1712

Half way up the elevator
shaft I met the barrel of
bricks coming down. The
encounter was brief and
spirited. I got the worst of
it but continued on my way
toward the roof—that is,
most of me went on, but
much of my epidermis clung
to the barrel and returned
to earth. Then I struck the

Letters of Complaint

The famous have been no more exempt than the rest of us from the imperfections of life. They have been obliged to write letters of complaint about their neighbors (F. Scott Fitzgerald and Mark Twain), about business transactions (Mary Todd Lincoln, Napoleon, Charles Dickens, Fred Allen), about the handling of their creative works (Elizabeth Gaskell, Ludwig van Beethoven, Christina Rossetti), and about their friends' behavior (Lady Mary Wortley Montagu).

P.G. Wodehouse once said of a character, "While not exactly disgruntled, he was far from feeling gruntled." The letter-writers in this chapter range from disgruntled to "far from feeling gruntled."

Charles Dickens to John Bennett, September 14, 1863:

My dear Sir,

Since my hall clock was sent to your establishment to be cleaned it has gone (as indeed it always has) perfectly well, but has struck the hours with great reluctance, and after enduring internal agonies of a most distressing nature, it has now ceased striking altogether. Though a happy release for the clock, this is not convenient to the household. If you can send down any confidential person with whom the clock can confer, I think it may have something on its works that it would be glad to make a clean breast of.

Groucho Marx to Confidential magazine, c. 1950:

Gentlemen:

If you continue to publish slanderous pieces about me, I shall feel compelled to cancel my subscription.

Lady Mary Wortley Montagu to Francesco Algarotti, April 1736:

My Lady Stafford and myself waited for you three hours. Three hours of expectation is no small trial of patience, and I believe some of your martyrs have been canonized for suffering less. If you have repentance enough to be inclined to ask pardon you may obtain it by coming here tomorrow at seven o'clock.

Let me have a line of answer.

F. *Scott Fitzgerald to Mrs. Neuville, his landlady, July 29, 1940:*

Dear Mrs. Neuville:

I thought the other day that a large rat had managed to insert itself into the plaster above my bedroom and workroom. I was, however, surprised that it apparently slept at night and worked in the day, causing its greatest din around high noon.

However, yesterday, much to my surprise, I deduced from the sounds it emitted that it was a dog, or rather several dogs, and evidently training for a race, for they ran round and round the tin roof. Now I don't know how these greyhounds climbed up the wall but I know dog-racing is against the law of California—so I thought you'd like to know. Beneath the arena where these races occur an old and harassed literary man is gradually going mad.

*M*ark *Twain to the gas company, February 12, 1891:*

Dear Sirs:

Some day you will move me almost to the verge of irritation by your chuckle-headed Goddamned fashion of shutting your Goddamned gas off without giving any notice to your Goddamned parishioners. Several times you have come within an ace of smothering half of this household in their beds and blowing up the other half by this idiotic, not to say criminal, custom of yours. And it has happened again today. Haven't you a telephone?

*F*ranklin *Delano Roosevelt to Captain John L. McCrea, Aug. 31, 1942:*

Will you tell the Navy Band that I don't like the way they play "The Star Spangled Banner"—it should not have a lot of frills in it?

F.D.R.

Ludwig van Beethoven to his music publishers, Breitkopf & Härtel, May 6, 1811:

> . . . Mistakes—mistakes—you yourselves are one great mistake—I have to keep my copyist and myself perpetually on the rush if I am to prevent my published work from consisting solely of mistakes: the Leipzig *Musiktribunal* seems unable to produce a single decent proofreader, and at that, you send off the work even before you receive the corrected proofs!. . .

E.B. White to J.H. Aiken, December 21, 1951:

Dear Mr. Aiken:

I am a stockholder in the Consolidated Edison Company, and I rent an apartment at 229 East 48 Street in which there is a gas refrigerator. So I have a double interest in your letter of December 19. It seems to me a very odd letter indeed.

You say that my refrigerator, even if it seems to be operating properly, may be producing poison gas, and you suggest that I open a window. I do not want to open a window. It would be a very unpopular move with the cook. Furthermore, I haven't the slightest intention of living under the same roof with a machine that discharges poison gas. Your recommendation is that I get plenty of fresh air—enough to counteract the effect of the gas. But I cannot believe that you are serious.

Will you be good enough to let me know what sort of poison gas is generated by a Servel gas refrigerator, and in what quantity, and how discharged. I know that there is a vent at the top of the machine and that some sort of warm air flows from the vent. I have always assumed it was hot air. Is it something else?

I also know that a gas refrigerator poses a carbon problem, and I ask the landlord to remove the carbon about once a year, which he does. But your letter makes me think that the matter is not so simple and I am anxious to be enlightened.

If gas refrigerators are, as your letter suggests, discharging poison gases into people's homes I don't want to own a gas refrigerator and I shall certainly sell my stock.

Frank Lloyd Wright to Mrs. Walker, May 21, 1951:

My dear Mrs. Walker:

The stone-work is very badly done. Evidently the mason has no feeling for this sort of thing. No feeling. . . .

I can hardly believe you have allowed the builder to make changes from the plans, as the affair of a house as a work of art is a sensitive affair, as you well know and the contractor does not. I say the outside entrance to the North violates the charm and practicability also, I may say, of your opus.

Once the builder gets out of hand the chance of perfection or anything approximate is gone.

Do be guided by the counsel of the boys trained by me in getting my work done.

Sincerely alarmed,
Frank Lloyd Wright

Christina G. Rossetti to Alexander Macmillan, December 9, 1861:

My dear Sir,

I received *Goblin Market* on Saturday; and found with dismay on reading through three errors, one of which I am sure was corrected in the proof. I have written without any delay to Messrs. Bradbury and Evans, hoping to be in time for redress. One of the three blunders is serious, so I shall be much vexed if the book appears as it stands.

Napoleon to M. de Champagny, December 31, 1811:

I have just seen the set of porcelain sent to the Empress as a present for New Year's Day. It is very ugly. See that it is prettier another year. Have a breakfast set made, in which every cup has portraits of the Empress and of the six princesses—my sisters and sisters-in-law. Make another set with portraits of the Empress's ladies-in-waiting.

Edna St. Vincent Millay to the League of American Penwomen, April 18, 1927:

Ladies:

I have received from you recently several communications, inviting me to be your Guest of Honor at a function to take place in Washington some time this month. I replied, not only that I was unable to attend, but that I regretted this inability; I said that I was sensible to the honor you did me, and that I hoped you would invite me again.

Your recent gross and shocking insolence to one of the most distinguished writers of our time has changed all that.

It is not in the power of an organization which has insulted Elinor Wylie to honor me.

And indeed I should feel it unbecoming on my part, to sit as Guest of Honor in a gathering of writers, where honor is tendered not so much for the excellence of one's literary accomplishment as for the circumspection of one's personal life.

Believe me, if the eminent object of your pusillanimous attack has not directed her movements in conformity with your timid philosophies, no more have I mine. I too am eligible for your disesteem. Strike me too from your lists, and permit me, I beg you, to share with Elinor Wylie a brilliant exile from your fusty province.

Very truly yours,

Elizabeth Cleghorn Gaskell to Edward Chapman, on her book eventually titled The Moorland Cottage, December 1850:

My dear Sir,

I do not at all like the title you have chosen. . . . May it, please, be December Days, which is much more suggestive of the quiet tone of the story. . . . I will disown that book if you call it The Fagot; the name of *my* book is December Days.

Claude Debussy to Maud Allan, July 30, 1916:

> Chère Miss Maud Allan,
>
> I have been sitting here for hours in front of the score of *Khamma* which is precisely tailored to a complement of 90 players. I am utterly at a loss as to how it could be reduced to suit an orchestra half the size. What would you do if you were asked to dance with just one arm and one leg? There is some analogy between such an insult and the amputation you are asking for. I can only leave you to act as you see fit, but I decline all responsibility in the matter. . . .
>
> With renewed regrets, I remain,
Yours sincerely,
C.D.

Alexander Woollcott to Malcolm Cowley, editor of The New Republic, December 7, 1934:

> My dear Mr. Cowley:
>
> I was deeply interested in your informed and sagacious piece on Proust which you were good enough to send me. But I am puzzled beyond expression by the following sentence: "But Mr. Woollcott, being so eager to have the job well done, should have done it himself or come forward with a better translator." Quite aside from the fact that no public notice was served about the fearful dearth which led to Dr. Blossom's selection as translator, I am puzzled by your implied conception of a reviewer's function. It recalls the happy, far off days when, as a dramatic critic, I ventured to regret in print that a prima donna had, throughout the premiere of an operetta, sung firmly off key. Her ringing riposte was a public statement to the effect that she would have liked to hear *me* sing that role. Of course, she wouldn't have liked it at all. People are so inexact in moments of stress.

Charles Dickens to Angus Fletcher, March 24, 1844:

My dear Fletcher,

You have (unconsciously) covered me with shame; and degraded me to an ignominious and deplorable level.

In an evil hour, I invited Fred, the McIans, and Maclise, to dine here last Wednesday the Twentieth—I repeat it in capitals, THE TWENTIETH. Said I, "Fletcher—a punctual man—is coming from Italy, and will turn up at half past five, sharp." I made use of the expression "sharp." They jeered; they sneered; they taunted me. "He will not appear,"—said they. "I know him better," said I. "We will dine," say they, "with pleasure. But Fletcher will not appear." Confiding in the rectitude and punctuality of my own heart, I ordered your knife and fork to be laid. John laid it. The guests arrived. At five and twenty minutes to six, they became restless. At twenty minutes to six, they remonstrated formally. At a quarter to six, they grew mutinous and insolent. At ten minutes to six, they proposed to leave me in a body, and dine together at the Star and Garter, Richmond. At five minutes to six, they rang the bell, and ordered John, on pain of death, to serve the Banquet. That wretched Innocent complied. Over my mortification and anguish, let me draw a decent veil. . . .

> Always, my dear Fletcher,
> Faithfully yours,

Abraham Lincoln to Governor John A. Andrew, August 12, 1862:

. . . Please say to these gentlemen that if they do not work quickly I will make quick work with them. In the name of all that is reasonable, how long does it take to pay a couple of regiments? . . .

*M*ark Twain to a neighbor on West Tenth Street, New York,
November 30, 1900:

Dear Madam,

I know I ought to respect my duty and perform it, but I am weak and faithless where boys are concerned, and I can't help secretly approving pretty bad and noisy ones, though I do object to the kind that ring doorbells. My family try to get me to stop the boys from holding conventions on the front steps, but I basely shirk out of it because I think the boys enjoy it.

My wife has been complaining to me this evening about the boys on the front steps and under compulsion I have made some promises. But I am very forgetful, now that I am old, and my sense of duty is getting spongy.

Very truly yours,
S.L. Clemens

*M*ary Todd Lincoln, telegram to James A. Kerr, January 9, 1865:

We must have the China tomorrow—send what you have. Our dinner comes off Monday, and on Saturday, the articles must be ready for use here. Mrs. Lincoln

*T*elegram the next day:

What is the meaning, that we do not have the China. *Answer* immediately.

Fred Allen to the State of New York Insurance Department, June 18, 1932:

Dear Sir:

The soullessness of corporations is something to stun you. . . . I went around last Sunday morning to a new house that is being built for me . . . on the top floor I found a pile of bricks which were not needed there. Feeling industrious, I decided to remove the bricks. In the elevator shaft there was a rope and a pulley, and on one end of the rope was a barrel. I pulled the barrel up to the top, after walking down the ladder, and then fastened the rope firmly at the bottom of the shaft. Then I climbed the ladder again and filled the barrel with bricks. Down the ladder I climbed again, five floors, mind you, and untied the rope to let the barrel down. The barrel was heavier than I was and before I had time to study over the proposition, I was going up the shaft with my speed increasing at every floor. I thought of letting go of the rope, but before I had decided to do so I was so high that it seemed more dangerous to let go than hold on, so I held on.

Half way up the elevator shaft I met the barrel of bricks coming down. The encounter was brief and spirited. I got the worst of it but continued on my way toward the roof—that is, most of me went on, but much of my epidermis clung to the barrel and returned to earth. Then I struck the roof the same time the barrel struck the cellar. The shock knocked the breath out of me and the bottom out of the barrel. Then I was heavier than the empty barrel, and I started down while the barrel started up. We went and met in the middle of our journey, and the barrel uppercut me, pounded my solar plexis, barked my shins, bruised my body and skinned my face. When we became untangled, I resumed my downward journey and the barrel went higher. I was soon at the bottom. I stopped so suddenly that I lost my presence of mind and let go of the rope. This released the barrel which was at the top of the elevator shaft and it fell five floors and landed squarely on top of me, and it landed hard too.

Now, here is where the heartlessness . . . comes in. I sustained five accidents in two minutes. One on my way up the shaft, when I met the barrel of bricks, the second when I met the roof, the third when I was descending and I met the empty barrel, the fourth when I struck the barrel, and the fifth when the barrel struck me. But the insurance man said that it was one accident not five and instead of receiving payment for injuries at the rate of five times $25.00, I only get one $25 payment. I, therefore, enclose my policy and ask that you cancel the same as I made up my mind that henceforth I am not to be skinned by either barrel or/and any insurance company.

Yours sincerely and regretfully,

*L*et me heartily congratulate you upon your phenomenal success at Atlanta—it was a word fitly spoken.

W.E.B. Du Bois, letter to Booker T. Washington, 1895

Your book came yesterday and I read it last night. It is undoubtedly in some ways the best thing you have done—the best planned, the best sustained, the best written. In fact, it amounts to a complete new departure in your work. The only bad feature of it is that the characters are mostly so

Congratulations

Lady Katie Magnus said that rejoicing with our neighbors' joys is no less a duty than grieving with their
griefs. We feel a compulsion to send a sympathy letter that we
often don't feel about the congratulatory note, which is one of
the most rewarding letters we can write. Its happy contagion
affects more than the recipient and often returns some pleasant
surprise to us months or years later.

One of the cardinal rules of congratulatory messages is to
focus on the other person's good news, leaving your own concerns for later. Friedrich Nietzsche's self-interested remarks on
his sister's marriage and his excuses for not attending her wedding illustrate how *not* to send congratulations.

John O'Hara to John Steinbeck, who had just received the Nobel Prize for Literature, October 25, 1962:

Congratulations. I can think of only one other author I'd rather see get it.

John Steinbeck to John O'Hara, a few days later:

Dear John:

Well, I'll tell you this. It wouldn't have been nearly as good without your greeting. Not nearly.

Thanks, John. The thing is meaningless alone. But if my friends like it—suddenly it has some dignity and desirability.

Yours,
John

Grover Cleveland to William Wyse, August 13, 1873:

I am amazed and dumbfounded, but I congratulate you from the bottom of my heart. A long life of perfect bliss and married contentment I hope may be yours. I go to find Bissell, with whom I drink the health of the newly-married. Please present my compliments to the other side of the firm.

Dorothy Parker, telegram to a friend who just had become a mother after a much-publicized pregnancy, 1915:

Good work, Mary. We all knew you had it in you.

Arna Bontemps to Langston Hughes, 1941:

Dear Lang,

You were grand on CBS Saturday! You have never read better, and the selection of poems was just right. Too bad *Shakespeare in Harlem* is not in the bookstores so that it can profit by the plug that this would surely give, but maybe there will be others. . . .

Your broadcast seems to have been widely listened to around here. Several people have already mentioned it to me. One did not like the preliminary chat between Frederick and Dillon, but I personally found it quite interesting. . . .

Willa Cather to the Nebraska State Journal, June 2, 1927:

Dear Mr. Jones,

Certainly I wish to send my congratulations to the *Journal* on its sixtieth birthday. I have many pleasant memories connected with it, with the *Journal*, I mean, not with its birthday. You see I still write as badly as ever. . . .

With pleasant memories of the past and good wishes for the future of the *Nebraska State Journal*, I am most cordially yours,

Albert Schweitzer to Léon M'Ba, 1961:

Dear Mr. President,

May I congratulate you on being elected president of the Republic of Gabon by the Gabonese people. It is my sincere wish that you may rule the destiny of this country for a long time and bring about whatever contributes to its development and its peace.

We owe it to you that peace reigns among us. Those who understand the role that you have played in establishing and maintaining peace are deeply grateful to you.

Best wishes,

Alexandra David-Neel to Amelia Earhart, May 12, 1932:

Dear Miss Earhart:

You are a mighty bird and I am but a pedestrian explorer. Nevertheless, I think that the first woman who has entered Lhasa the capital of Tibet may venture to offer her hearty congratulations to the first airwoman who has crossed the Atlantic.

I am most happy that success has crowned your intrepidity.

Anton Chekhov to A.N. Pleshtcheyev, February 15, 1890:

I answer you, dear Alexey Nikolaevitch, at once on receiving your letter. It was your nameday, and I forgot it!! Forgive me, dear friend, and accept my belated congratulations. . . .

Oscar Wilde to Frances Forbes-Robertson, June 1899:

My dear, sweet, beautiful Friend,

Eric has just sent me your charming letter, and I am delighted to have a chance of sending you my congratulations on your marriage, and all the good wishes of one who has always loved and admired you. I met Eric by chance, and he told me he had been over to the marriage. He was as picturesque and sweet as usual, but more than usually vague. I was quite furious with him. He could not quite remember who it was you had married, or whether he was fair or dark, young or old, tall or small. He could not remember where you were married, or what you wore, or whether you looked more than usually beautiful. He said there were a great many people at the wedding, but could not remember their names. He remembered, however, Johnston being present. He spoke of the whole thing as a sort of landscape in a morning mist. Your husband's name he could not for the moment recall: but said he thought he had it written down at home. He went dreamily away down the Boulevard followed by violent reproaches from me, but they were no more to him than the sound of flutes: he wore the sweet smile of those who are always looking for the moon at midday.

So, dear Frankie, you are married, and your husband is a "king of men"! That is as it should be: those who wed the daughters of the gods are kings, or become so. . . . Like dear St. Francis of Assisi I am wedded to Poverty: but in my case the marriage is not a success: I hate the Bride that has been given to me: I see no beauty in her hunger and her rags: I have not the soul of St. Francis: my thirst is for the beauty of life: my desire for its joy. But it was dear of you to ask me [to visit], and do tell the "king of men" how touched and grateful I am by the invitation you and he have sent me.

And, also, sometime send me a line to tell me of the beauty you have found in life. I live now on echoes, as I have little music of my own.

Your old friend,
Oscar

Edmund Wilson to F. Scott Fitzgerald, on The Great Gatsby, April 11, 1925:

> Dear Scott: Your book came yesterday and I read it last night. It is undoubtedly in some ways the best thing you have done—the best planned, the best sustained, the best written. In fact, it amounts to a complete new departure in your work. The only bad feature of it is that the characters are mostly so unpleasant in themselves that the story becomes rather a bitter dose before one has finished with it. However, the fact that you are able to get away with it is the proof of its brilliance. It is full of all sorts of happy touches—in fact, all the touches are happy—there is not a hole in it anywhere. I congratulate you—you have succeeded here in doing most of the things that people have always scolded you for not doing. . . .

> Yours as ever,
> EW

Edmund Wilson to Ernest Hemingway, on The Sun Also Rises, January 7, 1927:

> Dear Hemingway: I think your book is a knockout—perhaps the best piece of fiction that any American of this new crop has done. Croly, the editor of *The New Republic,* has also been extremely interested in it and has even written an editorial about it, which I am enclosing. We wish you would do something for *The New Republic.* Won't you send me something which you have on hand that you think there is even a remote chance of our being able to use? . . .

> Yours as ever,
> Edmund Wilson

Charles Darwin to J. W. Judd, June 27, 1878:

I am heartily glad to hear of your intended marriage. A good wife is the supreme blessing in this life, and I hope and believe from what you say that you will be as happy as I have been in this respect. May your future geological work be as valuable as that which you have already done; and more than this need not be wished for any man. . . .

Oscar W. Firkins to Ralph E. Dyar, July 10, 1909:

Dear Mr. Dyar:

The announcement of your marriage duly reached me, and I was glad to be remembered at a moment so important for yourself and so interesting to all your friends. It seems to me that you possess in a high degree the conditions for a happy married life—the wisdom to choose rightly and the power to cherish tenderly and faithfully. . . . I wish all good and joy to you and the new Mrs. Dyar. Nature has been generous with you; may the world and destiny be equally so.

Lady Mary Wortley Montagu to her daughter Lady Bute, May 22, 1759:

My dear Child,

I am always pleased to hear from you but particularly so when I have any occasion of congratulation. I sincerely wish you joy of your infant's having gone happily through the smallpox. . . .

*G*rover Cleveland to Queen Victoria, May 27, 1887:

Great and Good Friend:

In the name and on behalf of the people of the United States I present their sincere felicitations upon the arrival of the fiftieth anniversary of Your Majesty's accession to the crown of Great Britain. I but utter the general voice of my fellow countrymen in wishing for your people the prolongation of a reign so marked with advance in popular well-being, physical, moral, and intellectual. . . .

May your life be prolonged, and peace, honor and prosperity bless the people over whom you have been called to rule. May liberty flourish throughout your empire under just and equal laws and your government be strong in the affections of all who live under it, and I pray God to have Your Majesty in his holy keeping.

*F*ranklin K. Lane to Frank I. Cobb of the New York *World*, after Woodrow Wilson's election to the presidency, November 11, 1916:

My dear Cobb,

My very warm, earnest, and enthusiastic congratulations to you. You made the best editorial campaign that I have ever known to be made. I would give more for the editorial support of the New York *World* than for that of any two papers that I know of. . . .

Cordially yours,

Franklin K. Lane

Friedrich Nietzsche to his sister, Elisabeth Nietzsche, on the occasion of her marriage, May 20, 1884:

My dear Lama:

On the decisive day in your life (and the day on which nobody could wish you happiness and prosperity and good omens and good spirits more than I do)—on this day I must draw up a sort of account of my life. From now on, your mind and heart will be, first and foremost, taken up with quite other things than your brother's concerns, and that is right and good—and likewise it is natural that you will more and more come to share your husband's way of thinking—which is not my way at all, whatever I may find in it to honor and applaud. So that you may in the future have a kind of indication as to how far your brother's judgment will require from you much prudence and perhaps also forbearance, I am describing for you today, as a sign of great affection, the bad and difficult nature of my situation. I have found until now, from earliest childhood, *nobody* who had the same needs of heart and conscience as myself. This compels me still today, as at all times, to present myself, as best I can, and often with a lot of bad feeling, among one or another of the sorts of human beings who are permitted and understandable nowadays. But that one can only really grow among people of *like mind* and like will is for me an axiom of belief (even down to diet and the body's demands); that I have no such person is a misfortune. . . .

Do not therefore think me mad, my dear Lama, and especially forgive me for not coming to your wedding—such a "sick" philosopher would be a bad person to give away the bride! With a thousand affectionate good wishes,

Your F.

*H*ere is a copy of my book—published today—with the author's
compliments. . . . I haven't put any embarrassing
inscription, so you can give it to somebody as a birthday present. I should never know.

BARBARA PYM, LETTER TO HENRY HARVEY, 1950

If I had as much health as

zeal, I should go myself to

present to Your Majesty a

work of several years which

I dare offer you from so far;

and I should not suffer any

other hands than mine to

have the honor of bearing it

to the feet of the greatest

princess in the world. This

work, Madame, is a

Cover Letters

The writer of a cover letter—which is merely a device to identify and direct the reader's attention to something enclosed, attached, or sent under separate cover—bears in mind J.M. Barrie's "I do loathe explanations." The enclosure generally speaks for itself. However, even while keeping them simple, deft letterwriters manage to produce messages with a unique spin.

machine for making arith-metical calculations without pen or counters. Your Majesty is not ignorant of the cost of time and pains of ... ductions, above all when the inventors wish to bring them themselves to their highest perfection; this is why it would be useless to say how much I have labored upon this one, and I cannot better express myself than by saying that I have devoted myself to it with as

John O'Hara to his editor at the <u>New Yorker</u>, William Maxwell, 1939:

Dear William:

These pieces and a slice of raw onion will bring tears to your eyes. I want all three to be purchased immediately and check in full sent airmail special delivery, and no two ways about it. . . .

Happy new happy new happy new YEAR!

> PUREGOLD O'HARA,
> A Literary Toy
> for the Mind

Alexander Woollcott to Marian Stoll, January 21, 1942:

Dear Marian,

Under separate cover (which has always been our life in a nutshell) I have sent you two packs of playing cards because:

(a) you said you wanted some

(b) these, which were given me for Xmas, are not the kind I like and

(c) they can be washed with soap and water.

Personally I prefer washing my hands instead of the cards. I never soil cards because my hands are always pure, like my thoughts.

> Your old playmate,
> Alexander Woollcott

Charles Dickens to George Cruikshank, September 17, 1838:

My Dear Cruikshank,
      Will you look over this paper, and see if you like the subject?
      There is no Kidd in Ainsworth's book.
      I know you like short letters.
                       Faithfully yours,

King Henry VIII to Sir William Paget, December 4, 1542:

      Trusty and right well beloved, we greet you well. And herewithall we send unto you the copy of a declaration, which we have caused to be made and published to the world touching the grounds and causes of the war now open between us and Scotland. . . .

Frank Lloyd Wright to Rose Pauson, September 25, 1939:

My dear Miss Pauson:
      Here is a set of revised plans which I trust you will find as you want them. I've made the house a little larger all through—especially the bedrooms. We are ready to go. Are you? Please say when as the boys are "raring to go."
                       Sincerely,
                       Frank Lloyd Wright

Thornton Wilder to Gertrude Stein and Alice B. Toklas, February 7, 1936:

Dear Gertrude; dear Alicia:
> Just a word to enclose these letters for your file.
> No news here. . . .
> This is only a covering-letter and now squeaks to a close.
> Tout mon coeur,

> > > > T.N.

Charlotte Brontë to Thomas de Quincey, June 16, 1847:

Sir,
> My relatives, Ellis and Acton Bell, and myself, heedless of the repeated warnings of various respectable publishers, have committed the rash act of printing a volume of poems.
>
> The consequences predicted have, of course, overtaken us: our book is found to be a drug; no man needs it or heeds it. In the space of a year our publisher has disposed of but two copies, and by what painful efforts he succeeded in getting rid of these two, himself only knows.
>
> Before transferring the edition to the trunkmakers, we have decided on distributing as presents a few copies of what we cannot sell; and we beg to offer you one in acknowledgment of the pleasure and profit we have often and long derived from your works.
>
> I am, sir, yours very respectfully,

> > > > Currer Bell

Federico García Lorca to Sebastián Gasch, September 1928:

My dear Sebastián:

Enclosed are the two poems. I hope you like them. They answer to my new *spiritualist* manner, pure disembodied emotion, detached from logical control but—careful! careful!—with a tremendous poetic logic. It is not surrealism—careful!—the clearest self-awareness illuminates them. . . .

Adiós, Sebastián. Here's an affectionate hug from

Federico

Blaise Pascal to Queen Christina, 1650:

Madame,

If I had as much health as zeal, I should go myself to present to Your Majesty a work of several years which I dare offer you from so far; and I should not suffer any other hands than mine to have the honor of bearing it to the feet of the greatest princess in the world. This work, Madame, is a machine for making arithmetical calculations without pen or counters. Your Majesty is not ignorant of the cost of time and pains of new productions, above all when the inventors wish to bring them themselves to their highest perfection; this is why it would be useless to say how much I have labored upon this one, and I cannot better express myself than by saying that I have devoted myself to it with as much ardor as though I had foreseen that it would one day appear before so august a person. . . .

*C*atherine the Great to Voltaire, December 6, 1768:

Sir,

> . . . I would very much like to send you some verses in return for yours; but he who lacks brains to write good verse does better to work with his hands. That is what I have done. I have made a snuff-box, which I beg you to accept. It bears the image of someone who has the greatest respect for you; I do not need to name her, you will easily recognize her. . . .

Catherine

> P.S. I take up my pen again to beg you to use the fur-coat herewith enclosed, for protection against the north wind and the chill Alpine weather, which, I have been told, trouble you from time to time. . . .

*F*elix Mendelssohn to Friedrich Wilhelm IV, King of Prussia, October 17, 1847:

Your Royal Majesty,

> I am taking the liberty of laying with the utmost reverence the enclosed first copy of the score to my *Elijah* at your feet. It seems to me as if it were not only the deepest and innermost gratitude which makes this my duty, but as if I had no other means of proving to Your Majesty how continually I strive to be more and more worthy of all the generosity Your Majesty has shown me. . . .
>
> With deepest reverence, Your Majesty's most humble servant,

Felix Mendelssohn Bartholdy

John O'Hara to Albert Erskine, February 6, 1968:

Dear Albert:

The title of the forthcoming collection is *And Other Stories*. Here is the Foreword. The stories will be along later.

I think the title is so good that maybe it would be a good idea to institute a title search in case someone else has used it.

I am going to dedicate it to Bennett, as follows:

To Bennett Cerf

An Amiable Man

I will let you convey the news to him. I can't bear to see a grown man cry.

*W*e do not precisely enjoy liberty at the Figaro. M. de Latouche, our worthy *director (ha! you should know the fellow)*, is always hanging over us, cutting, pruning, right or wrong, imposing upon us his whims, his aberrations, his fancies, and we have to write as he bids.

GEORGE SAND, LETTER TO JULES BOUCOIRAN, 1831

You have a man in your employ that I have thought for a long time should be fired. I refer to Sherwood Anderson. He is a fellow of a good deal of ability but for a long time I have been convinced that his heart is not in his work. There is no question but that this man Anderson has in some ways

Letters Dealing with Employment

Work-related letters are so numerous that devoting only one chapter to them deserves an apology. Apologies. However, the letters here cover aspects of the work world ranging from job applications (Albert Schweitzer and Franz Schubert) to letters of resignation (Sherwood Anderson and Felix Mendelssohn). There are letters complaining about work, inquiries about a certain kind of work, as well as a report on an odd situation—an "election by poundings" (St. Teresa of Avila).

Sherwood Anderson to Bayard Barton, June 25, 1918:

Dear Barton:

You have a man in your employ that I have thought for a long time should be fired. I refer to Sherwood Anderson. He is a fellow of a good deal of ability but for a long time I have been convinced that his heart is not in his work. There is no question but that this man Anderson has in some ways been an ornament to our organization. His hair, for one thing, being long and mussy gives an artistic carelessness to his personal appearance that somewhat impresses such men as Frank Lloyd Wright and Mr. Curtiniez of Kalamazoo when they come into the office. But Anderson is not really productive, as I have said, his heart is not in his work. I think he should be fired, and if you will not do the job, I should like permission to fire him myself. I, therefore, suggest that Anderson be asked to sever his connections with the company on August 1st. He is a nice fellow. We will let him down easy, but let's can him.

Respectfully submitted,
Sherwood Anderson

George Orwell to his agent, Leonard Moore, November 19, 1932:

Dear Mr. Moore,

Many thanks for your letter. . . . As to a pseudonym, a name I always use when tramping etc. is P.S. Burton, but if you don't think this sounds a probable kind of name, what about
Kenneth Miles,
George Orwell,
H. Lewis Allways.
I rather favor George Orwell. . . .

Yours sincerely,
Eric A. Blair

Gertrude Stein to Thornton Wilder, September 10, 1936:

My dear Thornton,

I just read in this morning's paper that Wodehouse says that they give him $104,000 for doing nothing at Hollywood they keep him there but they do not use what they ask him to do, now that would just suit us fine . . . of course we are not valuable like he is, but for considerable less we would write dialogue and titles that they do not want to use, not at all do we insist that they use our works printed or unprinted not at all, we just want to run around and do nothing and be paid largely for it . . . so keep your eyes and ears open, if they want us we will come. . . .

Gtde.

Theodore Roosevelt, Civil Service Commissioner, to N.B. Pearce, June 3, 1892:

Sir:

In answer to your letter asking why your son was not appointed when Mr. Stark, his former teacher, was, and stating that in your opinion the examination was a farce, and that the appointment was given Mr. Stark and refused your son because the former was a Republican and the latter a Democrat, I have the honor to say that your letter is the first intimation the Commission has received as to the politics of either of the candidates. Mr. Stark was appointed in '88, while Mr. Cleveland was President. It is therefore quite obvious that he could not have been appointed because he was a Republican. He had an average of 88. Your son had an average of 75, which is low. The examination would indeed be a farce if a man passing it poorly had as good a chance as a man who passed it very well. During the time your son was on the Arkansas register no man was appointed with as low an average as he had. . . .

Felix Mendelssohn to Joseph von Fuchsius, October 12, 1834:

Your Excellency,

I must ask you, much as it grieves me to do so, to kindly relieve me of my duties as director of church music until circumstances allow for the appointment of a different organist to the one who rendered his services for today's mass at the Maximilianskirche. His incompetence makes impossible any successful performance, and it is thus so unpleasant for me to see the efforts of the other performers and of myself go entirely to waste that I hope you will graciously grant my request.

With utmost respect your most faithful
Felix Mendelssohn Bartholdy

Raymond Chandler to Charles Morton, associate editor at The Atlantic Monthly, *December 12, 1945:*

Dear Charles:

I've owed you a letter for so damn long that I suppose you wonder whether I'm still alive. So do I, at times. Before I delve into your two letters to see if there are any questions you wanted replies to, let me report that my blast at Hollywood ["Writers in Hollywood," *The Atlantic Monthly*, November 1945] was received here in frozen silence. . . . My agent was told by the Paramount story editor that it had done me a lot of harm with the producers at Paramount. Charlie Brackett, that fading wit, said: "Chandler's books are not good enough, nor his pictures bad enough, to justify that article." I wasted a little time trying to figure out what that meant. It seems to mean that the only guy who can speak his mind about Hollywood is either (a) a failure in Hollywood, or (b) a celebrity somewhere else. I would reply to Mr. Brackett that if my books had been any worse, I should not have been invited to Hollywood, and that if they had been any better, I should not have come. . . .

Franz Schubert to Francis II, 1826:

Your Majesty! Most gracious Emperor!

With the deepest submission the undersigned humbly begs Your Majesty graciously to bestow upon him the vacant position of Vice-Kapellmeister to the Court, and supports his application with the following qualifications:

(1) The undersigned was born in Vienna, is the son of a school-teacher, and is 29 years of age.

(2) He enjoyed the privilege of being for five years a Court Chorister at the Imperial and Royal College School.

(3) He received a complete course of instruction in Composition from the late Chief Kapellmeister to the Court, Herr Anton Salieri, and is fully qualified, therefore, to fill any post as Kapellmeister.

(4) His name is well known, not only in Vienna but throughout Germany, as a composer of songs and instrumental music.

(5) He has also written and arranged five Masses for both smaller and larger orchestras, and these have already been performed in various churches in Vienna.

(6) Finally, he is at the present time without employment, and hopes in the security of a permanent position to be able to realize at last those high musical aspirations which he has ever kept before him.

Should Your Majesty be graciously pleased to grant this request, the undersigned would strive to the utmost to give full satisfaction. . . .

Mari Sandoz to Alfred R. McIntyre, President, Little, Brown & Company, August 30, 1940:

Dear Mr. McIntyre:

Regarding your letter of August 28:

You can hold me to your option on my next book, but so long as you do, there will be no next one. . . .

Albert Schweitzer to the Reverend Alfred Boegner, director of the Paris Mission Society, July 9, 1905:

Dear Reverend and Colleague,

I am writing you today to inquire whether you might need someone for the Congo. I would be delighted to place myself at your disposal.

Allow me to introduce myself and to describe my qualifications. I have a doctorate in philosophy and a *license* in theology. I am the preacher at the Church of St. Nicholas, the supervisor of studies at the School of St. Thomas, and a lecturer at the theological faculty. I am thirty years old.

My plan to become a missionary is no sudden whim. I used to dream about it even in my childhood. . . . During my lectures I keep telling myself: Others could perform this job just as well as you can. You could easily be replaced here, but there is a shortage of people over there! . . .

Louisa May Alcott to her publishers, December 28, 1869:

Many thanks for the check which made my Christmas an unusually merry one.

After toiling so many years along the uphill road—always a hard one to women writers—it is peculiarly grateful to me to find the way growing easier at last, with pleasant little surprises blossoming on either side, and the rough places made smooth by the courtesy and kindness of those who have proved themselves friends as well as publishers.

With best wishes for the coming year,

Paul Cézanne to Victor Chocquet, January 28, 1879:

My dear Monsieur Chocquet,

May I ask you to be kind enough to get some information for me?. . . . I should like to know how to set about having a picture reach the administration of the Beaux Arts for the purpose of submitting it to the approval of the jury, and then if, as I am afraid, the picture is rejected whether the kind administration will undertake to return the above-mentioned work of art to its author. . . .

Teresa of Avila to Madre María de San José, October 1577:

. . . I must tell your Reverence about something which has been happening here at the Incarnation, the like of which, I should think, has never been seen before. On the order of Tostado, the Provincial of the Calced came here a fortnight ago to conduct the election, and threatened all those who voted for me with severe reprimands and excommunication. But, in spite of all that, they took no notice, and fifty-five of the nuns voted for me just as though he had said no such thing. And as each of them handed the Provincial her vote he excommunicated her, and abused her, and pounded the voting-papers with his fist and struck them and burned them. And for exactly a fortnight he has left these nuns without Communion and forbidden them to hear Mass or enter the choir even when the Divine office is not being said. And nobody is allowed to speak to them, not even their confessor or their own parents. And the most amusing thing is that, on the day after this election by poundings, the Provincial summoned these nuns to a fresh election; to which they replied that there was no need to hold another as they had held one already. On hearing this, he excommunicated them again. . . .

Learned men declare that they are not excommunicated at all and that the friars are going against the council in declaring anyone elected prioress who has a minority of votes. The nuns who voted for me have sent to tell Tostado that they want me to be Prioress. He says no; I can go and live quietly at the Incarnation if I like but they cannot tolerate me as Prioress. I don't know how it will end. . . .

Y ou deserve a longer letter than this;
but it is my unhappy fate seldom to
treat people so well as they deserve.

JANE AUSTEN, LETTER TO HER SISTER CASSANDRA, 1798

I do want you to be quite sure that I am all right. I am sorry that I was not allowed to write to you sooner, but I was all right during the first ten days too. Strangely enough, the discomforts that one generally associates with prison life, the physical hardships, hardly bother me at all.

Letters to Family

One can even have enough to eat in the mornings with dry bread (I get a variety of extras too). . . . A violent mental upheaval such as is produced by a sudden arrest brings with it the need to take one's mental bearings and come to terms with an entirely new situation—all this means that physical things take a back seat and lose their importance, and it is something that I find to be a real enrichment of my

In another letter, Jane tells Cassandra, "You cannot write too often." That is almost always true of letters to family. The best ones display a gift for making intriguing reading out of everyday events. Jane wrote Cassandra, "We met . . . Dr. Hall in such very deep mourning that either his mother, his wife, or himself must be dead." Lady Mary Wortley Montagu had a less dependable correspondence with her sister; the complaint in her letter was one of many.

Theodore Roosevelt, that inveterate letterwriter, was twenty years old when he wrote the note in this chapter, but his boyish style lasted as long as his mother lived (he also called her "Darling Little Pet," "Darling Little Muffie," and "Darling Motherling").

Lady Mary Wortley Montagu to her sister the Countess of Mar,
December 25, 1722:

> I have writ to you at least five-and-forty letters, dear sister,
> without receiving any answer, and resolved not to confide in post-
> house fidelity any more; being firmly persuaded that they never came
> to your hands, or you would not refuse one line to let me know how
> you do, which is and ever will be of great importance to me. . . .

Hannah Whitall Smith to her daughter Mary Berenson, January 1, 1905:

> I *shall* be glad to see thee back, daughter, for I miss thee dread-
> fully. I wish I did not! I was taking a nap in my chair today, and I thought
> I heard thee rustling thy papers, and I looked over at thy table expecting to
> see thee, and alas! thee was not there, and it was dreadful. . . .

George Eliot to her stepdaughter Elma Stuart, November 19, 1875:

> Dearest Elma,
> I am too busy to write a letter. This is not a letter—it is a wail
> at your silence. How can you leave your parent so long in ignorance
> about you?. . .
> Write me a few words at least, to assure me that you are well—
> that Roland is causing you no anxiety—that all things are peaceful with
> you.
> We long to have some assurance that you love us still. But
> whether or not, I am as ever,
>
> > Your faithfully affectionate
> > Mother

Franz Kafka to his sister Ottilie, February 1, 1919:

Dear Ottla,

Last night, at midnight between January 31 and February 1, I woke at about five and heard you at the door of the room calling "Franz," softly, but I heard it distinctly. I answered at once but nothing more happened. What did you want?

George Armstrong Custer, last letter to his wife Elizabeth Custer, from camp at the junction of the Yellowstone and Rosebud rivers, Montana Territory, June 22, 1876:

My Darling,

I have but a few moments to write as we start at twelve, and I have my hands full of preparations for the scout. Do not be anxious about me. You would be surprised how closely I obey your instructions about keeping with the column. I hope to have a good report to send you by the next mail. . . .

Your devoted boy Autie

Lillian Carter to her daughter Gloria Carter Spann, c. 1967:

I had four letters yesterday from different people. All of them said, "I guess Gloria wrote you about what happened to Dan." Then a letter from you—no mention of Dan. Dan who? A bird? A plane? A man? A dog? I have thought of every Dan I ever knew and can't figure which one! What happened to him? Did his wife shoot him? Did he drown? Wreck his car? Break his leg? Catch a fish? Get bit by a dog? For God's sake—what happened to Dan, whoever or whatever he is???

*E*dna St. Vincent Millay to her mother Cora B. Millay, July 21, 1921:

Dearest Mother,

You do write the sweetest and the most wonderful letters! They are so lovely that very often I read parts of them aloud to people, just as literature. . . .

With all the love of my heart,
Vincent

P.S. Do you suppose, when you and I are dead, dear, they will publish the *Love Letters of Edna St. Vincent Millay and Her Mother?*

*V*áclav Havel to his wife Olga Havel, June 4, 1979:

Dear Olga,

It appears the astrologers were right when they predicted prison for me again this year and when they said the summer would be a hot one. As a matter of fact, it's stifling hot here, like being in a perpetual sauna. I feel sorry about the many complications my new stint in jail will probably cause you. . . . Prison as such is, of course, a terrible bore; it's no fun staring at the walls day after day, but with each stay I find it easier to bear because a lot that I once found disturbing no longer surprises or upsets me. What bothers me the most is the thought that some people outside might be harassed on my account. . . . If you send me a parcel, make it the usual: powdered juice, lemons, cheese slices, cigars, a little instant cocoa and so on. And above all, write me a lot; you know how important every scrap of information is here, even news about how our lawn is surviving the dry spell. . . .

Kisses,
Vašek

Paul Laurence Dunbar to his mother Matilda Dunbar, May 4, 1893:

Dear Mother:

It is now half past eleven but it is with pleasure I sit down to answer your welcome letter which I received on getting home this evening. The flowers came this morning all in good condition and I was so thankful for them. It was so thoughtful of you to send them, Ma, knowing how I had longed to see those bushes in bloom. But that's just like my own little mother. . . .

Amelia Earhart to her mother, to be opened in case of her death, May 20, 1928:

Even though I have lost, the adventure was worth while. Our family tends to be too secure. My life has really been very happy, and I didn't mind contemplating its end in the midst of it.

Dietrich Bonhoeffer to his parents, April 14, 1943:

My dear Parents,

I do want you to be quite sure that I am all right. I am sorry that I was not allowed to write to you sooner, but I was all right during the first ten days too. Strangely enough, the discomforts that one generally associates with prison life, the physical hardships, hardly bother me at all. One can even have enough to eat in the mornings with dry bread (I get a variety of extras too). . . . A violent mental upheaval such as is produced by a sudden arrest brings with it the need to take one's mental bearings and come to terms with an entirely new situation—all this means that physical things take a back seat and lose their importance, and it is something that I find to be a real enrichment of my experience. I am not so unused to being alone as other people are, and it is certainly a good spiritual Turkish bath. The only thing that bothers me or would bother me is the thought that you are being tormented by anxiety about me, and are not sleeping or eating properly. Forgive me for causing you so much worry. . . .

Meriwether Lewis to his mother Lucy Marks, June 2, 1803:

Dear Mother,

The day after tomorrow I shall set out for the Western Country; I had calculated on the pleasure of visiting you before my departure but circumstances have rendered this impossible; my absence will probably be equal to fifteen or eighteen months; the nature of this expedition is by no means dangerous . . . therefore consider the chances of life just as much in my favor on this trip as I should conceive them were I to remain at home for the same length of time; the charge of this expedition is as honorable to myself as it is important to my country. For its fatigues I feel myself perfectly prepared, nor do I doubt my health and strength of constitution to bear me through it; I go with the most perfect preconviction in my own mind of returning safe and hope therefore that you will not suffer yourself to indulge any anxiety for my safety. . . .

Paula Modersohn-Becker to her sister Milly Rohland-Becker, May 1906:

I'm becoming somebody—I'm living the most intensely happy period of my life. Pray for me. Send me sixty francs for models' fees. Thank you.

Never lose faith in me.

Your Paula

Jane Austen to her sister Cassandra, September 1, 1796:

My dearest Cassandra,

The letter which I have this moment received from you has diverted me beyond moderation. I could die of laughter at it, as they used to say at school. You are indeed the finest comic writer of the present age. . . .

I am very affectionately yours,

Empress Josephine to her daughter Queen Hortense of Holland, July 15, 1806:

Since you left I have been ill, sad, and unhappy; I have even been feverish and have had to keep to my bed. I am now well again, but my sorrow remains. How could it be otherwise when I am separated from a daughter like you, loving, gentle, and amiable, who was the charm of my life?. . . How is your husband? Are my grandchildren well? Heavens, how sad it makes me not to see them! and how is your health, dear Hortense? If you are ever ill, let me know, and I will hasten to you at once. . . . Goodbye, my dear Hortense, think often of your mother, and be sure that never was a daughter more loved than you are. Many kind messages to your husband; kiss the children for me. . . .

Theodore Roosevelt to his mother Martha Bulloch Roosevelt, October 8, 1878:

Darling, beloved, little Motherling,

I have just *loved* your dear, funny pathetic little letter; and I am now going to write you the longest letter I ever wrote—and if it is still rather short, you must recollect that it takes Teddy-boy a long time to write. . . .

With best love to all I am *Your Loving Son,*

Fanny Longfellow to her sister-in-law Anne Longfellow Pierce, January 17, 1844:

Dear Anne,

. . . I referred above to my health in a way which may puzzle you. I will explain myself by informing you then, in plain terms, of what you have a right to know, viz., that somewhere between May and June I hope to give you a little nephew or niece, for you to exercise all your auntly capacities of affection and interest upon. You can read our hearts, although so much separated from us, and therefore need not to be told how grateful we feel to God for this promised addition to our happiness.

J.R.R. Tolkien to his son Christopher Tolkien, October 25, 1944:

Dearest man,

Here is a little more of "the Ring" for your delectation (I hope) and criticism. . . . Two more chapters to complete the "Fourth Book" and then I hope to finish the "Fifth" and last of the Ring. I have written a long airletter today, and shall write again (of course) before your birthday. I am afraid this little packet won't get to you in time for it. . . . God bless you, beloved. Do you think "The Ring" will come off, and reach the thirsty?

Your own Father

Marjorie Fleming, age 6, to her mother, 1809:

My Dear Mud,

I hope you are well: give my love to Isa and Baby, and I will send them something. I have been often at Ravelstone and once at Aunt Fleming and Mrs. Miller. I've been acquainted with many very genteel girls, and Janetta is a fine one. . . .

I saw the most prettyist two tame pidgeons you ever saw and two very wee small kittens like our cat.

I am very much acquainted with a young gentleman called Mordecai that I am quite in love with, another called Captain Bell, and Jamie Keith, and Willie's my great tormentor.

A good-natured girl gave me a song book, and I am very happy.

I'll go down and be thinking when I'm eating my dinner more to tell you, Mud. . . .

Remember your dear Madgie.

Amen.

Finis.

M.F. Six years old.

Karen Blixen to her mother Ingeborg Dinesen, October 25, 1921:

My own beloved Mother,

. . . I am going to beg you, dearest Mother, not to write to me any more concerning my marriage or Bror. Of course I know you do it with the best intentions; but sometimes even things done in this spirit can fail, and what costs you effort and pain to write, costs me effort and pain to read, and I do not think anything is gained by it other than my realization of how little you understand me. . . . My little Mother, you must not think that I am writing in anger or bitterness; but I think that this is the reason for even *you* writing as you do, and I do so deeply wish that it would stop. . . .

There are two things that none of you understand: how different from you I am and always have been. What makes me happy or unhappy is completely different from what makes you happy or unhappy. . . . You must not think this is written out of hard-heartedness. I would really rather leave it alone; but it *cannot* be avoided when you write as you do, and I think that you have written things to me now that have hurt me still more, and this is the only way that I can think of to put a stop to it from both sides. . . .

Goodnight, my above all else beloved Mother,

Your Tanne

Friedrich Nietzsche to his mother Franziska Nietzsche, October 18, 1887:

My dear Mother:

Your letter, arriving on my birthday, found me doing a thing which would have pleased you: I was writing a little letter to the South American Lama [his sister Elisabeth]. Your letter and birthday greetings were, by the way, the only ones that I received, which gives me a good idea of the "independence" to which I have now attained; the latter is the *foremost condition* for a philosopher. . . .

With warmest and most grateful greetings,
your old creature

Friedrich Nietzsche to his sister Elisabeth Nietzsche, December 1888:

My sister:

I received your letter, and after reading it several times I see that I am compelled to part company with you for ever. Now that my destiny is certain, I feel every word of yours with tenfold sharpness; you have not the remotest conception of what it means to be most closely related to the man and to the destiny in whom the question of millennia has been decided—I hold, quite literally, the future of mankind in the palm of my hand. . . . I play with the burden which would crush any other mortal. . . . For what I have to do is *terrible*, in any sense of the word; I do not challenge individuals—I am challenging humanity as a whole with my terrible accusation; whichever way the decision may go, *for* me or *against* me, in any case there attaches to my name a quantity of doom that is beyond telling. . . .

In asking you, with all my heart, not to see any hardness in this letter, but the reverse—a real humanity, which is trying to prevent any unnecessary damage—I ask you, over and above this necessity, to keep on loving me.

Your brother

Jean Rhys to her granddaughter Ellen Ruth Moerman, January 11, 1960:

My darling Ruthie,

I was so very pleased to get your Christmas card. Which do you play? Violin or piano? Piano isn't it? I used to long ago. One night when I was about your age I played at a concert and was so nervous before I started. Then when I had finished without mishap I was very pleased. I can remember it now—the lights, and the people clapping and the palm trees, for this was of course in the West Indies. I do hope you aren't too cold in Holland. I imagine you skating in a fur cap and a little muff to keep your hands warm. But I expect that's imagination so I will add a bright red coat to make my picture complete. . . .

Hugs and a big kiss from
Ooma

Theodore Roosevelt to his mother-in-law Gertrude Elizabeth Tyler Carow, October 18, 1890:

My dear Mrs. Carow,

I have rarely seen Edith enjoy anything more than she did the six days at my ranch, and the trip through the Yellowstone Park; and she looks just as well and young and pretty and happy as she did four years ago when I married her—indeed I sometimes almost think she looks if possible even sweeter and prettier, and she is as healthy as possible, and so young looking and slender to be the mother of those two sturdy little scamps, Ted and Kermit. . . .

The children are darlings. Alice has grown more and more affectionate, and is devoted to, and worshipped by, both the boys; Kermie holds out his little arms to her whenever she comes near, and she really takes care of him like a little mother. Ted eyes him with some suspicion; and when I take the wee fellow up in my arms Ted clings tightly to one of my legs, so that I can hardly walk. Kermie crawls with the utmost rapidity; and when he is getting towards some forbidden spot and we call to him to stop Ted always joins in officiously and overtaking the small yellow-haired wanderer seizes him with his chubby hands round the neck and tries to drag him back—while the enraged Kermie endeavors in vain to retaliate. . . .

Samuel Johnson to his dying mother, January 16, 1759:

Dear honored Mother,

Your weakness afflicts me beyond what I am willing to communicate to you. I do not think you unfit to face death, but I know not how to bear the thought of losing you. Endeavor to do all you can for yourself. Eat as much as you can.

I pray often for you; do you pray for me. I have nothing to add to my last letter.

I am, dear, dear mother,
Your dutiful son,
Sam. Johnson

Helen Hunt Jackson to her husband William Sharpless Jackson, March 29, 1885:

Dearest,

I am sure I am not going to get well and I want to bid you goodbye while my mind is clear.

At first, I did not want to die. I would have liked to do a few more of the things that I had planned—but now I am more than willing. It is of no consequence about the few words more I could say. If *Ramona* and *The Century of Dishonor* have not helped—one more would have made little odds. But they *will* tell in the long run. The thought of this is my only consolation as I look back over the last ten years and realize how I have failed to be to you what I longed and hoped to be. But it is not too late yet, my beloved, for you to have wife and children and live the life that will satisfy your longings.

It is the greatest hope of my heart that you will desire to marry our Helen. She will make you a pure devoted loving wife and a splendid mother for your children and will meet your wishes and views far better than I have done. I have left her the bulk of my property, feeling that it would be wrong for me to let my grandfather's money go away from his heirs, and that you do not need it. I hope you will think this was right. If you marry Helen, it will be a happiness to me, in whatever world I am in, to see her and her children heirs to all I had. If you do not feel drawn to her, let me implore you, darling, to marry some one else *very soon*. Do not live the life of a homeless tieless man any longer than you must, but be *sure*, this time, dearest, to marry some one whose tastes and standards in all matters of living are like your own— don't make a second mistake, love. You will wonder I can write so calmly of this. I am writing as if I spoke to you from another world. Will, you have never known how deep my realization has been of the fact that I was not the *right* wife for you—much as I have loved you. With a different woman and with children at your knees, you would have been a different man—and a happier one. . . . I am glad to go for your sake, my beloved one. Forgive every pain and vexation I have ever given you, and only remember that I loved you as few men are ever loved. In this world, *nobody* will ever love you so well. . . .

Your Peggy

Claude A. Barnett and Etta M. Barnett to Maria Barnett Tinnin, October 14, 1954:

Dear Maria Barnett Tinnin:

Your grandmother and I send you the warmest sort of welcome. We are so glad you came to join our family circle. Both of us are anxious to see you and will do so at the very earliest moment. . . .

As I think of all the little girls of our hue who come into the world, I am especially happy for you. You have been born to two parents who will love and cherish you, who will surround you not only with affection but with their brilliance of mind and infinite charm of personality.

They will guide you in paths which will make your life one of happiness and beauty and offside your grandmother and grandfather and all your other relatives will be praying that only that which is good and lovely may ever traverse your path.

Welcome again and tell your broad-shouldered Brother Freeman that we give him the special trust of looking after you.

With all our love,

Your Grandma and Grandpa

George Sand to Alexandre Dumas Fils, on the birth of her grandson, July 14, 1863:

Marc-Antoine Sand was born this morning, the anniversary of the taking of the Bastille. He is big and strong and he looked me in the eyes with an attentive and deliberate air when I received him all warm into my apron. I think we know each other already and he looked as if he wanted to say to me: "Hullo. There you are!" He was dipped into a bath of Bordeaux wine in which he kicked about with marked satisfaction. . . . Rejoice with us . . . and come and see us soon.

G. Sand

Marjorie Kinnan Rawlings to her ex-husband Charles A. Rawlings, Jr., November 11, 1933:

Dear Chuck:

The divorce was granted yesterday—

You're free as the wind, big boy, and I hope you'll make the most of it. . . .

Had a frightfully nice letter from your mother, in answer to mine—glad she and I can go our ways with mutual respect and affection.

Hope you get your mail all right. . . .

Let me know when you want your odds & ends.

Best of luck—and hope your material is pouring out nicely.

Marjorie

Frederic Chopin to his family, August 12, 1829:

You know from my last letter, dearest Parents, that I have been persuaded to give a concert. So yesterday, that is, Tuesday evening at 7, in the Imperial-and-Royal Opera-house, I made my entry into the world!. . . As soon as I appeared on the stage, the bravos began; after each variation the applause was so loud that I couldn't hear the orchestra's *tutti*. When I finished, they clapped so much that I had to come out and bow a second time. . . . When I come home, I'll tell you more about it than I can write; but you need have no anxiety for me and my reputation. . . .

Maria Edgeworth to Miss Beaufort, soon to be her stepmother, May 16, 1798:

Whilst you, my dear Miss Beaufort, have been toiling in Dublin, my father has been delighting himself in preparations for June. The little boudoir looks as if it intends to be pretty. This is the only room in the house which my father will allow to be finished, as he wishes that your taste should finish the rest. . . .

You call yourself, dear Miss Beaufort, my friend and companion; I hope you will never have reason to repent beginning in this style towards me. I think you will not find me encroach upon you. The overflowings of your kindness, if I know anything of my own heart, will fertilize the land, but will not destroy the landmarks. . . . You need not, dear Miss Beaufort, fence yourself round with very strong palings in this family, where all have been early accustomed to mind their boundaries. As for me, you see my intentions, or at least my theories, are good enough; if my practice be but half as good, you will be content, will you not? . . .

John James Audubon to his wife Lucy Audubon, May 19, 1833:

My Dearest Friend,

I had the pleasure of receiving thy own dear letter of the 12th instant today; I was fretting in real earnest at not hearing from thee, for now in almost complete state of idleness I find the days and *the nights* more particularly sadly too long without thy company—

I have no news to relate—we have drawn one bird only, and although we have searched diligently for more, no more have we met with. . . . God bless thee my sweet wife and preserve us all to the completion at least of our great work.

> Good night, my Love
> Thine Friend and Husband,
> John J. Audubon

Rudyard Kipling to his daughter Elsie, July 29, 1908:

My dear Miss Kipling,

Your Little Brother returned from school yesterday. I repaired to Rottingdean in the Motor via Brighton stopping at the Queen of Watering Places to pay a pleasant and instructive visit to a Dentist of my acquaintance who kindly walked round my Beaming Smile with spanners, wrenches, thumbscrews and similar pleasant tools.

At 3:30 p.m. I reached Master Kipling's seminary and found your Poor Brother dissolved in tears at the thought of parting with his Dearly Loved Companions, his affectionate Matron and his Respected Head Master. When his sobs had abated somewhat, he flung himself at Mrs. Stanford's feet and pleaded most eloquently to be allowed to Remain and pursue his studies—if necessary on Bread and Water! Such were his simple words. I carried him, still weeping, to the house of Lady Burne-Jones where at 4:15 p.m. he made a Delicate Tea of not more than six or seven slices of Bread and Butter, several hot tea-cakes and a few pounds of chocolate cake. At 5 he consented to get into the motor and with many a regretful glance at St. Aubyns (the home of so many pleasant Reminiscences) I carried him away, the prey of uncontrollable emotion. Seldom have I seen one so young so loath to revisit his Ancestral home. He complained that no time would now be allowed him to continue his studies in Latin and Mathematics—the objects of his deepest interest. He further stated that his sister was a Slacker and at Lewes (his sobs being less frequent) staggered to the Post Office to send her a telegram to this effect.

(The true version)

The young imp sang nearly all the way home and struck up "The church's one foundation" at the head of Lewes High Street! I had to remind him it wasn't the Heathfield road! When we got home he ran about till he got the bat and stumps and made me bowl to him. He sat up to dinner 7:30 and went to bed at 8:30 about as blissfully happy a young mortal as I've ever seen. He is now (9 a.m.) rampaging round my room, after having washed out my old stilo, wondering what he shall do next. I foresee my days will be evil and hectic 'til you come back. I am trying to get him to send you a few lines but he shies off the subject. He has all his exam papers with him which he wants Miss Blaikie to look at.

Now he has hauled up a chair to my table and says he will write to you. Oh Lor! Don't you *ever* be a father, my Bird. He's shaking my table like an earthquake!

With love,
Dad

Henry Wadsworth Longfellow to his sister Anne Longfellow Pierce, October 15, 1839:

My dear Annie,

To tell the truth, I was a little surprised to get so long a letter from you, knowing your various occupations. It does you the more credit, and I reply in an unusually short space of time, for me, as you will bear witness. The chief news I have to write are very disagreeable news to me; namely, that I am growing corpulent (you know my amiable weakness)—and consequently unhappy. I have the most entire aversion to rotundity. You shall judge for yourself next week, as I intend to come. . . .

Affectionately yours,
Henry

It is now eight days since I asked you to send me ten burnt lakes no. 7 and I have had no reply. What is the matter? Let me have an answer and as quickly as possible, please.

PAUL CÉZANNE, LETTER TO AN ARTISTS' SUPPLY SHOP, 1906

Your mother says she does not know what engagements you have but she wishes you might come & persuade Will to come & dine with her on Monday at 3:30 & bring your babies, if you will. She has invited Aunt Elizabeth & I believe Mr. Hotham of Walden Pond, to her quasi Christmas mince pie on that day, &, I *fancy, Mr. Channing. She does not wish to give her fete any importance in your eyes, in case it should be inconvenient to you, but it would gratify her much.*

Follow-up Letters

She adds that you need not come till the 2:15 train, for she does not need aid.

F
ollow-up letters, which are usually brief and specific, include reminders, second requests, or thoughts that occurred to the writer after mailing the first letter. Lincoln, always a model of brevity, outdoes himself in his letter in this chapter. Emerson's second letter to his daughter is a literal example of the follow-up letter.

As some of us are not sure whether my note today

Sometimes letters in the "second requests" category wax a little testy. Nobody likes having to remind others of their promises or, as in Chandler's situation, their manners.

named the right date of Mamma's mince pie, you are to know that it is Monday

Elizabeth Cleghorn Gaskell to George Smith, October 30, 1855:

Dear Sir,

Relying on your promise of putting at my disposal any papers or letters in your possession which might assist me in writing my memoir of Miss Brontë, I wrote to you *ten days* ago to claim its fulfillment; and I have been both surprised and disappointed that so long a time has elapsed without your forwarding me the promised materials.

Believe me, dear Sir,

Yours truly,

Raymond Chandler to William W. Seward, May 27, 1946:

Dear Professor Seward:

Some time ago, at your request, I sent you one of my books. I am wondering if you ever received it. It seems rather curious that you should not have acknowledged it, if it arrived.

I don't exactly know why I am writing this note. It is not a matter of great consequence either way. I suppose I find the incident rather shocking.

Henry Wadsworth Longfellow to Nathaniel Hawthorne, March 19, 1843:

Dearest Hawthornius,

Don't forget that you are to dine with me on Tuesday next—that is to say, the day after tomorrow—at 3 o'clock.

I want very much to see you, and to tell you how truly delighted I was with your last story, "The Birth Mark." Not the comet himself can unfold a more glorious *tail*. . . .

H.W.L.

Theodore Roosevelt, telegram to Jane Addams, August 8, 1912:

Did I put into telegram the flat-footed statement without quali-
fication or equivocation that I was for woman suffrage, that the Progressive Party is for woman suffrage, and that I believe within half a
dozen years we shall have no one in the United States against it. If not,
please insert this, making it as strong as you can, and also wire me if
there is anything further of any kind you wish me to put in.

P.T. Barnum to Spencer F. Baird, June 21, 1884:

Dear Prof. Baird,

I neglected to say in my last letter that my managers & self
think Jumbo's skin or skeleton should go to your institution—you taking your choice, & then the "Barnum" Museum at Tufts College take
the other. That seems under the circumstances to be the way to do the
most good & to best hand down our names.

Truly yours,
P.T. Barnum

P.S. We hope, however, that Jumbo may yet live many years, but think it
as well to decide now as ever where he shall be *distributed* when he
ceases to breathe.

William Faulkner to the Four Seas Company, November 1923:

Some time ago I sent you a book of verse in ms. entitled
"Orpheus, and Other Poems." Will you be kind enough to inform me if
such a ms. was received; and if so, what disposition has been made of
it? I am under the impression that I enclosed postage for its return.

Ralph Waldo Emerson to his daughter Edith Emerson Forbes, December 24, 1868:

Dear Edith,

Your mother says she does not know what engagements you have but she wishes you might come & persuade Will to come & dine with her on Monday at 3:30 & bring your babies, if you will. She has invited Aunt Elizabeth & I believe Mr. Hotham of Walden Pond, to her *quasi* Christmas mince pie on that day, &, I fancy, Mr. Channing. She does not wish to give her fete any importance in your eyes, in case it should be inconvenient to you, but it would gratify her much. She adds that you need not come till the 2:15 train, for she does not need aid.

Later the same day:

Dear Edith,

As some of us are not sure whether my note today named the right date of Mamma's mince pie, you are to know that it is *Monday* at 3:30 that was & remains determined.

RWE

Abraham Lincoln to Hamilton Rowan Gamble, Governor of Missouri, November 15, 1862:

I have not yet been able to get the document but have the Secretary of War hunting for it.

A. Lincoln

George Eliot to John Blackwood, August 16, 1859:

My dear Sir,

When you last wrote to me—about three weeks ago—you mentioned that you should shortly be sending me a check for the second edition of "Scenes of Clerical Life."

I have no doubt the subject has escaped your memory among the many things that claim it, but as it is urged upon mine by the fact that my exchequer is rather low at present, I feel sure you will pardon me for not being patient enough to wait until the matter recurred to you, as it inevitably would before long.

Alexander Woollcott to Harpo Marx, March 24, 1937:

Dear Harpo,

This is the reminder I promised about Helen Keller. She and Polly Thompson will sail April 1st from San Francisco on the *Asamu Maru*. For two days ahead of that they will be at the St. Francis Hotel. If you have it in mind to send flowers, remember that for a blind person one flower that smells like all get out is better than the most costly bouquet which may be merely something to look at. . . .

The Prince Chap

P.S. Come to think of it, Helen would prefer a bottle of bourbon or scotch to a mere bouquet any day.

A.W.

Do let me hear from you even if it's only a twenty-page letter.

GROUCHO MARX, LETTER TO GOODMAN ACE, 1960

Recently I have been corresponding with your daughter. She wrote me a long exuberant letter. In reply I wrote her a short curt note. She then wrote me a letter twice as long as the original one so I gave up and sent her a copy of "War and Peace." This, I hope, will keep her quiet until

Letters to Friends

GeORGE Sand wrote to Gustave Flaubert, "You don't have to write to me if you don't feel like it. There's no real friendship without *absolute* freedom." That sense of freedom—along with affection, good humor, and frankness—seems to define long-running correspondences between mutually supportive and admiring friends.

Friends also have a great deal to say to each other; the last letter in this chapter—the longest letter in the book—is still only an excerpt of its complete gossipy self.

*G*roucho Marx to Arthur Sheekman, December 16, 1954:

Dear Sheek:

Recently I have been corresponding with your daughter. She wrote me a long exuberant letter. In reply I wrote her a short curt note. She then wrote me a letter twice as long as the original one so I gave up and sent her a copy of "War and Peace." This, I hope, will keep her quiet until after the holidays.

I just read in the Reporter that Irving Berlin's bite out of his last two pictures was $1,300,000. Is it any wonder he keeps singing, "There's no business like Show Business"? There is also no business-man like Irving Berlin. Not that I begrudge him this. He is a giant talent worth every nickel he gets. Single-handed, if he were interested, I believe he could pay off the British debt.

I could write you many more items but we're both busy, have very little interest in each other and as I always say, why try to keep a friendship alive that has been dying on the vine for twenty-five years. . . .

Your loving friend,

*G*ertrude Stein to Thornton Wilder, January 10, 1940:

My dearest Thornton,

Oh where oh where are you, not a Christmas greeting not a New Years greeting, shall auld acquaintance be forgot in the glory of a New York residence or are you sick in bed, Thornton where are you. With us it is easy because we are here, we just are, we set before the fire we brave the frosty air, we go in and we go out, we have the visits of all the permissionnaires, we have lots of new friends some nice English among others, and we have just finished our book Paris, France and everybody seems to like it and it will very soon be out but we have no Thornton, where oh where is Thornton, are you on your way over, where is Thornton,

lots of love,
Gtrde

Gustave Flaubert to Ivan Turgenev, 1878:

> You reduce me to *tears*, my good Turgenev. It's not possible to
> be nicer. What a friend I have in you! I embrace you.
> I'll see you tomorrow, won't I?

P. G. Wodehouse to William Townend, January 11, 1946:

> Dear Bill,
> Hooray! The French Government have now assured me official-
> ly and in writing that I am no longer a danger to the Republic. I never
> was, a matter of fact. Actually, I was very fond of the Republic and
> wouldn't have laid a finger on it if you had brought it to me asleep on
> a chair, but they did not know this and I suppose you couldn't blame
> them for feeling nervous. . . .

*Oscar Wilde, telegram to James McNeill Whistler, about an article
in Punch describing them gossiping about Sarah Bernhardt and Miss Anderson,
November 10, 1883:*

> *Punch* too ridiculous. When you and I are together we never
> talk about anything except ourselves.

James McNeill Whistler, telegram to Oscar Wilde, later that day:

> No, no, Oscar, you forget. When you and I are together, we
> never talk about anything except me.

Charles Dickens to Washington Irving, March 21, 1842:

My dear Irving,

We passed through—literally passed through—this place again today. I did not come to see you, for I really have not the heart to say "good-bye" again, and felt more than I can tell you when we shook hands last Wednesday. . . .

Wherever you go, God bless you! What pleasure I have had in seeing and talking with you, I will not attempt to say. I shall never forget it as long as I live. What *would* I give if we could have but a quiet week together! Spain is a lazy place, and its climate an indolent one. But if you have ever leisure under its sunny skies, to think of a man who loves you, and holds communion with your spirit oftener, perhaps, than any other person alive—leisure from listlessness, I mean—and will write to me in London, you will give me an inexpressible amount of pleasure.

Your affectionate friend,

Beatrice Stella Campbell to George Bernard Shaw, November 1, 1912:

. . . Oh dear me—its too late to do anything but *accept* you and *love* you—but when you were quite a little boy somebody ought to have said "hush" just once!

Ernest Hemingway to F. Scott Fitzgerald, December 24, 1925:

Dear Scott:

Have sent the $400 to your concierge. You can keep it yourself or give it to Harold Stearns. You write a swell letter. Glad somebody spells worse than I do. . . .

Yours always,
Yogi Liveright

M.F.K. Fisher to Helen Marshall, March 28, 1973:

Dearest Helen,

. . . I hope you find life more good than bad and that you stay more strong than weak, or at least more up than down. . . . *Really*, it's so hard to say anything sensible to anyone who is fairly elderly and has a bad heart and and and, but you know what I am *trying* to say . . . it all comes down to the basic fact that I want the salt to keep its savor for you.

*K*atherine Mansfield, who suffered from—and died at the age of 35 from—tuber-culosis, to S.S. Kotelianski, April 7, 1919:

I wish you would come in now, this moment, and let us have tea and talk. There is no one here except my cough. It is like a big wild dog who followed me home one day and has taken a most unpleasant fancy to me. If only he would be tame! But he has been this last week wilder than ever. . . .

P.G. Wodehouse to William Townend, September 3, 1929:

Dear Bill,

Sorry not to have written before, but I have been tied up with a very difficult story (short). "Company for Gertrude" I'm calling it. It's one of those maddening yarns where you get the beginning and end all right and can't think what to put in the middle. . . .

Cheering news from India. My press clipping agency has sent me a letter from the correspondence column of an Indian paper about a cow that came into the bungalow of a Mr. Verrier Elwyn, who lives at Patengarth, Mandla District, and ate his copy of *Carry On, Jeeves*, "selecting it from a shelf which contained, among other works, books by Shakespeare, Thomas Hardy and Henry Fielding." A pretty striking tribute I look on that as. . . .

Sylvia Townsend Warner to Nancy Cunard, September 4, 1960:

Dearest Nancy,

I am appalled by your news. I had heard nothing about it, read nothing about it. What date was the case, which court were you had up in? If they decided you were drunk, it would have been in order to send you to jail, but I cannot understand why you should be where you are. Are you being given any form of treatment—I think this would be the usual procedure—or are you just "in reclusion"? And what for? What form of insanity are you said to be suffering from?. . .

I will think more—your letter only came an hour ago, and I am still feeling as if it were the earthquake in Chile—and do everything and anything I can, my darling, to help you out of this hideous entanglement.

Franz Schubert to Anselm Hüttenbrenner, January 21, 1819:

Dear old friend,

Are you still alive? When I consider how long it is since you have been away and since you have written and how faithlessly you have abandoned us, I really feel obliged to ask. . . .

You have composed two symphonies: that is good. You let us see nothing of them: that is not good. You really should let your old friend hear something of you now and again.

What has become of all those supremely happy hours that we once spent together? Perhaps you do not think of them any more. But how often do I! You will have heard that otherwise everything is going very well with me.

I wish you with all my heart the same.

Be my friend always and do not forget

> Your
> Schubert

Write to me really soon.

F. Scott Fitzgerald to Edmund Wilson, August 15, 1919:

> Dear Bunny:
>
>   Delighted to get your letter. I am deep in the throes of a new novel. Which is the best title
>   (1) The Education of a Personage
>   (2) The Romantic Egotist
>   (3) This Side of Paradise
>   I am sending it to Scribner. They liked my first one. . . .

Flannery O'Connor to Cecil Dawkins, July 17, 1959:

> Well my novel is finished. . . .
>   The current ordeal is that my mother is now in the process of reading it. She reads about two pages, gets up and goes to the back door for a conference with Shot [the dog], comes back, reads two more pages, gets up and goes to the barn. Yesterday she read a whole chapter. There are twelve chapters. All the time she is reading, I know she would like to be in the yard digging. I think the reason I am a short-story writer is so my mother can read my work in one sitting. . . .

Harriet Martineau to Anna Jameson, June 15, 1841:

> My dear Mrs. Jameson,
>   Your letter gave me very great pleasure. . . .
>   Miss Fox . . . had a fearful illness in February, from which I think she has hardly recovered. She is excellent at heart, and as full of energy as of kindness; but I fear she wears herself out—chiefly with *talking*. She cannot now moderate the habit; but I really fear she will shorten her days by it. On this account, it is well that she lives alone. . . .
>   Excuse my scrawl. I shall always be truly pleased to hear from you; but I know you are always busy. . . .

Joseph Conrad to Marguerite Poradowska, August 2, 1906:

Dear Marguerite,

Another boy, whose name is John Alexander Conrad, and for whom I ask a small place in your heart.

He is not very large, but he is well formed. It all went off very well. At six o'clock I got up to go for the doctor, and at nine-thirty I made the acquaintance of my second son. He looked at me with kindliness, and now (at four in the afternoon) I already feel considerable friendship for him. His mother is very well and embraces you warmly. She is calm and very happy. There is no reason to fear complications. She feels perfectly well.

Borys was quite surprised, but he extended to his brother the kindest possible welcome. He has already made a fair division of his toys and has given him half his dog, which is a real proof of affection, I assure you. So the most perfect harmony reigns in the family. . . .

H.L. Mencken to Dorothy Hergesheimer, July 28, 1930:

Dearest Dorothy:

If any scandal-mongers call you up and try to make you believe that Sara and I are to be joined in connubial bonds on August 27th don't deny it, for it is a fact. The solemn announcement will issue from Confederate G.H.Q. in Montgomery in about a week. Your congratulations I take for granted, for you know Sara, and so you know what a lovely gal she is. If you write to her please say nothing about my heavy drinking, or about the trouble with that girl in Red Lion, Pa., in 1917. I still maintain that I was innocent of any unlawful or immoral purpose. . . .

I kiss your hand. Recall me to the Mister.

Yours,
H.L.M.

Dylan Thomas to Rayner Heppenstall, December 31, 1935:

I owe you a lot of apologies, five shillings, and a long letter. I haven't got enough news to make a long letter, I certainly haven't five shillings, but I do apologize for my delay in answering your letter, quite half of which I nearly understood. . . . From what I could gather, you'd come back either from the Rectory or the Fitzroy and were gassed hard. Purposely you were in a strong and came out only for impudent purposes. What a time you've been having. But thanks again, I'm frightfully glad to hear from you. . . . I want to go abroad this summer but I don't know where. Do you know anything about Spain? Can you get along without Spanish and without money?. . .

Raymond Chandler to Deirdre Gartrell, on his thirty years of marriage to Cissy, April 23, 1957:

Deirdre Darling:
     . . . Most people make do with what is available and seemingly appropriate to their condition. Ferocious romantics of my sort never make do with anything. They demand the impossible and on very rare occasions they achieve it, much to their surprise. I was one of those, one of the perhaps two percent, who are blessed with a marriage which is forever a courtship. I can't, as I think back, find any reason why I should have been so favored. . . . To answer one question, I never proposed marriage formally to anyone. My wife and I just seemed to melt into each other's hearts without the need of words.

                              With much love,
                              Ray

*C*elia Thaxter to Annie Fields, November 14, 1877:

Dearest Annie,

This morning, at half past seven, the sweetest mother in the world went, God alone knows where, away from us! There is no comfort for us anywhere except by the gradual hand of time. The "consolations of religion" I cannot bear. I can bear my anguish better than their emptiness, though I am crushed breathless by my sorrow. It seems as if I could never fill my lungs with air again, as if I never wished to look upon the light of day.

She lies close by me, like a lily flower, her snow-white hair under her snow-white cap of delicate lace, and her sweet hands folded, her pillow strewn with the brightest flowers that blow—scarlet geraniums, gold chrysanthemums, and blood-red roses and bright blush roses. She is white enough to cool their ardent colors, and beautiful she looks. . . . I never left her a moment this last week; she clung to my hand day and night. We had no stranger. Mina and I did everything ourselves, night and day. This morning, when she died, we did for her all that was necessary, and made her comely and beautiful for her coffin, with only our own hands. She breathed her life away so softly she looks like a dear, quiet child. . . .

*W*illiam Cowper to Lady Hesketh, January 31, 1786:

. . . I have almost conceived a design to send up half a dozen stout country fellows, to tie by the leg to their respective bed-posts the company that so abridges your opportunity of writing to me. Your letters are the joy of my heart; and I cannot endure to be robbed, by I know not whom, of half my treasure. . . .

W.D. *Howells to Sarah Orne Jewett, September 25, 1901:*

My dear Miss Jewett:

I am almost wounded more by your supposition that I could let anything in the way of work keep me from answering you than I am by the fact that *I never got your letter.*

I am going home with an arrow in my breast that sticks through the back of my coat in a way that will excite universal comment.* But I hope to pull it before next summer, and we all hope to see you, for we expect to be back next summer, for York has done Mrs. Howells good. She joins Pilla and me in lasting affection to you and yours.

Sincerely yours,
W.D. Howells

*I shall just say, "Oh! That? Miss Jewett did it."

*I*gnatius Sancho to Mr. Meheux, February 9, 1777:

Zounds! If alive—what ails you? if dead—why did you not send me word?. . . I have only time to thank you for the leaves, and to lament your want of perspicuity in writing. My love to George when you see him—and two loves to Nancy—tell her I could fold her to my bosom with the same tender pressure I do my girls—shut my eyes—draw her to my heart—and call her Daughter!—and thou, monkey-face, write me a decent letter—or you shall have another trimming from yours,

I. Sancho

Oscar Wilde to E.W. Godwin, May 20, 1885:

Dear Godwino,

I am delighted to know you are somewhere. We thought you were nowhere, and searched for you everywhere, but could not find you anywhere. . . .

"My wife has a cold" but in about a month will be over it. I hope it is a boy cold, but will love whatever the gods send. . . .

Ever yours,

O.W.

Sylvia Townsend Warner to William Maxwell, July 10, 1972:

Dear William,

Your letter came this morning. I was still thinking about it, and washing my hair, when the telephone rang. My cousin Rachel, to tell me she had long suspected she was under a curse, and had now been assured by an expert that she was—and that it was a curse of long standing, extending through generations, and did I think it had come in from the Highland side of the family. She was perfectly convinced, and, like all the demented, perfectly convincing. Reason would have been heartless. On the principle of Feed a Fever, I supplied some more instances of hereditary doom and recommended trying an exorcist. After her, my hair still dank about me, came the parson, to ask how I was keeping and could I let him have a large kettle for the Youth Club's canteen. I couldn't but console him with strawberries. The next telephone call was to ask me if I could adopt two frogs—a nature conservationist, and frogs are a dying race because of farming poisons. Again I had to refuse, three cats made this garden unsuitable for frog conservation. All this before midday. This island is inflexibly lunatic.

Mark Twain to W.D. Howells, July 3, 1899:

Dear Howells,

 . . . I've a lot of things to write you, but it's no use—I can't get time for anything these days. I must break off and write a postscript to Canon Wilberforce before I go to bed. This afternoon he left a luncheon-party half an hour ahead of the rest, and carried off my hat (which has *Mark Twain* in a big hand written in it). When the rest of us came out there was but one hat that would go on my head—it fitted exactly, too. So I wore it away. It had no name in it, but the Canon was the only man who was absent. I wrote him a note at 8 p.m.; saying that for four hours I had not been able to take anything that did not belong to me, nor stretch a fact beyond the frontiers of truth, and my family were getting alarmed. Could he explain my trouble? And now at 8:30 p.m. comes a note from him to say that all the afternoon he has been exhibiting a wonder-compelling mental vivacity and grace of expression, etc., etc., and have I missed a hat? Our letters have crossed.

Arna Bontemps to Langston Hughes, March 6, 1962:

Dear Lang,

 The indications are that you have reached a point vis-à-vis your public comparable to that which some years ago drove Hemingway to Cuba and which this week caused Thornton Wilder to announce that he is moving to Arizona. . . . So that seems to be the price one pays for becoming an institution, a part of the culture, a classic in his own time. One thing is sure: there's no turning back. This has been in the cards ever since you wrote "The Negro Speaks of Rivers." Since you did not pause at that moment to count the cost, you are now in this fix: biographers, bibliographers, researchers and all such as that sitting on your steps!. . .

Best ever,
Arna

Pliny to Cornelius Tacitus, c. 100 A.D.:

Certainly you will laugh (and laugh you may) when I tell you that your old acquaintance is turned sportsman, and has taken three noble boars. What! (methinks I hear you say with astonishment) Pliny!—*Even he.* However, I indulged at the same time my beloved inactivity, and while I sat at my nets, you would have found me, not with my spear, but my pen by my side. I mused and wrote, being resolved, if I returned with my hands empty, at least to come home with my papers full. Believe me, this manner of studying is not to be despised: you cannot conceive how greatly exercise contributes to enliven the imagination. There is, beside, something in the solemnity of the venerable woods with which one is surrounded, together with that awful silence which is observed on these occasions, that strongly inclines the mind to meditation. For the future, therefore, let me advise you, whenever you hunt, to take along with you your pen and paper, as well as your basket and bottle. . . .

Voltaire to Catherine the Great, August 9, 1774:

Madam,

I am positively in disgrace at your court. Your Imperial Majesty has abandoned me for Diderot, or Grimm, or some other favorite: you have had no consideration for my age; this would be understandable if your Majesty were a French coquette; but how can a victorious and law-making Empress be so fickle? I have taken on all the Turks for your sake, and even the Marquis de Pugachov; and your neglect is all the reward I receive. Well, that is that. I shall never love another empress as long as I live. . . .

Elizabeth Cady Stanton to Susan B. Anthony, June 20, 1853:

Dear Susan,

Say not one word to me about another convention. I forbid you to ask me to send one thought or one line to any convention, any paper, or any individual; for I swear by all the saints that whilst I am nursing this baby I will not be tormented with suffering humanity. I am determined to make no effort to do anything beyond my imperative home duties until I can bring about the following conditions: 1st, Relieve myself of housekeeping altogether; 2nd, Secure some capable teacher for my children; 3rd, See my present baby on her feet. My ceaseless cares begin to wear upon my spirit. I feel it in my innermost soul and am resolved to seek some relief. Therefore, I say adieu to the public for a time, for I must give all my moments and my thoughts to my children. But above all this I am so full of dreams of the true associative life that all the reforms of the day beside that seem to me superficial and fragmentary. You ask me if I am not plunged in grief at my defeat at the recent convention for the presidency of our society. Not at all. I am only too happy in all the relief I feel from this additional care. I accomplished at Rochester all I desired by having the divorce question brought up and so eloquently supported by dear little Lucy Stone. How proud I felt of her that night! We have no woman who compares with her. Now, Susan, I do beg of you to let the past be past, and to waste no powder on the Woman's State Temperance Society. We have other and bigger fish to fry.

Gustav Mahler to Friedrich Löhr, on his Second Symphony, June 29, 1894:

This is to announce the auspicious birth of a strong, healthy last movement for the 2nd. Father and child are doing as well as can be expected; the latter is not yet out of danger. It is to be baptized with the name *Lux lucet in tenebris.* . . .

Evelyn Waugh to Diana Cooper, February 1952:

I have been wretchedly unwell since I last wrote but today have dragged myself from bed to table to say: did you notice the coincidence that the King died (so far as one knows) at the very moment when Princess Elizabeth was donning "slacks" for the first time. I hope you will be warned and pass on your nether garments to the lady gardener. . . . W. Churchill made an excruciating speech on BBC about the King's death. Platitudes enlivened by gaffes. The most painful was (roughly) "During the war I made a point of keeping the King informed. He showed quite an intelligent interest. I even told him military secrets and he never once blabbed.". . .

> Love from
> Bo

Bessie Head to Randolph Vigne, August 22, 1969:

Dear Randolph,

How can you damage my eyesight like this! To say I can't read your handwriting is an understatement!. . .

Frédéric Chopin to Julien Fontana, December 3, 1838:

My Julien,

I have been as sick as a dog for the last fortnight. I had caught cold in spite of the eighteen degrees centigrade, the roses, the orange-trees, the palms and the fig-trees. Three doctors—the most celebrated on this island—examined me. . . . The first said I was going to die, the second that I was actually dying, the third that I was dead already. . . . I had great difficulty in escaping from their bleedings, vesicatories and packsheets, but thanks be to providence, I am myself again. But my illness was unfavorable to the *Preludes*, which will reach you God knows when. . . .

Oscar Wilde, in Rome, to Robert Ross, April 21, 1900:

My dear Robbie,

A thousand thanks for all your trouble. The check arrived safely this morning.

Of course I got your telegram, from Milan, and wrote to you at the Hôtel Cavour—a long, interesting, and of course seriously compromising letter. Should it fall into the hands of the authorities you will be immortal.

I have not seen the Holy Father since Thursday, but am bearing up wonderfully well. I am sorry to say he has approved of a dreadful handkerchief, with a portrait of himself in the middle, and basilicas at the corners. It is very curious the connection between Faith and bad art. . . .

I have given up Armando, a very smart elegant young Roman Sporus. He was beautiful, but his requests for raiment and neckties were incessant: he really bayed for boots, as a dog moonwards. I now like Arnaldo: he was Armando's greatest friend, but the friendship is over. Armando is jealous apparently, and is suspected of having stolen a lovely covert-coat in which he patrols the Corso. The coat is so delightful, and he looks so handsome in it, that, although the coat wasn't mine, I have forgiven him the theft. . . .

Albert Schweitzer to Albert Einstein, February 28, 1951:

Dear Friend,

Let me call you that, for it expresses my feelings about you and the hopes and anxieties we share about the future of mankind. I know how kindly you spoke about me on the occasion of my seventy-fifth birthday, and I would like to tell you how good it made me feel. I was so sorry that I could find no opportunity to meet with you during the three weeks I spent in the United States during the summer of 1949. I am not giving up hope that we can get together eventually.

With my best wishes for your health and your work,

Your devoted,

Albert Schweitzer

William Cowper to William Unwin, October 31, 1779:

My dear Friend,

I wrote my last letter merely to inform you that I had nothing to say; in answer to which you have said nothing. I admire the propriety of your conduct though I am a loser by it. I will endeavor to say something now, and shall hope for something in return.

I have been well entertained with Johnson's biography, for which I thank you: with one exception, and that a swingeing one, I think he has acquitted himself with his usual good sense and sufficiency. His treatment of Milton is unmerciful to the last degree. . . . Was there ever anything so delightful as the music of the Paradise Lost? It is like that of a fine organ; has the fullest and the deepest tones of majesty, with all the softness and elegance of the Dorian flute: variety without end, and never equalled, unless perhaps by Virgil. Yet the Doctor has little or nothing to say upon this copious theme, but talks something about the unfitness of the English language for blank verse, and how apt it is, in the mouth of some readers, to degenerate into declamation. Oh! I could thrash his old jacket till I made his pension jingle in his pockets. . . .

Charlotte Brontë to Elizabeth Gaskell, August 27, 1850:

Papa and I have just had tea; he is sitting quietly in his room, and I in mine: "storms of rain" are sweeping over the garden and churchyard: as to the moors, they are hidden in the thick fog. Though alone I am not unhappy; I have a thousand things to be thankful for, and, amongst the rest, that this morning I received a letter from you, and that this evening I have the privilege of answering it. . . .

I shall be glad to hear from you whenever you have time to write to me, *but you are never on any account to do this except when inclination prompts and leisure permits.* I should never thank you for a letter which you had felt it a task to write.

George Gordon, Lord Byron, to Thomas Moore, September 20, 1814:

My dear Moore,

I am going to be married—that is, I am accepted, and one usually hopes the rest will follow. . . . Miss Milbanke is the lady, and I have her father's invitation to proceed there in my elect capacity—which, however, I cannot do till I have settled some business in London and got a blue coat.

She is said to be an heiress, but of that I really know nothing certainly, and shall not enquire. But I do know that she has talents and excellent qualities; and you will not deny her judgment, after having refused six suitors and taken me.

Now, if you have any thing to say against this, pray do; my mind's made up, positively fixed, determined, and therefore I will listen to reason, because now it can do no harm. Things may occur to break it off, but I will hope not. . . . I must, of course, reform thoroughly; and, seriously, if I can contribute to her happiness, I shall secure my own. She is so good a person, that—that—in short, I wish I was a better.

Susan Hale to Mrs. William G. Weld, September 19, 1897:

Dearest Caroline,

. . . I had to go to town on account of my celebrated back-tooth, which has been a source of income to dentists since 1833. It finally broke off and came out one day lately, and I repaired to Piper to have it repaired. He got into my mouth along with a pickaxe and telescope, battering-ram and other instruments, and drove a lawn-cutting machine up and down my jaws for a couple of hours. When he came out he said he meant wonderful improvements, and it seems I'm to have a bridge and a mill-wheel and summit and crown of gold, and harps, and Lord knows what, better than new. . . . This may reach you at Prague or Vienna. My! can't I get into the envelope myself? *Write, write.*

Your loving Susie

Mrs. C. Burgoyne to the Duchess of Argyll, October 7, 1773:

My dear Duchess,

When you thought it necessary to make an apology for not answering my letter sooner what can I say in excuse for myself, who have been double the time silent? . . .

I am afraid it is too true that Miss P. lost in one night £500 and the next £1500, and paid it all the next day. I am almost afraid to tell you what I hear at so many hundred miles distance, lest my letter should be lost, but they say she (Miss P.) borrows the money of her sister Mary, having lost everything of her own except *Terra firma*. If so how shocking must be her situation. I agree with you, she will one time or another put an end to herself. . . .

I can give you no account of the proceedings of the Conway family. Now I am no longer useful, I see Lady H. about once in five or six weeks, just so as to keep up a civility; the visit does not consist of above 15 minutes, and during that time I learn nothing that is going on, but my own opinion is that Lord L. never had nor ever will have serious thoughts of Lady F. The young ladies must for this winter look upon the D. of Devonshire as a lost man, for he has taken Charlotte Spencer (a lady I presume you know by sight) into keeping selon toutes les formes. I hear she says she has received the *most passionate* letters from him that ever she read in her Life. He is not at Chatsworth, and it was once reported she was going down to him, but that is not true.

I have really deferred writing a few posts till Col. Phillipson came to town that I might be able to ascertain the truth of the above story, and come likewise at the knowledge of the Duke of Kingston's will, for as Mr. Burgoyne has been in the North near a month, and *we* never go to London, it is difficult to come at any news that may be depended upon, and I hate to write a parcel of lies. After hearing various stories I believe the following may be depended on. All his estate he has left the Duchess for her Life . . . after her decease to the Meadows, excluding the eldest son, whose conduct had disobliged him, and therefore he only left him a legacy of £500. If the two younger Meadows die without issue it goes to Lord Thomas Clinton. There was £1200 per year settled upon Mr. Brand which he could not hinder him of, and the same sum to Mr. W. Montagu (Lady Bute's brother). Some people say the words of the will run thus: I leave to the Duchess of Kingston, alias Mrs. Hervey, alias Miss Chudleigh; but I do not pretend to vouch the truth of it, but for curiosity I will get some friend to go and read the will, which anybody may do for a shilling. I hear she is going into Saxony to spend the remainder of her days with her *dear* Electress. I think she has judged very wisely, for those very few who took notice of her in the Duke's lifetime will now desert her I make no doubt; abroad her money will get her friends, and she will make a noble figure at Dresden on £12,000 per year which they say the estate is.

By the by we hear strange accounts of your ladies in Scotland; it is not one or two men that satisfy them, even though they are married. If there is any truth in the story you will know who I mean without mentioning names. I heard the D. of Dorset passed through Preston on his way to Scotland. I fancy *I smell a rat.* My love to Lady Betty. I don't apprehend the Queen has been ill, at least as fame would make one believe; she has miss'd her Drawing Rooms sometimes, and I fancy by what I hear she is with child again, but it is certain she looks very well, for Miss Stanley was at Court on the 22nd of last month, and said she never saw her look better or more in health than she appeared to be. It can be no news to tell you Miss Keck is to be married to Lord Hereford, and that there is great joy in the Carlisle family on the birth of a son. I must enquire of you if Lady Gower is brought to bed, I wish she may have a son.

Adieu, Dear Duchess, indulge me with the pleasure of hearing from you soon. . . .

*H*ere's hoping that your tonsils are on the track again. Why are we constantly tortured with such ills? What low, bar-room comedian is boss of this world?

H.L. MENCKEN, LETTER TO WILLARD HUNTINGTON WRIGHT, 1913

You can imagine how sad all your friends felt when they got that first story of your illness. It came in such a way that it was hard to dis-believe, and although we all hoped that it might be a telegraphic sensational over-statement, the relief was very great and the rejoicing most hearty when we

Get Well Letters

"Everyone who is born holds dual citizenship, in the kingdom of the well and in the kingdom of the sick. Although we all prefer to use only the good passport, sooner or later each of us is obliged, at least for a spell, to identify ourselves as citizens of that other place." (Susan Sontag, *Illness As Metaphor*)

The get well letter is an attempt to bridge the distance, to enter the other kingdom without surrendering our own passport in the kingdom of the well. Perhaps the most heartfelt letters are written by the newly convalescent to the still ailing. Louisa May Alcott reports she is just beginning to feel a little less "like a sick oyster at low tide."

Groucho Marx to T.S. Eliot, January 25, 1963:

Dear Mr. Eliot:

I read in the current *Time* magazine that you are ill. I just want you to know that I am rooting for your quick recovery. First because of your contributions to literature and, then, the fact that under the most trying conditions you never stopped smoking cigars.

Hurry up and get well.

Samuel Johnson to Mrs. Montagu, December 15, 1775:

Madame,

Having, after my return from a little ramble to France, passed some time in the country, I did not hear, till I was told by Miss Reynolds, that you were in town; and when I did hear it, I heard likewise that you were ill. To have you detained among us by sickness is to enjoy your presence at too dear a rate. I suffer myself to be flattered with hope that only half the intelligence is now true, and that you are now so well as to be able to leave us, and so kind as not to be willing.

St. Teresa of Avila to Padre Jerónimo Gracián, October 1575:

. . . I must tell you that I am cross about these falls you have been having. It would be as well if they were to tie you on your mount, and then you could not fall. I don't know what sort of a donkey you have, nor why your Paternity has to do ten leagues a day; on a pack-saddle that is suicidal. . . .

Mark Twain to the W.D. Howells, January 7, 1884:

My dear Howells,

"O my goodn's" as Jean says. You have now encountered at last the heaviest calamity that can befall an author. The scarlet fever, once domesticated, is a permanent member of the family. Money may desert you, friends forsake you, enemies grow indifferent to you, but the scarlet fever will be true to you, through thick and thin, till you be all saved or damned, down to the last one. I say these things to cheer you. . . . You folks have our most sincere sympathy. . . .

Oliver Wendell Holmes, Sr. to John Lothrop Motley, August 26, 1873:

My dear Motley,

You can imagine how sad all your friends felt when they got that first story of your illness. It came in such a way that it was hard to disbelieve, and although we all hoped that it might be a telegraphic sensational over-statement, the relief was very great and the rejoicing most hearty when we received the second message, that your complaint had been magnified in an "absurdly exaggeraged" story, and that it did not threaten your life or your continued usefulness and enjoyment. There are few men better loved by their friends than yourself; and who are there of whom their country is prouder as representing its noblest literary attainment and achievement? Such was the feeling produced by that first telegram that it seemed almost like a resurrection to picture you again in health, and in the full exercise of all your active powers. . . .

Pray do not think of troubling yourself to *answer* this letter, no matter how well you feel.

Emily Dickinson to Charles H. Clark on the illness of his brother James, May 1883:

Dear Friend,

The temptation to inquire every morning for your sufferer is almost irresistible, but our own invalid taught us that a sick room is at times too sacred a place for a friend's knock, timid as that is.

I trust this sweet May morning is not without its peace to your brother and you, though the richest peace is of sorrow. With constant and fervent anxiousness, and the hope of an early word, please be sure we share your suspense.

Louisa May Alcott to Mrs. Bond, March 15, 1887:

Dear Auntie,

I have been hoping to get out and see you all winter, but have been so ill I could only live on hope as a relish to my gruel—that being my only food, and not of a nature to give me strength. Now I am beginning to live a little, and feel less like a sick oyster at low tide. . . .

I was sorry to hear that you were poorly again. Isn't it hard to sit serenely in one's soul when one's body is in a dilapidated state? I find it a great bore, but try to do it patiently, and hope to see the why by and by, when this mysterious life is made clear to me. . . .

Ever yours,
L.M.A.

Sigmund Freud to Wilhelm Fliess, October 18, 1893:

Dearest friend,

I hope that my confidence in the speediest recovery of your dear wife arrives at your house after that recovery has itself taken place. It cannot be her desire to be ill, so I shall not dwell on that at all. . . .

Ouida (Louise de la Ramée), author of <u>A Dog of Flanders</u>, to Mrs. Patrick Campbell on her broken kneecap, January 10, 1905:

Dear Madam,

I am unknown to you, but I venture to thank you for the admirable example you give of affection for your dogs. It is most valuable in a world which is so cruelly indifferent to the canine race.

I was grieved to read of your accident, and hope your captivity will be sooner over than the doctors think. It is a very great misfortune to befall one so gifted and admired.

With my sincere sympathy I remain, faithfully yours,
Ouida

Oscar W. Firkins to Bess Dvorsky, April 11, 1930:

Dear Miss Dvorsky:

I am told you are ill in the hospital. I hope the stay will be short and the pain gentle and that you will soon be back among us ready to join Molière and Mr. Shaw in laughing at doctors. One pleasant little thing about a sickbed is that from its hardships one's daily burdens come to look like pleasures; one never dreamed that they could look so cheerful. You are not to worry about your work in Drama; the make-up shall be made as light as possible.

May I extend to you the greetings of the New Year. May you have a continuous and abiding and keen sense that you are doing good, likewise doing well.

FRANKLIN K. LANE, LETTER TO LATHROP BROWN, 1921

I cannot let Christmas come without sending you both my love and greeting. I love Christmas. . . . In that other world where wishes are laws, there would be a great shining wreath of holly on the door knocker, lights at all the windows, and a real party going on inside. We meet in the hall

Holiday Letters

Although commercial holiday cards are popular, most of us agree with Oscar Firkins: "I was glad to get a letter instead of a Christmas card. A Christmas card is a rather innutritious thing." Tradition says holidays are happy times for everyone but the curmudgeons among us (W.C. Fields wrote, "A Merry Christmas to all my friends except two"), but this isn't always true. Margaret Oliphant's letter acknowledges that holidays can be painful. Katherine Mansfield's hopeful holiday letter contrasts dramatically with Hart Crane's bleak one. Mansfield's letter was written during her struggle with tuberculosis; she was to die less than two years later at the age of 35. Crane committed suicide less than six years after writing his letter.

Paul Celan to Nelly Sachs, September 13, 1961:

> My dear Nelly,
>
> It is Jewish New Year—accept our warmest wishes for all the best in this new year. May it bring you everything you long for, peace and health and poems!. . .

Charles Dickens to Mr. John Forster, December 27, 1846:

> My very dear Forster,
>
> Amen, amen. Many merry Christmases, many happy new years, unbroken friendship, great accumulation of cheerful recollections, affection on earth, and heaven at last for all of us. . . .

Grover Cleveland to E.C. Benedict, December 31, 1897:

> . . . I am the only one out of bed in the house; and in about half an hour the year 1897 will disappear in the darkness of the past. I want to wish you a Happy New Year before I go to bed, and to write you the only letter I have written today. I said to my wife when she bade me "good night" that "old '97" had treated us very well and I felt thankful. I want you to know that in thinking of the pleasant things of the year, you are prominently present; and that your kindnesses and those of your household are gratefully remembered; and we fervently hope that the coming year will be full of happiness and comfort for you and all you hold dear. . . .

Oliver Wendell Holmes, Sr. to Mrs. Kellogg, January 1883:

A happy New Year, my dear Mrs. Kellogg, and as many such as you can count until you reach a hundred, and then begin again, if you like the planet well enough.

Christina Stead to Ko-Ko and Bruno (c/o Dorothy and Ron Geering), December 9, 1979:

Dear Ko-Ko and Dear Bruno,
Merry Christmas and Many Happy Mew Years,
from
Your Constant Admirer—
Would write in Purrsian but don't know what you may be mewsing about the present goings-on over there—where the fur is flying.
Never mind, you are very lucky to be with the Duke and Duchess.

P(US)S. Enc. small gift of smoked oysters; as purr usual. Xris

Margaret Oliphant to Mr. W. Blackwood, December 26, 1880:

. . . Christmas is just over with all its many memories, and I am glad of it. It will not have been very merry for you, and it is the worst of such anniversaries that they bring so strongly before us the consciousness of every empty place. Accept my best wishes for the new year on which we are so soon to enter, and give my kindest messages to your mother and sisters. I trust Mrs. Blackwood, surrounded as she is with the devotion of the good children who remain to her, is strengthened to bear the griefs of which I know she has had no small share. . . .

Dorothea Dix to Millard Fillmore, January 3, 1854:

My dear Sir and Friend,

. . . I wish you a Happy New Year—many happy years—God bless you now and always. And as the days of life on earth are measured may the seeds fall on sunny hills and green valleys where cheerful contentment and useful existences are measured. . . .

Sincerely in the alliance of a cordial friendship,
D.L. Dix

Samuel Johnson to James Boswell, January 24, 1778:

Dear Sir,

To a letter so interesting as your last, it is proper to return some answer, however little I may be disposed to write. . . .

You always seem to call for tenderness. Know, then, that in the first month of the present year I very highly esteem and very cordially love you. I hope to tell you this at the beginning of every year as long as we live; and why should we trouble ourselves to tell or hear it oftener?

I am, dear Sir, yours affectionately,

Ellen Glasgow to Eleanor and Van Wyck Brooks, December 22, 1940:

Dear Eleanor and Van Wyck,

You have been much in my thoughts, and I send you my affectionate greeting and a blessing for each separate day in the New Year. . . .

Are you coming South again? How I should love to see you! That afternoon in New York makes a bright place in my thoughts. . . .

My love to you both,
Ellen

Katherine Mansfield to Thomas and Bessie Moult, December 20, 1921:

I cannot let Christmas come without sending you both my love and greeting. I love Christmas. . . . In that other world where wishes are laws, there would be a great shining wreath of holly on the door knocker, lights at all the windows, and a real party going on inside. We meet in the hall and warmly re-clasp hands. Good Heavens! *I'm* not above a tree, colored candles and crackers—are you? Wait. We shall have it all—or something better! I will never despair of a real gay meeting, one of these days, for us all. It's always only an accident that the day is not fine, that one happens for the moment to be under an umbrella. It will all flash and sparkle, I truly *believe* that, sooner than we expect. The very fact that we rebel at our little terms of imprisonment is proof that freedom is our real element. . . .

Hart Crane to Wilbur Underwood, December 16, 1926:

I'm laid up with tonsillitis—but must somehow thank you for your pleasant N.Y. letter and wish you as amusing a New Year as possible. As for myself—I don't expect much.

Nothing but illness and mental disorder in my family—and I am expected by all the middle-class ethics and dogmas to rush myself to Cleveland and devote myself interminably to nursing, sympathizing with woes which I have no sympathy for because they are all unnecessary, and bolstering up the faith in others toward concepts which I long ago discarded as crass and cheap.

Whether I can do it or not is the question. It means tortures and immolations which are hard to conceive, impossible to describe. There seems to be no place left in the world for love or the innocence of a single spontaneous act. Write me here.

Hart

P.S. Have you read Norman Douglas' *South Wind?* It almost makes one jolly—

Grover Cleveland to Mrs. E. L. Yeomans, December 23, 1907:

I hope that my infrequent letters never suggest the thought in your mind that advancing years or any other thing has in the least abated my brotherly love for you. I think of you as often and as affectionately as ever; but you know, as well as I do, how easily the letter-writing habit becomes interrupted.

I am determined, in any event, that this holiday season shall not come and go without especially wishing you a "Merry Christmas" and "Happy New Year." And from the bottom of my heart I hope the future holds in store for you many of these holidays full of comfort and the best gifts of God.

Our four children do not permit us to forget that Christmas is near; and there is an air of busy mystery about the house that cannot be misinterpreted. . . .

Claude Debussy to his wife Emma (one of the notes he used to send up to her in her bedroom, on the story above his study), December 24, 1916:

In this year of 1916 Father Christmas is at the front and communications are so difficult, he hasn't been able to respond to my requests. I've no flowers or music. . . . Nothing but my poor anxious heart and an urgent desire to see the end of this marking time which is like a premature burial.

This waiting for better days is enough to drive one crazy and if your courage wasn't here with me I would long ago have gone off to read the communiqués on another planet.

Never has your love been more precious or more necessary to me. I worry when you go away! Noël! Noël! The bells are cracked. Noël! Noël! They have wept too long! . . .

If I didn't know your spirit was so strong, I'd be afraid for you, living this life with an invalid. But you will be the source of my ease from all the cares that oppress me.

Forgive me for loving you . . . Wait for me.
Your Claude

Barbara Pym to Robert Liddell, January 12, 1940:

Dear Jock,

How can you possibly know that I was delighted with your letters when I do not write to tell you so? I feel I should write nearly a whole novel to make up for my neglect. "Oh, surely that will not be necessary," I can hear you saying, in a high nervous tone. "I really do not think you need put yourself to such trouble. Is it not true that the Government is exhorting us to save paper?". . .

A very happy New Year to you and may it be not quite as bad as we expect, and even bring the end of the war in sight. . . .

BMCP

*C*an you come and take a cutlet with us
today at five?

Let me know and we'll add a bit of fish.

CHARLES DICKENS, LETTER TO JOHN FORSTER, 1837

I got back from the country to find your card sparkling like a jewel in a diadem of unpaid bills, poison pen letters, and rusty old telephone messages. We would like very much to see you but there is no earthly reason why you should have to bend over a hot stove (with flushed cheeks, occasionally

Invitations

tucking up a wisp of hair on the nape of your neck) to prepare dinner for us. I think it would be much better if Mrs. Wilson and you came in and had dinner with us. This invitation does not extend to your baby, who I understand has a tendency to fall asleep about six o'clock after gorging himself belching and generally behaving in the worst possible taste.

Do you have a sitter whom

ormal invitations have standardized arrangements, and even the wittiest or most versatile letterwriter can't do much to personalize them. The invitations and letters about invitations in this chapter are therefore the informal type, with the exception of Mark Twain's ersatz formal creation.

In *The Story of My Life* (1900), Augustus J.C. Hare reprints an invitation from a friend: "Will you be so very kind as to allow me to take the liberty of entreating you to have the kindness to confer the favor upon me of giving me the happiness of your company on Friday?" Hare was justified in complaining of the excess verbiage. However, it is interesting to note that his autobiography runs to six volumes.

S. *J. Perelman to Edmund Wilson, February 9, 1939:*

Dear Edmondo,

 I got back from the country to find your card sparkling like a jewel in a diadem of unpaid bills, poison pen letters, and rusty old telephone messages. We would like very much to see you but there is no earthly reason why you should have to bend over a hot stove (with flushed cheeks, occasionally tucking up a wisp of hair on the nape of your neck) to prepare dinner for us. I think it would be much better if Mrs. Wilson and you came in and had dinner with us. This invitation does not extend to your baby, who I understand has a tendency to fall asleep about six o'clock after gorging himself, belching and generally behaving in the worst possible taste.

 Do you have a sitter whom you could call in for the occasion? A father of two since I saw you last, you will find my conversation studded with references to Snuggle-duckies, pablum, and strollers. But why depress you in advance?

 We look forward to seeing you just as soon as possible.

              Ever,

*M*ark *Twain to Harry and Mary Benjamin Rogers, Spring 1907:*

The pleasure of the company of
Mr. and Mrs. H.H. Rogers, Jr.
is requested at the Voss domicile on Wednesday 1:30 p.m.
to meet Mr. Clemens, the celebrated humorist.

Informal.
Dress not necessary.
Only clothes.

Charles Dickens to W. Harrison Ainsworth, December 28, 1838:

My Dear Ainsworth,

Cruikshank has been here to say how that he thought your dinner was *last* Saturday, how that he now finds it is *next* Saturday, and how he means to come with me and surprise you. As the surprise, however agreeable, might be too much for Mrs. Touchet, I have thought it best to send you this warning. Mind, you must assume the virtue though you have it not, and feign extravagant astonishment at the sight of the Illustrious George.

Gertrude Stein to Thornton Wilder, July 6, 1940:

My dearest Thornton,

Well come and we will tell you everything and as we sit on the terrace we will tell you so many stories, when will you come, there is so much to tell that you can see that all we can say is that we are here, and that Bilignin was beautiful through it all, my dearest Thornton love to you

Gtrde and Alice

Grover Cleveland to Postmaster-General Vilas, May 28, 1886:

On Wednesday next at seven o'clock in the evening I shall be married to Miss Folsom at the White House.

We shall have a very quiet wedding, but I earnestly desire that you and Mrs. Vilas will be present on that occasion.

Lydia Maria Child to Mrs. S.B. Shaw, 1859:

      I would gladly come to meet you, to save you trouble; but for no other reason. As for turning us out of our chamber, we transfer only our bodies; and should you consider that any great trouble, for the sight of a precious friend? Moreover, suppose it was any trouble, be it known to you that I would turn myself out of my house, and live in a tree, any time, for you. Please put quite out of your head all idea that your coming will give me trouble. In the first place, I will promise not to take trouble. In the next place, I would inform you that the world is divided into two classes: those who love to minister to others, and those who like to be ministered unto. I think I belong to the first class.

   . . .

Ralph Waldo Emerson, James Russell Lowell, and Oliver Wendell Holmes to Edward Everett, April 6, 1864:

Dear Sir,

      The "Saturday Club," a party of gentlemen, most and perhaps all of whom are individually known to you, propose to hold their monthly meeting for April on the 23rd instant and to invite a few friends of Shakespeare to dine with them. In their behalf we request the honor of your company at dinner at the Revere House at 6 o'clock on that evening.

                        R.W. Emerson
                        J.R. Lowell
                        O.W. Holmes

Alexander Woollcott to Beatrice Kaufman, May 31, 1933:

Beatrice:

You must come here some part of this and every summer. It is my favorite place in all the world. I am simply exhausted from buttering so many griddle cakes and can write no more.

A.W.

P.T. Barnum to Mark Twain, August 13, 1874:

My dear Clemens,

Suppose you come down here Saturday next, stop over Sunday and remain a few days next week, have a clambake, etc.? Bring wife and babies if agreeable. I mean if agreeable to *you* and *them*, and not if they are agreeable. . . .

Truly yours,
P. T. Barnum

Charles Dickens to Samuel Lover, December 6, 1837:

My dear Lover,

We christen an infant phenomenon on Saturday, and expect a few friends in the evening in honor of the occasion. If you will join us at about eight o'clock you will give both myself and Mrs. Dickens very sincere pleasure. . . .

Believe me, always,
Faithfully yours,
Charles Dickens

Oliver Wendell Holmes, Sr. to James Thomas Fields, February 11, 1862:

My dear Mr. Fields,

On Friday evening last I white-cravated myself, took a carriage, and found myself at your door at eight of the clock p.m. A cautious female responded to my ring, and opened the chained portal about as far as a clam opens his shell to see what is going on in Cambridge Street, where he is waiting for a customer.

Her first glance impressed her with the conviction that I was a burglar. The mild address with which I accosted her removed that impression, and I rose in the moral scale to the comparatively elevated position of what the unfeeling world calls a "sneak-thief."

By dint, however, of soft words, and that look of ingenuous simplicity by which I am so well known to you and all my friends, I coaxed her into the belief that I was nothing worse than a rejected contributor, an autograph collector, an author with a volume of poems to dispose of, or other disagreeable but not dangerous character.

She unfastened the chain, and I stood before her.

"I calmed her fears, and she was calm
And told"

me how you and Mrs. F. had gone to New York, and how she knew nothing of any literary debauch that was to come off under your roof, but would go and call another unprotected female who knew the past, present, and future, and could tell me why this was thus, that I had been lured from my fireside by the *ignis fatuus* of a deceptive invitation.

It was my turn to be afraid, alone in the house with two of the stronger sex; and I retired.

On reaching home, I read my note and found it was Friday the 16th, not the 9th, I was invited for. . . .

Always truly yours,
O. W. Holmes

P.*G. Wodehouse to William Townend, February 25, 1931:*

Dear Bill,

Since I last wrote, I have been spending a week at Hearst's ranch. He owns 400,000 acres, more than the whole of Long Island. . . .

Meals take place in an enormous room hung with banners, and are served at a long table, with Hearst sitting in the middle on one side and Marion Davies in the middle on the other. The longer you're there, the further you get from the middle. I sat on Marion's right the first night, then found myself getting edged further and further away, till I got to the extreme end, when I thought it time to leave. Another day and I should have been feeding on the floor. . . .

Mr. J. Armour-Milne refers to "the amount of drivel that is to be found in the Letters to the Editor." Whether or not you, in fact, publish drivel is not for me to decide, but a sure method of raising the standard of letters that you receive would be not only to publish your usual selection of letters, but also to print, each day, a complete list of the names of those correspondents whose letters you have rejected. The thought of possibly being included in your Rejects List, and then to have one's acquaintances saying, "I see that you have had yet another letter refused by The Times," would be too much of a risk for most people.

P.H.H. MOORE, LETTER TO THE LONDON TIMES, 1970

After reading Sir Almroth Wright's able and weighty exposition of women as he knows them, the question seems no longer to be "Should women have votes?" but "Ought women not to be abolished altogether?" I have been so much impressed by Sir Almroth Wright's disquisition . . . .

that I have come to the conclusion that women should be put a stop to. We learn from him that in their youth they are unbalanced, that from time to time they suffer from unreasonableness and hypersensitiveness . . . and . . . later on in life they are subject to grave and long-continued mental disorders, and, if not quite insane, many of them have to be shut up. Now this being so, how

Letters to the Editor

Some letters to the editor deal with life-and-death issues; others are humorous or even frivolous. Some—like Clementine Churchill's—delight with their sarcasm and well-weighted language.

Clementine Churchill to the London Times, March 30, 1912:

Sir,

After reading Sir Almroth Wright's able and weighty exposition of women as he knows them, the question seems no longer to be "Should women have votes?" but "Ought women not to be abolished altogether?"

I have been so much impressed by Sir Almroth Wright's disquisition . . . that I have come to the conclusion that women should be put a stop to.

We learn from him that in their youth they are unbalanced, that from time to time they suffer from unreasonableness and hypersensitiveness . . . and . . . later on in life they are subject to grave and long-continued mental disorders, and, if not quite insane, many of them have to be shut up.

Now this being so, how much happier and better would the world not be if only it could be purged of women?. . . Is the case really hopeless?. . . Cannot science give us some assurance, or at least some ground of hope, that we are on the eve of the greatest discovery of all— i.e., how to maintain a race of males by purely scientific means?

And may we not look to Sir Almroth Wright to crown his many achievements by delivering mankind from the parasitic, demented, and immoral species which has infested the world for so long?

Yours obediently,

Clementine S. Churchill

"One of the Doomed"

Mark Twain to W.D. Howells, October 4, 1907:

To the Editor,

Sir to you, I would like to know what kind of a goddam govment this is that discriminates between two common carriers & makes a goddam railroad charge everybody equal & lets a goddam man charge any goddam price he wants to for his goddam opera box.

W D Howells
Tuxedo Park Oct 4
(goddam it)

Howells, it is an outrage the way the govment is acting so I sent this complaint to N.Y. Times with your name signed because it would have more weight. Mark

Patrick White to Time magazine, February 17, 1974:

Dear Sir,

It isn't my habit to write to papers after reading reviews of my books, but after coming across Martha Duffy (whoever she is) on my novel *The Eye of the Storm* where she refers to me as "living in Sydney with several dogs and a male housekeeper" I feel I must draw your attention to an incorrect, and I should have thought gratuitous, biographical detail. The distinguished, and universally respected man who has given me his friendship and moral support over a period of thirty-four years, has never been a housekeeper. *I* am that, and shall continue playing the role at least till I am paralyzed: it keeps me in touch with a reality often remote from those who dish up their superficial, slovenly pieces for *Time* magazine.

Alexander Woollcott to the Omaha World Herald, December 19, 1935:

Dear Sir:

May I not, as the late Woodrow Wilson used to say, call your attention to an editorial which appeared in your issue of December 9th under the caption "The Woollcott Menace"? It has found its way out to me here in San Mateo, out in the great open spaces where men are menace. . . .

It is the substance of this editorial that as a recommender of books over the radio, I take advantage of a nationwide network to further the sale of soft, sentimental works. "Marshmallows" was the term employed. Since this series of broadcasts began, I have cast my oral vote for the following works. . . . It is quite impossible for any literate adult to think that this list represents pink publications for pale people. If these be "marshmallows," then I am the Grand Duchess Marie.

. . . If that editorial was written by someone who would think of that list as so many marshmallows, it was the work of a fool. If it was written by someone who was not even familiar with what books I had recommended, it was the work of a knave. Neither alternative is agreeable for a colleague to contemplate. Of course, there is always the third possibility that your editorial writer is a nicely balanced mixture of the two.

Bassett Digby to the London Times, February 17, 1915:

Sir,

A little light might be shed, with advantage, upon the high-handed methods of the Passports Department at the Foreign Office. On the form provided for the purpose I described my face as "intelligent." Instead of finding this characterization entered, I have received a passport on which some official utterly unknown to me, has taken it upon himself to call my face "oval."

Yours very truly,
Bassett Digby

E.B. White to the New York Herald Tribune, November 29, 1947:

I am a member of a party of one, and I live in an age of fear. Nothing lately has unsettled my party and raised my fears so much as your editorial, on Thanksgiving Day, suggesting that employees should be required to state their beliefs in order to hold their jobs. The idea is inconsistent with our Constitutional theory and has been stubbornly opposed by watchful men since the early days of the Republic. . . . I can only assume that your editorial writer, in a hurry to get home for Thanksgiving, tripped over the First Amendment and thought it was the office cat. . . .

I hold that it would be improper for any committee or any employer to examine my conscience. They wouldn't know how to get into it, they wouldn't know what to do when they got in there, and I wouldn't let them in anyway. Like other Americans, my acts and my words are open to inspection—not my thoughts or my political affiliation. . . .

It is not a crime to believe anything at all in America. To date it has not been declared illegal to belong to the Communist party. Yet ten men have been convicted not of wrongdoing but of wrong believing. That is news in this country, and if I have not misread history, it is bad news.

Susan B. Anthony to Sidepaths, 1898:

I think it [the bicycle] has done a great deal to emancipate women. I stand and rejoice every time I see a woman ride by on a wheel. It gives her a feeling of freedom, self-reliance and independence. The moment she takes her seat she knows she can't get into harm while she is on her bicycle, and away she goes, the picture of free, untrammeled womanhood. . . .

Philip Freneau to the Aurora, 1799:

Mr. Editor,

      Having heard that there was a tavern at about the distance of a mile or so from my favorite country spot, where now and then a few neighbors meet to spit, smoke cegars, drink apple whiskey, cider, or cider-royal, and read the news—a few evenings ago, I put on my best coat, combed out my wig, put my spectacles in my pocket, and a quarter dollar—This I thought was right; for although Mrs. Slender told me eleven-pence was enough, says I, I'll e'en take the quarter dollar, for a man always feels himself of more consequence when he has got good money in his pocket—so out I walks, with a good stout stick in my hand, which I always make a point to carry with me, lest the dogs should make rather freer with my legs than I could wish. But I had not gone more than half the way, when, by making a false step, I splashed my stocking from the knee to the ankle—Odds my heart, said I, see what a hand I have made of my stocking; I'll be bail, added I, I'll hear of this in both sides of my head—but it can't now be helped—this, and a thousand worse accidents, which daily happen, are all occasioned by public neglect, and the misapplication of the public's money—Had I, said I (talking to myself all the while) the disposal of but half the income of the United States, I could at least so order matters, that a man might walk to his next neighbor's without splashing his stockings, or being in danger of breaking his legs in ruts, holes, gutts, and gullies. . . .

George Eliot to the London Times, June 25, 1859:

Sir,

Will you kindly admit one final effort on my part to save benevolent persons from imposture? In spite of all that has been affirmed on the word of honorable gentlemen, like Messrs. Blackwood, there are still numbers who believe that the "Scenes of Clerical Life" and "Adam Bede" were written by a Mr. Joseph Liggins; and I hear from various well-informed persons, interested in the matter, that money has actually been accepted by Mr. Liggens, as their author. . .

Mr. Liggins is, I know, perfectly aware of the delusion which exists concerning his claim to the authorship and aware of the efforts made by myself and publishers to dispel it. Common honesty, one would think, would lead him to use every effort to undeceive his neighbors and supporters. . . . If Mr. Liggins, or any one bearing a name at all resembling Liggins, has in any way stated, or suggested, or by implication of smile, shrug, or tone, allowed any one to believe that he wrote the "Scenes of Clerical Life" or "Adam Bede"—or even contributed a single detail to those works—or ever saw a page of the ms.—*he is an imposter.* And if he received money knowing at the time the money was intended for the author of those works—*he is a swindler.* . . . If there are persons who will continue to believe in his authorship after this letter, they must be willing dupes. I can do no more to undeceive them.

_L_etters were first invented for consoling such solitary wretches as myself. Having lost the substantial pleasures of seeing and possessing you, I shall in some measure compensate this loss by the satisfaction I shall find in your writing.

HÉLOÏSE, LETTER TO ABELARD, 12TH CENTURY

In your letter from Madras you wrote some words very dear to me, about my having enriched your life. I cannot tell you what pleasure this gave me, because I always feel so overwhelmingly in your debt, if there can be accounts in love. It was sweet of you to write this to me, and I hope and pray I

Love Letters

Letters in this chapter are longer than those in other chapters. As Judith Viorst said, "Brevity may be the soul of wit, but not when someone's saying, 'I love you.'" Although most love letters are written in pairs (Elizabeth and George Custer, Robert and Elizabeth Browning, Charles and Anne Morrow Lindbergh), there are occasionally three sides to love letters. Two men (Gustav Mahler and Oskar Kokoschka) write love letters to the same woman. One man (King Henry VIII) writes love letters to two women, although the second letter, to his sixth wife Katharine Parr, appears less fervent and romantic than his letter to his second wife, Anne Boleyn. There may be a point of diminishing enthusiasm in the writing of love letters.

*W*inston *Churchill to Clementine Churchill, January 23, 1935:*

My darling Clemmie,

      In your letter from Madras you wrote some words very dear to me, about my having enriched your life. I cannot tell you what pleasure this gave me, because I always feel so overwhelmingly in your debt, if there can be accounts in love. It was sweet of you to write this to me, and I hope and pray I shall be able to make you happy and secure during my remaining years, and cherish you, my darling one, as you deserve, and leave you in comfort when my race is run. What it has been to me to live all these years in your heart and companionship no phrases can convey. Time passes swiftly, but is it not joyous to see how great and growing is the treasure we have gathered together, amid the storms and stresses of so many eventful and to millions tragic and terrible years?

                          Your loving husband,
                          W

*G*eorge *Bernard Shaw to Beatrice Stella Campbell, February 6, 1913:*

Stella,

      Stella what is there left to say? . . . How did I get it ground into me that happiness is always picked up on the way and must not be sought? Yet there is something in it: it came nobly off today. Stella: I WAS happy. Was! I *am*. I shall never be unhappy again. . . . oh Stella Stella Stella Stella Stella Stella

                          G.B.S.

*H*enry VIII *to Anne Boleyn, c. 1527:*

> Mine own Sweetheart, this shall be to advertise you of the great
> melancholy that I find here since your departing; for, I ensure you,
> methinketh the time longer since your departing now last than I was
> wont to do a whole fortnight. I think your kindness and my fervency of
> love causeth it; for, otherwise I would not have thought it possible that
> for so little a while it should have grieved me. But now I am coming
> towards you, methinketh my pains by half removed. . . . Wishing
> myself (especially an evening) in my sweetheart's arms whose pretty
> duckies I trust shortly to kiss. Written by the hand of him that was, is,
> and shall be yours by his own will,
>
> H.R.

*K*ing Henry VIII *to Katharine Parr, September 8, 1544:*

> Most dearly and most entirely beloved wife, we recommend us
> heartily unto you, and thank you as well for your letter written unto us
> by your servant Robert Warner as for the venison which you sent then
> by him, and now last by Fowler, servant unto our dearest son the
> Prince, for the which we give unto you our hearty thanks, and would
> have written unto you again a letter with our own hand, but that we be
> so occupied, and have so much to do in foreseeing and caring for
> everything ourself, as we have almost no manner rest or leisure to do
> any other thing. . . .

Charles R. Drew to Lenore Robbins Drew, April 9, 1939:

Lenore,

With a heart that's full with a newfound joy my thoughts turn to you as the day closes, and a sigh rises as an evening prayer to ask whatever gods there be to keep you safe for me. Since first seeing you I have moved through the days as one in a dream, lost in reverie, awed by the speed with which the moving finger of fate has pointed out the way I should go. As the miles of countryside sped by on our return trip I sat silent and pondered on the power that lies in a smile to change the course of a life; the magic in the tilt of a head, the beauty of your carriage and the gentleness that struck so deeply.

Later, when I become more coherent, I shall say perhaps many things but tonight this one thing alone seems to ring clearly,

I love you.

Charlie

Wolfgang Amadeus Mozart to Constanze Mozart, April 13, 1789:

Dearest, best little Wife!

. . . if only I had a letter from you! If I were to tell you all the things I do with your dear portrait you would often laugh, I think! For instance, when I take it out of its case, I say, "Good morrow, Stanzerl! Good day, little rogue—pussy-wussy! saucy one!—good-for-nothing!— dainty morsel!" And when I put it back I slip it in little by little saying all the time, "Ny—nu—nu—nu" with just the peculiar emphasis that this very meaningful word demands, and then, just at the last, quickly, "Good night, little pet—sleep sound!" Well, I suppose that what I have written is folly (to the world, at least) but to us, loving each other as devotedly as we do, it is *not* folly. Today is the sixth since I left you, and, by God, it seems a year!

Ogden Nash to his future wife Frances Rider Leonard, August 25, 1929:

Frances darling,

Have you heard that I love you? I'm not sure that I made it clear to you, and I don't want to have any misunderstanding. It's such a young love yet—just nine and a half months old, born November 13th, 1928 at about nine o'clock in the evening. But it's big for its age, and seems much older. . . .

This is a peculiarly gifted and intelligent pen. Look what it's writing now: I love you. That's a phrase I can't get out of my head—but I don't want to. I've wanted to try it out for a long time; I like the look of it and the sound of it and the meaning of it.

It's past one now and I've got to have some sleep before I face Nelson Doubleday tomorrow. But tell me something before I leave. I was told tonight on what seemed to me the best authority that you are fond of me. Can you confirm this rumor?

Then there's another problem. As long as I'm thinking about you I can't go to sleep; and I'd rather think about you than go to sleep; how am I to sleep?

Oh, Frances, do tell me that everything really happened, that it wasn't just something that I wanted so much that it crystallized in my imagination. . . .

I do love you.

John Muir to Louie Wanda Strentzel Muir, Sitka, Alaska, August 10, 1880:

My own dear Louie,

I'm now about as far from you as I will be this year—only this wee sail to the North and then to thee, my lassie. And I'm not away at all, you know, for only they who do not love may ever be apart. There is no true separation for those whose hearts and souls are together. . . .

Affectionately, your husband,
John Muir

Zelda Sayre to F. Scott Fitzgerald, 1919:

Sweetheart,

Please, please don't be so depressed. We'll be married soon, and then these lonesome nights will be over forever—and until we are, I am loving, loving every tiny minute of the day and night. Maybe you won't understand this, but sometimes when I miss you most, it's hardest to write—and you always know when I make myself—Just the ache of it all—and I can't tell you. . . .

Scott—there's nothing in all the world I want but you—and your precious love. All the material things are nothing. I'd just hate to live a sordid, colorless existence—because you'd soon love me less—and less—and I'd do anything—anything—to keep your heart for my own—I don't want to live—I want to love first, and live incidentally. . . .

All my heart. I love you,

Robert Schumann to Clara Wieck, March 17, 1838:

. . . I have discovered that nothing lends wings to the imagination so much as suspense and longing for something, as happened again in the last few days when, waiting for your letter, I composed whole volumes—strange, crazy, even cheerful stuff. It will make you open your eyes if you ever come to play it—indeed, nowadays I am often ready to burst with sheer music. And I must not forget to tell you what I composed. Perhaps it was a kind of echo of one of your letters, where you wrote that "I sometimes seemed to you to be like a child too"—at any rate I felt just as though I were in short frocks again, and I wrote some 30 little droll things, from which I have chosen about 12 and called them *Scenes from Childhood.* . . .

Dolly Madison to James Madison, October 26, 1805:

My dearest Husband,

> Peter returned safe with your dear letter, and cheered me with a favorable account of the prospects of your getting home in the stage. . . . I am getting well as fast as I can, for I have the reward in view of then seeing my beloved. . . . Farewell, until to-morrow, my best friend; think of thy wife, who thinks and dreams of thee.

> > Dolly

Paul Laurence Dunbar to his future wife Alice Ruth Moore, March 7, 1897:

Alice:

> My darling, someday, when I can hold you in my arms and punctuate every sentence with a kiss and an embrace I may be able to tell you how happy your letter has made me. . . .

> Will I love you tenderly and faithfully? Darling, darling, can you ask! You who are my heart, my all, my life. I will love you as no man has ever loved before. Already I am living for you and working for you and through the gray days and the long nights I am longing and yearning for you—for the sound of your voice, the touch of your hand, the magic of your presence, the thrill of your kiss. . . .

> Love me, dear, and tell me so. Write to me often and believe me ever

> > Your devoted lover,
> > Paul

A melia Earhart to George Putnam the morning of their wedding, February 7, 1931:

Dear GP,

There are some things which should be writ before we are married. Things we have talked over before—most of them.

You must know again my reluctance to marry, my feeling that I shatter thereby chances in work which means so much to me. I feel the move just now as foolish as anything I could do. I know there may be compensations, but have no heart to look ahead.

In our life together I shall not hold you to any medieval code of faithfulness to me, nor shall I consider myself bound to you similarly. If we can be honest I think the differences which arise may best be avoided.

Please let us not interfere with each other's work or play, nor let the world see private joys or disagreements. In this connection I may have to keep some place where I can go to be myself now and then, for I cannot guarantee to endure at all times the confinement of even an attractive cage.

I must exact a cruel promise, and this is that you will let me go in a year if we find no happiness together.

I will try to do my best in every way.

AE

S imone de Beauvoir to Paul Sartre, September 25, 1939:

My love, my dear love,

My heart's just mush this evening, I'm consumed by passion for you and it couldn't be more painful. This has been brewing all day and it came down on me like a tornado in the streets of Douarnenez, where I broke into sobs. Luckily it was moonlight! . . . O my love, I do so long for your tenderness this evening! I feel I've never told you enough how I loved you, that I've never been nice enough to you. . . . I love you passionately.

Your charming Beaver

Gustav Mahler to Alma Mahler, December 15, 1901:

> So, dearest, now comes the best part of my day. I sit down and talk to you. I've been tormenting and worrying the hall-porter all day. I thought one line at least was sure to come, and so I've been hoping and hoping all day and now set my hopes on the first post tomorrow morning. Yes, a man can become so greedy and exacting in eight days that he cannot hold out for one day without a letter. . . . A thousand kisses and what I had better not think of in case I die of longing! My beloved, my friend, my Alma!
>
> Your
Gustav

Oskar Kokoschka to Alma Mahler, January 6, 1915:

Dear Goddess from last night's dream!

I was being chased by an enraged little man, and I fled to you across extraordinary Italian landscapes which were illuminated by a fire; and you were not like a person, however, but like a word that I heard all the time inside me, while the other inhabitants of this nocturnal planet conducted loud conversations without any warmth. I awoke strengthened, and heard again your soft, darling admonitions in your darling letters. I telephoned you today, in order to hear your angelic voice once more, and as a result I shall be very good for the rest of the day.

The enraged little man was the major, who screamed a shrill "No!" at me yesterday, when I asked for permission to go and see you. . . .

I belong to you.

Oskar

Bean Brummell (George Bryan Brummell) in one of many similar letters written to various women, 1818:

Yesterday morning, I was subdued almost to insanity, but your note in the evening restored me to peace and equanimity, and, as if I had been redeemed from earthly purgatory, placed me in heaven. Thank you, thank you, dearest of beings; how can I retribute all this benevolent open-heartedness, this delightful proof and avowal of my not being indifferent to you? I cannot, by inanimate words, then, with indulgent admission and forbearance, the simple boon, a sacred pledge of my heart's deepest affections for you; they are rooted in my very soul and existence; they will never deviate; they will never die away. . . .

I have known few that could equal, none that could excel you; yet they possessed not your charms of countenance, your form, your heart, in my estimation. Certainly they did not possess that unaffected and fervent homage, which in my constant memory—in my heart's blood—and in my devoted soul I bear to you.

Ever most affectionately yours,
George Brummell

Elizabeth Custer to George Armstrong Custer, July 1873:

My Darling Boy,

Your magnificent letter of 42 pages sent me in the seventh heaven of bliss. I had declined an invitation to the Lake, preferring to wait for the one o'clock train with mail. Ten years have so changed me in some respects that though I enjoy even the simple pleasures of Monroe I no longer go into ecstasies over anything but your letters. How we have managed to preserve the romance . . . after nine years of married life and all our vicissitudes. . . . But, though we have had our trials, you have the blessed faculty of looking on the sunny side of things. Dear Autie, you are the richest of men. . . . God keep you, my precious darling. I kiss you a hundred times.

George Armstrong Custer to Elizabeth Custer, April 17, 1876:

My Darling Sunbeam,

If you only knew how truly a sunbeam you are to me!. . . The lines you sent me are lovely. I showed them to a lady at this hotel. She said, "Your sweetheart sent them. Never your wife." I told her "Both are one." "What? How long have you been married?" "Twelve years." "And haven't got over that?" "No. And never shall.". . .

Your devoted Autie

Heinrich von Kleist to Henrietta Vogel, 1810:

My little Henrietta, my little heart, my dear thing, my dovelet, my life, my dear sweet life, my life-light, my all, my goods and chattels, my castles, acres, lawns, and vineyards, O sun of my life, Sun, Moon, and Stars, Heaven and Earth, my Past and Future, my bride, my girl, my dear friend, my inmost being, my heart-blood, my entrails, star of my eyes, O dearest, what shall I call you?

My golden child, my pearl, my precious stone, my crown, my queen and empress. You dear darling of my heart, my highest and most precious, my all and everything, my wife, my wedding, the baptism of my children, my tragic play, my posthumous reputation. Ach! you are my second better self, my virtues, my merits, my hope, the forgiveness of my sins, my future and sanctity, O little daughter of Heaven, my child of God, my intercessor, my guardian angel, my Cherubim and Seraph, how I love you!

Sir Richard Steele to Mrs. Scurlock, August 30, 1707:

Madam,

I beg pardon that my paper is not finer; but I am forced to write from a coffeehouse where I am attending about business. There is a dirty crowd of busy faces all around me, talking of money; while all my ambition, all my wealth, is love! Love, which animates my heart, sweetens my humor, enlarges my soul, and affects every action of my life. It is to my lovely charmer I owe, that many noble ideas are continually affixed to my words and actions; it is the natural effect of that generous passion, to create in the admirer some similitude of the object admired. Thus, my dear, am I every day to improve from so sweet a companion. . . . I am forever your faithful servant.

The next day:

Madam,

It is the hardest thing in the world to be in love, and yet attend business. As for me, all who speak to me find out, and I must lock myself up, or other people will do it for me. A gentleman asked me this morning, What news from Lisbon? and I answered, She's exquisitely handsome. Another desired to know when I had last been at Hampton Court; I replied, 'Twill be on Tuesday come se'nnight. Prithee, allow me at least to kiss your hand before that day, that my mind may be in some composure. O Love!. . . Methinks I could write a volume to you, but all the language on earth would fail in saying how much, and with what disinterested passion, I am ever yours,

Rich. Steele

Three years later:

Dear Prue,

I am very sleepy and tired, but could not think of closing my eyes till I had told you I am, dearest creature,

Your most affectionate and faithful husband,
Richard Steele

Queen Christina of Sweden to Prince Karl Gustaf, whom she did not marry but whom she named her successor when she abdicated the throne, January 5, 1644:

Beloved Cousin,

I see by your letter that you do not trust your thoughts to the pen. We may, however, correspond with all freedom, if you send me the key to a cipher, and compose your letters according to it, and change the seals, as I do with mine. Then the letters may be sent to your sister, the Princess Maria. You must take every precaution, for never were people here so much against us as now; but they shall never get their way, so long as you remain firm. . . . My love is so strong that it can only be overcome by death, and if, which God forbid, you should die before me, my heart shall remain dead for every other, and my mind and affection shall follow you to eternity, there to dwell with you.

Perhaps some will advise you to demand my hand openly; but I beseech you, by all that is holy, to have patience for some time, until you have acquired some reputation in the war, and until I have the crown on my head. I entreat you not to consider this time long, but to think of the old saying: "He does not wait too long who waits for something good." I hope, by God's blessing, that it is a good thing we both are waiting for.

Charles A. Lindbergh to Anne Morrow Lindbergh, April 28, 1942:

Dear Anne:

 . . . The hours you were here have slipped through my fingers like water, and are gone. When you are gone, I feel your absence all around me and I am acutely conscious of the passage of time. When you were here, I was so surrounded by the warmth and satisfaction of your presence that time slipped by unnoticed behind my back. I was keenly aware of you before you came. I am keenly aware that you *were here*. Possibly tomorrow, or even next week I may realize it; but now I can only think how little I have saved of your visit. Our search for a house, our discussions of the future, all those routine details remain clear and tangible enough. When I think of them, these last four days stand out like posts against the sky. But you—the essence of you—have not remained in that landscape. I think it is because you do not belong there, because the essence of you is not a part of these routine problems of life—it is something far above and far beyond, and when you touch life you leave a feeling of immortality behind, a feeling that is deeper and stronger than the memory of your presence. It is what I meant when I wrote you that you had a touch of divinity in your pen. It is what I have felt ever since I have known you. I feel it more strongly with every year that passes.

 After leaving you and Jon at the station, I came back to the Inn planning on reading and studying through the evening; but I found that I had to write this letter, that I had to try to tell you in a letter what I have never been able to tell you quite adequately in words. Not that I have told it adequately here, but I have been able to say more, and say it in a different way, and in so doing to bring you more closely to me, for you seemed farther away in the hour after you left than you were in the days before you came.

   With all the love I can send you,

   C.A.L.

Anne Morrow Lindbergh to Charles A. Lindbergh, May 3, 1942:

Dear C.,

Jon and I arrived last night after a long but not too difficult day
on the train. I wrote you from the train but now I feel days removed
from it. . . . I still have not answered your letter. It was a love letter. One
does not say "thank you" for a love letter. One thinks only, "Why
should I ever ask for anything else if I have this?"

Lydia Maria Child to David Lee Child, August 8, 1830:

Dearest Husband,

Here I am in a snug little old-fashioned parlor, at a round
table, in a rocking chair, writing to you, and the greatest comfort I have
is the pen-knife you sharpened for me just before I came away. As you
tell me sometimes, it makes my heart leap to see anything you have
touched. . . . I went down to a little cove between two lines of rocks
this morning, and having taken off my stockings, I let the saucy waves
come dashing and sparkling into my lap. I was a little sad, because it
made me think of the beautiful time we had, when we washed our feet
together in the mountain waterfall. How I do wish you were here! It is
nonsense for me to go a "pleasuring" without you. It does me no good,
and every pleasant sight makes my heart yearn for you to be with me. I
am very homesick for you; and my private opinion is, that I shall not
be able to stand it a whole week. . . .

*R*obert Browning, excerpt of first letter to Elizabeth Barrett Browning, January 10, 1845:

I love your verses with all my heart, dear Miss Barrett . . . this great living poetry of yours, not a flower of which but took root and grew—Oh, how different that is from lying to be dried and pressed flat, and prized highly, and put in a book with a proper account at top and bottom, and shut up and put away. . . . I do, as I say, love these books with all my heart—and I love you too. Do you know I was once not very far from seeing—really seeing you? Mr. Kenyon said to me one morning, "Would you like to see Miss Barrett?" Then he went to announce me—then he returned . . . you were too unwell, and now it is years ago, and I feel as at some untoward passage in my travels, as if I had been close, so close, to some world's-wonder in chapel or crypt, only a screen to push and I might have entered, but there was some slight, so it now seems, slight and just sufficient bar to admission, and the half-opened door shut, and I went home my thousands of miles, and the sight was never to be.

Well, these poems were to be, and this true thankful joy and pride with which I feel myself,

Yours ever faithfully,
Robert Browning

*E*lizabeth Barrett Browning to Robert Browning, August 17, 1846:

How I thank you for your letter, ever beloved. You were made perfectly to be loved—and surely I have loved you, in the idea of you, my whole life long. Did I tell you *that* before, so often as I have thought it? It is *that* which makes me take it all as visionary good—for when one's Ideal comes down to one, and walks beside one suddenly, what is it possible to do but to cry out, "A dream?" You are the best. . . . You have lifted my very soul up into the light of your soul, and I am not ever likely to mistake it for the common daylight. May God bless you, ever ever dearest! I am your own.

Rachel Carson to Dorothy Freeman, February 20, 1954:

My precious darling,

What lovely surprises this week!. . . Friday, I found myself watching for the mailman—habit, do you suppose?—although I told myself firmly that of course there wouldn't be anything from you—there just wouldn't! But the irresponsible half of me answered back that there just *might* be, and kept watching. And was so, so rewarded when there was your dear handwriting after all! Today I wouldn't let myself watch but when I heard the rattle at the mailbox my heart leaped as if it knew. As one little measure of how much those letters meant, I'll tell you that hours later I suddenly realized that the rest of the mail was still lying unopened. . . .

My darling, there is no end to the things that might be said now that what you call "The Revelation" has been put on paper. How blind I was not to realize sooner that I should say it! Do you remember now that I did at least skirt around the edge of the subject that day as we were sitting in the car watching the ducks? But so tentatively, I suppose, that you, darling, didn't know what I meant! And while the essence of it all was in my heart then, probably it's true that I hadn't thought it all out. Yes, we were a little shy, weren't we, especially at first—but it was rather sweet that way and perhaps as it should have been for the first time you and I were together!. . .

But, oh darling, I want to be with you so terribly that it hurts! . . . I love you darling—I don't need to tell you but I shall anyway.

*F*or me, being rich means to possess—
apart from the tenderness of a loved
one and my friends—a bit of ground, a car that runs,
good health, and the freedom not to work when I
don't want to, or cannot.

COLETTE, LETTER TO MARGUERITE MORENO, 1927

Your request for eighty dollars I do not think it best to comply with now. At the various times when I have helped you a little you have said to me, "We can get along very well now," but in a very short time I find you in the same difficulty again. . . . Let father and your boys take charge of your

Letters About Money

"People keep telling us about their love affairs," says Mignon McLaughlin, "when what we really want to know is how much money they make and how they manage on it." One way to find out is to read their letters. Many of the most creative and productive individuals in history did not, in fact, "manage" on their money. Their letters are riven with money anxieties, desperate appeals to family and friends, and reports of fruitless efforts to produce income. Another class of money letters are those that have always traveled between the younger generation's empty pockets and the older generation's supposedly deep pockets. Abraham Lincoln dispenses mercy, advice, and justice—the first two not to offspring but to his father and brother.

P.G. Wodehouse to George Horace Lorrimer at the <u>Saturday Evening Post</u>, 1936:

> Dear Mr. Lorrimer,
>
> I am so intensely spiritual that money means nothing to me, but I must confess that that $2,000 was a bit of a sock on the jaw, as I had been expecting $4,000.

*M*adame de Staël to Monsieur Dupont de Nemours, June 5, 1804:

> My dear du Pont,
>
> I know nothing sadder than having business affairs between friends, but . . . if you cannot pay on the due date, I must ask you to send me a note for a year from this date with the guarantee of someone that you will name. . . .

*G*rover Cleveland to Mrs. Minnie Scott, April 4, 1886:

> Your letter, portraying a condition which greatly excites my sympathy, is received. I have many such and find it utterly impossible to comply with the requests for aid which they contain in a great many cases. I am so well convinced of your truthfulness and good faith that I am constrained to send you a small sum, which I hope will add to your comfort and that of the young triplets. I am so unaccustomed to matters of the kind that I must ask to be excused from the attempt to give names to the three little girls.

Bean Brummell to fellow gambler Scrope Davies, May 16, 1816:

> My dear Scrope,
>   Lend me two hundred pounds. The banks are shut, and all my money is in the three percents. It shall be repaid tomorrow.
>   Yours,
>   George Brummell

Immediate reply from Scrope Davies:

> My dear George,
>   'Tis very unfortunate; but all my money is in the three percents.
>   Yours,
>   S. Davies

Silla-Labbum and Elani to Puzur-Assur, Amua, and Assur-samsi, c. 2000 B.C.:

> Thirty years ago you left the city of Assur. You have never made a deposit since, and we have not recovered one shekel of silver from you, but we have never made you feel bad about this. Our tablets have been going to you with caravan after caravan, but no report from you has ever come here. We have addressed claims to your father but we have not been claiming one shekel of your private silver. Please, do come back right away; should you be too busy with your business, deposit the silver for us. . . . If not, we will send you a notice from the local ruler and the police, and thus put you to shame in the assembly of the merchants. You will also cease to be one of us.

Henri de Toulouse-Lautrec to his mother, January 1899:

My dear Mama,

I have wired you to send me 100 francs so I won't be obliged to beg from the concierge, who is a rude man. . . .

Wolfgang Amadeus Mozart to his friend Michael Puchberg, June 1788:

Dear Brother,

Your true friendship and brotherly love embolden me to ask you for a great favor: I still owe you 8 ducats—and not only am I unable at the moment to repay them, but my confidence in you is so great that I venture to beg you to help me, only until next week (when my concerts at the Casino begin), with the loan of 100 fl.; the subscription money cannot fail to be in my hands by that time, and I can quite easily repay you 136 fl., with my warmest thanks. . . .

Zora Neale Hurston to her white patron Mrs. R. Osgood Mason, April 27, 1932:

. . . I really need a pair of shoes. You remember that we discussed the matter in the fall and agreed that I should own only one pair at a time. I bought a pair in mid-December and they have held up until now. My big toe is about to burst out of my right shoe and so I must do something about it.

Charles Dickens to Henry Fielding Dickens, October 15, 1868:

My dear Harry:

I have your letter here this morning. I enclose you another check for twenty-five pounds. . . .

Now, observe attentively. We must have no shadow of debt. Square up everything whatsoever that it has been necessary to buy. Let not a farthing be outstanding on any account, when we begin together with your allowance. . . . It appears to me that an allowance of two hundred and fifty pounds a year will be handsome for all your wants. . . .

Whatever you do, above all other things keep out of debt and confide in me. . . .

Ever your affectionate Father,

Groucho Marx to his son, 1941:

Dear Arthur:

I can't understand why you don't get any mail from me. Perhaps it's because I haven't been writing. However, now that you've broken your silence, I will do the same, despite the fact that you probably wouldn't have written if you hadn't needed money. Well, that's one of the nice things about holding the purse strings. Eventually, children come around to seeing things your way. . . .

Love,
Padre

Henry D. Thoreau to Henry G. Denny, accompanying his contribution to the fund for the public library of Harvard College, February 1859:

Dear Sir,

Enclosed please find five dollars, for the object above described. I would gladly give more, but this exceeds my income from all sources together for the last four months.

Y'rs respectfully,
Henry D. Thoreau

Abraham Lincoln to his father Thomas Lincoln, December 24, 1848:

My dear Father:

Your letter of the 7th was received night before last. I very cheerfully send you the twenty dollars, which sum you say is necessary to save your land from sale. It is singular that you should have forgotten a judgment against you; and it is more singular that the plaintiff should have let you forget it so long, particularly as I suppose you have always had property enough to satisfy a judgment of that amount. Before you pay it, it would be well to be sure you have not paid it; or, at least, that you can not prove you have paid it.

Give my love to Mother and all the connections.

Affectionately your Son,

*A*braham *Lincoln to his stepbrother John D. Johnston, January 2, 1851:*

Dear Johnston:

Your request for eighty dollars I do not think it best to comply with now. At the various times when I have helped you a little you have said to me, "We can get along very well now," but in a very short time I find you in the same difficulty again. . . . Let father and your boys take charge of your things at home, prepare for a crop, and make the crop, and you go to work for the best money wages, or in discharge of any debt you owe, that you can get; and, to secure you a fair reward for your labor, I now promise you, that for every dollar you will, between this and the first of May, get for your own labor, either in money, or as your own indebtedness, I will then give you one other dollar. . . . Now, if you will do this, you will soon be out of debt, and, what is better, you will have a habit that will keep you from getting in debt again. But, if I should now clear you out, next year you will be just as deep in as ever. . . . You have always been kind to me, and I do not mean to be unkind to you. On the contrary, if you will but follow my advice, you will find it worth more than eighty times eighty dollars to you.

Affectionately your brother,

*A*braham *Lincoln to George P. Floyd, February 21, 1856:*

Dear Sir:

I have just received yours of 16th, with check on Flagg & Savage for twenty-five dollars. You must think I am a high-priced man. You are too liberal with your money.

Fifteen dollars is enough for the job. I send you a receipt for fifteen dollars, and return to you a ten-dollar bill.

Yours truly,

Mark Twain to Frank E. Bliss, November 4, 1897:

Dear Bliss,

Your cablegram informing me that a report is in circulation which purports to come from me and which says I have recently made $82,000 and paid all my debts has just reached me, and I have cabled back my regret to you that it is not true. I wrote a letter—a private letter—a short time ago, in which I expressed the belief that I should be out of debt within the next twelvemonth. . . .

It is out of that moderate letter that the Eighty-Two-Thousand-Dollar mare's nest has developed. But why do you worry about the various reports? . . . It has been reported that I was seriously ill—it was another man; dying—it was another man; dead—the other man again. It has been reported that I have received a legacy—it was another man; that I am out of debt—it was another man; and now comes this $82,000—still another man. It has been reported that I am writing books—for publication; I am not doing anything of the kind. It would surprise (and gratify) me if I should be able to get another book ready for the press within the next three years. You can see, yourself, that there isn't anything more to be reported—invention is exhausted. Therefore, don't worry, Bliss—the long night is breaking. . . .

Truly yours,
Mark Twain

P.S. This is not a private letter. I am getting tired of private letters.

Hannah Whitall Smith to her sister, March 28, 1885:

Sarah, I want to ask thee a solemn question. Did thee ever one single time have thy Bank book balance and thy own check book balance agree exactly? Do not tell, but *I* never did. . . .

Katharine Hathaway to her husband Dan Hathaway, 1933:

Dearest Mr. Muffet,

. . . Sometimes I have hurt you without meaning to at all. . . .
Especially so on the subject of money, which is something I am
absolutely determined shall not make us unhappy together. . . . I think
if you understood really and truly the thing I feel about money, you
would believe once and for all that I am never trying to hurt you, or
deprive you or coerce you.

To me, money is alive. It is almost human. If you treat it with
real sympathy and kindness and consideration, it will be a good servant
and work hard for you, and stay with you and take care of you. If you
treat it arrogantly and contemptuously, as if it were not human, as if it
were only a slave and could work without limit, it will turn on you
with a great revenge and leave you to look after yourself alone. . . .
Look at the history of the past year in our checkbooks and look at us
now. It is our own fault, nobody else's. We had a very, very good servant in the beginning, and we let it get absolutely out of control. . . .

It is obvious that we can't live without our servant, and we
can't live tranquilly if it is threatening to leave every few months.

Mrs. Muffet loves Mr. Muffet very, very much. That alone is the
whole reason for everything. The reason I am passionate, obstinate, and
sometimes angry about money is because our life together depends on
it. It depends not only on having it, but on not being tormented every
day by little conflicts about it. . . .

*W*hen I spoke of the Progressive Party as having a lunatic fringe, I specifically had you in mind. On the supposition that you are of entire sound mind, I should be obliged to say that you are absolutely dishonorable and untruthful. I prefer to accept the former alternative.

THEODORE ROOSEVELT, LETTER TO AMOS RICHARDS ENO PINCHOT, 1916

I am no fool, neither are you, but you might pass for one, if in good earnest you did not understand my letter. You tell me what is self-evident—that I have no right to inherit Colonel Needham's property. . . . Do not be afraid that I am going to give you any fresh trouble about this affair,

Outspoken Letters

When told she was outspoken, Dorothy Parker quickly demanded, "By whom?" She would like this chapter. C.E. Vulliamy says "letters are valuable and entertaining in proportion to the wit and ability, and above all to the imprudence, of those who write them." To come across plain-speaking—to say nothing of high dudgeon and anger—in a person's letters is to stop for a moment of pure admiration and envy. Some people seem more prone to the choleric letter (see a second letter from Theodore Roosevelt that follows). But, in general, letterwriters have moderated their language as society has become more litigious. Mignon McLaughlin said it took us thousands of years to put words down on paper, and our lawyers still wish we wouldn't.

*T*heodore Roosevelt to John Watson Foster, June 13, 1911:

Dear Sir:

Your statements are false, and you know them to be false. Mr. Henry White, recently Ambassador to France, was speaking to me of the matter the other day. He knows all the facts of the case, and was the man through whom the intimate and decisive negotiations were carried on. He can corroborate every statement I made about the Alaska negotiations. As for your statement that Mr. Hay did not refer to you in a contemptuous manner, or criticize your conduct, that is mere nonsense. Mr. Hay, in talking of you to me, habitually alluded to you by the name of Chin-pen-fee. Such a nickname is incompatible with his belief that your conduct was proper.

*L*ady Hester Stanhope to Sir Francis Burdett, July 20, 1838:

My dear Burdett,

I am no fool, neither are you, but you might pass for one, if in good earnest you did not understand my letter. You tell me what is self-evident—that I have no right to inherit Colonel Needham's property. . . . Do not be afraid that I am going to give you any fresh trouble about this affair, notwithstanding I believe you were some time hatching this stupid answer, but I do not owe you any grudge, as I know it does not come from you; I know where it comes from.

A lion of the desert, being caught in the huntsman's net, called in vain to the beasts in the field to assist him, and received from them about as shuffling an answer as I have received from you, and previously from Lord Hardwicke. A little field-mouse gnawed the master-knot and called to the lion to make a great effort, which burst the noose, and out came the lion stronger than ever.

I am now about building up every avenue to my premises, and there shall wait with patience, immured within the walls, till it please God to send me a little mouse. . . .

Elizabeth I to Dr. Richard Cox, Bishop of Ely, 1573:

Proud Prelate,

You know what you were before I made you what you are now. If you do not immediately comply with my request, I will unfrock you, by God.

Grover Cleveland to William P. Larkins, April 14, 1888:

I must ask you to excuse me from my engagement with you this morning. When I made it I did not know who you were nor the object of your request. I have learned both from Mr. Martin's letter and am satisfied I can improve my time much more profitably at this extremely busy period than by talking politics with you.

Ludwig van Beethoven to Nikolaus Simrock, October 4, 1804:

Dear, most excellent Herr Simrock,

For a long time already I have been waiting impatiently for a copy of the sonata which I gave you, but in vain. Kindly let me know what exactly is being done about it and whether you acquired it from me only to give the moths a feast. . . . What is happening to the slow devil who is to see that my sonata is published? Usually you are the quick devil, are notorious for being in league with the black devil, as Faust was once, and are not less loved for it by your fellows. Once again: where is the devil, and what sort of a devil is it, who is sitting on my sonata. . .?

S.J. Perelman to Arthur H. Rosen, president of the National Committee on United States-China Relations, Inc., July 17, 1978:

Dear Sir:

I am in receipt of your boorish little note in which you dub me "an alte knacker" (whatever you conceive that to mean) and a "meshugener" (misspelled though the intent is clear), and equate me with folk seeking to perform rock on the Great Wall and to canoe on the Yangtse. Not content with these gibes at a person unknown to you, you then demand with a cackle whether I consider myself a comedian. All the foregoing, please note, on the basis of a telephone inquiry reported to you by a subordinate, the details of which you know nothing about.

Let me, therefore, reply as succinctly as I can. I have never before heard of you, but if the above is indicative of your skill at furthering relations between the United States and China, you are lamentably miscast. . . .

Samuel Johnson to James Macpherson, January 20, 1775:

Mr. James Macpherson,

I received your foolish and impudent letter. Any violence offered me I shall do my best to repel; and what I cannot do for myself, the law shall do for me. I hope I shall never be deterred from detecting what I think a cheat by the menaces of a ruffian.

What would you have me retract? I thought your book an imposture; I think it an imposture still. For this opinion I have given my reason to the public, which I here dare you to refute. Your rage I defy. Your abilities . . . are not so formidable; and what I hear of your morals inclines me to pay regard not to what you shall say, but to what you shall prove. You may print this if you will.

Frank Lloyd Wright to Mrs. Walker, February 28, 1951:

My dear Mrs. Walker:

Again we are up in the air. Looks very much as though the "Cabin on the Rocks" was on the rocks in more senses than one. You were once of my mind about the cabin. You gave me reason to think so and I was happy to build it as I put my best mind and heart into producing a little masterpiece appropriate to the unique site.

An ordinary little door and window house on that site would look as foolish as a hen resting where you ought to find a seagull.

I am unwilling to spoil my charming seabird and substitute the hen. You don't need me for that. Anyone can do it.

E. E. Cummings to James Light, January 8, 1951:

Dear Jimmy—

Could A A perhaps do something quick for Joe Gould? He's almost on it now. Seems to totter between Minetta Tavern & Goody's Bar, with occasional stumblings in the direction of Dorothy Day
—here's hoping.

Three days later to Joe Gould:

Dear Joe—

you and I've been friends for quite some time. But we're not going to be friends much longer unless you sober up and stay sober. . . .

*S*herwood Anderson to Thomas Wolfe, December 17, 1937:

Dear Tom:

I do hope, Tom, you didn't take seriously the queer row we seemed to have got into that night at Mary's house. I am a bit uncertain yet what it was all about. . . .

I phoned you about the cocktail party Mary Emmett is giving from 5 to 7 next Tuesday afternoon. She is doing it as some kind of scheme to raise money for the Spanish Loyalists; people are going to chip in $2 each.

Dreiser and a lot of others are coming, and I hope you can come, as I'd like to see you again.

Sincerely,

P.S. Why not have dinner with us afterwards at some nearby restaurant?

*T*he next day:

Dear Tom:

When I wrote you yesterday, suggesting that you have dinner with me Tuesday evening, I had no notion how you felt. As you have expressed such a hearty desire to chuck our acquaintance, why not?

Ursula Nordstrom to Hilary Knight, September 18, 1964:

Dear Hilary,

I hesitate to worry you, but I thought I should tell you that some enemy of yours is writing me very angry letters, and signing your name to them.

John O'Hara to his editor, Bennett Cerf, on Arthur Mizener who had reviewed From the Terrace *unfavorably, November 2, 1963:*

Dear Bennett:

I cannot find words to express my anger at seeing the Signet edition of *Appointment in Samarra*, with an "Afterward" by Arthur Mizener.

I want you to go to the telephone on receipt of this letter, and tell the New American Library that the Mizener comments must be killed immediately. I don't give a God damn whether it means killing the whole edition.

At this moment you are very close to losing an author. This is one of the most outrageous performances I have ever known, and in future, if there is to be any future, no deal is to be made for reprint of anything of mine without my being consulted in all details.

As for the present, you know what I want done. I have made myself clear. I don't care how you do it, but I want that "afterword" killed.

*M*ari Sandoz to Mrs. Ray C. Wiles, October 29, 1959:

Dear Mrs. Wiles:

After eight months of research in the west and speaking from Colorado to Swampscott, Mass., I returned here to find boxes of mail that never caught up with me. Your postcard about the placement of the word *only* in a sentence in *Hostiles and Friendlies* was among the accumulation.

All I can say is that I am sorry my writing reached your purist's eye. . . .

Your card reminded me of the letter Dr. Weseen, head of Business English, University of Nebraska, once wrote to Willa Cather, one of the world's great stylists. He listed over 400 grammatical errors in one of her books. Her reply, paraphrased, was, "Only that many?" . . .

*S*ergei Prokofiev to Paul Bowler, August 27, 1930:

Dear Mr. Bowler:

It isn't that your Minuet is old-fashioned, but it is written in a rather uninteresting way. This is why: it consists of 24 measures, then three closing chords, but in these 24 measures there are only 5 measures of music (1-4, and 9). The rest is nothing but repetition of these five measures.

Now suppose I were to compose a symphony lasting 24 minutes in which there were only 5 minutes of music, and the remainder nothing but repetition of the preceding part. How boring!

You will say that the reason this happened was that you haven't learned how to compose, and that you sent me the manuscript to find out whether it was worth the trouble of learning. Well, my friend, I have never been able to judge a composer on the basis of 5 measures, and no composer has ever sent me 5 measures for me to give my opinion of his music.

Sincerely yours,

Arnold Schoenberg to Otto Klemperer, September 25, 1940:

Dear Klemperer,

You have been misinformed. I did not say that you "do not like some of my works." On the contrary:

I quoted verbatim what you said to me in a discussion that I am sure you have not forgotten:

"Your music has become alien to me."

That is: not "some" of my works, but *all* my works.

There should therefore be no need for any further explanation why I then consider that you should cease to conduct my works. For what can a performance be like if the music has become alien to one?

How it can possibly be insulting to you for me to quote your words requires elucidation.

The fact that you have become estranged from my music has not caused me to feel insulted, though it has certainly estranged me. I do not mean to say that I shall take no further interest in you; although I have no notion how the broken (artistic) bridge is ever to function again.

With best wishes for your health,

Yours sincerely,

*O*n behalf of the women of this
nation—one half of the entire peo-
ple—*I ask you to put a plank in your platform that*
shall assert the duty of the National Government to
protect women citizens in the exercise of their right
to vote. . . .

SUSAN B. ANTHONY, LETTER TO THE COMMITTEE ON PLATFORM AND
RESOLUTIONS OF THE NATIONAL REPUBLICAN CONVENTION, 1872

My friend over in Terebone
Parish received a $1,000
check from the government
this year for not raising hogs.
So I am going into the not-
raising hogs business next
year.
What I want to know is, in
your opinion, what is the
best kind of farm not to
raise hogs on and the best

Letters to Public Officials

kind of hogs not to raise? I would prefer not to raise Razorbacks, but if that is not a good breed not to raise, I will just as gladly not raise Berkshires or Durocs.

The hardest work in this business is going to be in keeping an inventory of how many hogs I haven't raised. My friend is very joyful about the future of his business. He has been raising hogs for more than 30 years

Marian Wright Edelman says, "Democracy is not a spectator sport." The thousands of letters written each year to officeholders and public officials indicate that many people do not watch passively from the political sidelines.

In the letters in this chapter, Albert Schweitzer conveys his concerns to President Kennedy about nuclear disarmament, Frida Kahlo writes the President of Mexico about the concealing of Diego Rivera's murals, and F.D.R. discusses wartime spying with Churchill.

The letters dealing with women's rights illustrate the value of getting involved—and of writing letters about the issues we consider important.

J.B. Lee, Jr. to Congressman Ed Foreman, March 20, 1963:

Dear Sir:

My friend over in Terebone Parish received a $1,000 check from the government this year for not raising hogs. So I am going into the not-raising hogs business next year.

What I want to know is, in your opinion, what is the best kind of farm not to raise hogs on and the best kind of hogs not to raise? I would prefer not to raise Razorbacks, but if that is not a good breed not to raise, I will just as gladly not raise any Berkshires or Durocs.

The hardest work in this business is going to be in keeping an inventory of how many hogs I haven't raised.

My friend is very joyful about the future of his business. He has been raising hogs for more than 30 years and the best he ever made was $400, until this year; when he got $1,000 for not raising hogs.

If I can get $1,000 for not raising 50 hogs, then will I get $2,000 for not raising 100 hogs? I plan to operate on a small scale at first, holding myself down to 4,000 hogs which means I will have $80,000 coming from the government.

Now, another thing: these hogs I will not raise will not eat 100,000 bushels of corn. So will you pay me anything for not raising 100,000 bushels of corn not to feed the hogs I am not raising?

I want to get started as soon as possible as this seems to be a good time of the year for not raising hogs.

One thing more, can I raise 10 or 12 hogs on the side while I am in the not-raising-hog-business, just enough to get a few sides of bacon to eat?

Very truly yours,
J.B. Lee, Jr.
Potential Hog Raiser

Benjamin Franklin to William Strahan, July 5, 1775:

Mr. Strahan,

You are a Member of Parliament, and one of that majority, which has doomed my country to destruction. You have begun to burn our towns and murder our people. Look upon your hands! They are stained with the blood of your relations! You and I were long friends. You are now my enemy, and I am

Yours,

B. Franklin

Albert Schweitzer to John F. Kennedy, April 20, 1962:

Dear President Kennedy,

Would you have the great kindness to forgive me, old as I am, for taking the courage to write you about the tests, which the United States together with England, wants to carry out if Russia does not accede to your request that international inspection on their territory takes care that no tests will take place. . . .

An urgent necessity for the world is that the atomic powers agree as soon as possible on disarmament under effective international control. . . .

The Reverend Martin Luther King, Jr. to Harold Courlander, October 30, 1961:

Public relations is a very necessary part of any protest of civil disobedience. The main objective is to bring moral pressure to bear upon an unjust system or a particularly unjust law. The public at large must be aware of the inequities involved in such a system. . . .

Franklin Delano Roosevelt to Winston Churchill, November 10, 1944:

My dear Winston:

I realize that it is very trying for many people that we should continue to prevent information from leaking out about our submarine methods; but our own submarine campaign in the Pacific is playing such an important role that the Barbarian will seize desperately on any information that will help him in anti-submarine measures. I do hope, therefore, that we may continue to do all that we can to keep anyone from talking too much. I have no doubt that indiscretions are committed in our press but the enclosed has recently appeared under a London date-line.

I will do what I can to keep the lid on here and I know I may count on you for similar measures.

Franklin K. Lane to Woodrow Wilson, March 11, 1914:

My dear Mr. President,

I have your note of yesterday referring to me the correspondence between yourself and the Civil Service Commission on the question of the participation of women Civil Service employees in woman suffrage organizations. I think perhaps I am a prejudiced partisan in this matter for I believe that the women should have the right to agitate for the suffrage. Furthermore, I think they are going to get the suffrage, and that it would be politically unwise for the administration to create the impression that it was attempting to block the movement. I should think it the part of wisdom for you personally to make the announcement that women Civil Service employees will be protected in the right to join woman suffrage organizations and to participate in woman suffrage parades or meetings. This is practically what the Civil Service Commission says, but in a more careful, lawyer-like manner, whereas what is said should be said in a rather robust, forthright style. . . .

E.*B. White to Margaret Chase Smith, August 15, 1966:*

Dear Senator Smith:

I think the Dirksen amendment on voluntary prayer should be defeated. The Constitution is clear on the subject: there shall be no establishment of religion.

Any religious ceremony in a public school is an exercise in orthodoxy—the orthodoxy of the Christian faith, which is correct for most of us, unacceptable to some. In an atmosphere of "voluntary" prayer, pupils coming from homes where other faiths prevail will feel an embarrassment by their non-participation; in the eyes of their schoolmates they will be "queer" or "different" or "irreligious." Such a stigma for a child can be emotionally disturbing, and although we no longer hang and burn our infidels and our witches, a schoolchild who is left out in the cold during a prayer session suffers scars that are very real. . . .

Frida Kahlo to the President of Mexico, Miguel Alemán, October 20, 1948:

Miguel Alemán:

This letter is a protest of just indignation that I want to communicate to you, against a cowardly and humiliating crime that is being perpetrated in this country.

I am referring to an intolerable act without precedent that the owners of the Hotel del Prado are committing by covering up with wooden boards the mural painting by Diego Rivera in the dining hall of this hotel. . . .

That type of crime against the culture of a country, against the right that every man has to express his ideas—those criminal attacks against freedom have only been committed in regimes like Hitler's and are still being committed under Francisco Franco, and in the past, during the dark and negative age of the "Holy" Inquisition.

It is not possible that you . . . can allow a few investors, in complicity with a few ill-willed Mexicans, to cover up the words that tell *the History of Mexico* and the work of a Mexican citizen whom the civilized world recognizes as one of the most illustrious painters of our times.

John Muir to Theodore Roosevelt, April 21, 1908:

Dear Mr. President,

      I am anxious that the Yosemite National Park may be saved from all sorts of commercialism and marks of man's work other than the roads, hotels, etc., required to make its wonders and blessings available. For as far as I have seen there is not in all the wonderful Sierra, or indeed in the world, another so grand and wonderful and useful a block of Nature's mountain handiwork.

      There is now under consideration, as doubtless you well know, an application of San Francisco supervisors for the use of the Hetch-Hetchy Valley and Lake Eleanor as storage reservoirs for a city water supply. This application should, I think, be denied, especially the Hetch-Hetchy part, for this Valley, as you will see by the enclosed descriptions, is a counterpart of Yosemite, and one of the most sublime and beautiful and important features of the Park, and to dam and submerge it would be hardly less destructive and deplorable in its effect on the Park in general than would be the damming of Yosemite itself. . . .

Wilbur and Orville Wright to Congressman Robert M. Nevin, January 18, 1905:

      The series of aeronautical experiments upon which we have been engaged for the past five years has ended in the production of a flying-machine of a type fitted for practical use. It not only flies through the air at high speed, but it also lands without being wrecked. . . .

      If you can find it convenient to ascertain whether this is a subject of interest to our own government, it would oblige us greatly, as early information on this point will aid us in making our plans for the future.

Georgia O'Keeffe to Eleanor Roosevelt, February 10, 1944:

Having noticed in the N.Y. Times of Feb. 1st that you are against the Equal Rights Amendment may I say to you that it is the women who have studied the idea of Equal Rights and worked for Equal Rights that make it possible for you, today, to be the power that you are in our country, to work as you work and to have the kind of public life that you have.

The Equal Rights Amendment would write into the highest law of our country, legal equality for all. At present women do not have it. . . .

It seems to me very important to the idea of true democracy—to my country—and to the world eventually—that all men and women stand equal under the sky—

I wish that you could be with us in the fight. You could be a real help to this change that must come.

Susan B. Anthony to Mrs. Rutherford B. Hayes, 1879:

My dear Mrs. Hayes,

May I not address you, and ask you to help your dear husband the President—to *remember not to forget to sign* the bill to admit Women Lawyers to the Supreme Court? I cannot tell you how my heart leaped for joy yesterday morning as I read the report of the splendid Senate vote of 40 to 20 for that bill! I feel sure the President will not fail to sign it. . . . It is not, I am sure, asking too much of the woman whose good fortune places her in the highest position in the nation, that she shall give the influence, nay, the prestige and power of that position, to crown the life efforts of the few for the full completion of the experiment of a genuine republic on this continent. . . .

*H*ere is my story about a witch, that you were kind enough to say you would like to read. If you like it well enough to think it worth publishing I shall be extremely pleased. If you don't, I shan't be much surprised.

SYLVIA TOWNSEND WARNER, LETTER TO CHARLES PRENTICE, 1929

This is a query. I have a project. It is a work of about 20,000 words and more on the order of my novel than like these stories I've been doing. But it's the sort of thing that will require a full month's work and as The New Republic, Scribner's and possibly the Atlantic

Query Letters

Early in the life of almost every great book or article, its author labored over the most difficult writing of all: the query letter. "A query letter," says Lisel Eisenheimer, "is really a sales letter without the hype." The "sales letters" that brought you *Moby Dick* and *Wuthering Heights* are included here.

While struggling to "get the words right" (Hemingway) for a query letter, the anxious writer may feel, along with Dorothy Parker, "The writer's way is rough and lonely, and who would choose it while there are vacancies in more gracious professions, such as, say, cleaning out ferryboats?"

F. Scott Fitzgerald to an editor at Charles Scribner's Sons, October 25, 1919:

Dear Mr. Bridges:

This is a query. I have a project. It is a work of about 20,000 words and more on the order of my novel than like these stories I've been doing. But it's the sort of thing that will require a full month's work and as *The New Republic*, *Scribner's* and possibly the *Atlantic Monthly* are the only magazines that would publish it I don't want to start until you assure me that there's *nothing* in the project which seems to bar it from *Scribner's* if it be *sufficiently* interesting and well done.

It is a literary forgery purporting to be selections from the notebooks of a man who is a complete literary radical. . . .

It will be in turns cynical, ingenuous, life-saturated, critical and bitter. It will be racy and startling with opinions and personalities. . . .

Of course you can't possibly commit yourself until you've seen it but as I say I'd want to know before I start if a work of that nature would be intrinsically hostile to the policy of *Scribner's Magazine.* . . .

Edmund Wilson to F. Scott Fitzgerald, August 28, 1915:

Dear Fitz:

I wrote a whole first act, lyrics and all; some of it was exquisitely humorous and some of it was very weak. I sent it to Lane and told him to forward it to you, when he had finished with it, because I was too lazy to make another copy. He returned it to me with a long letter explaining that he liked it but that there were a number of important changes he wanted me to make. My impression was that he had failed to appreciate the exquisite humor of the exquisitely humorous parts but had fully appreciated the weakness of the weak parts. . . . At any rate, I'll have the MS sent to you at once.

Yours etc.,

E.W.

*M*ari Sandoz to the New York Times, January 21, 1931:

> Would you be interested in a 3,000 to 4,000 word article, "Stalking the Ghost of Crazy Horse," to be used as you see fit, and with a large number of good illustrations, photographs taken in 1930?
>
> Last summer Miss Hinman . . . and I made a 3,000 mile trip in a $45 Ford through the old Sioux country. . . . We camped on the ridge along which Custer's men retreated, burned out our clutch band in Reno Creek, and saw the canyon where the battle of the Rosebud took place, reported to be both "deep, dark, and tortuous," and "at no place less than two miles wide," which we found to be neither.
>
> But our main interest was Crazy Horse, the Ogalala war chief said to be the first to break the lines of Custer and later bayoneted through the kidney at Fort Robinson after he had been promised security, the victim, we suspected, of betrayal by his own people. . . . We uncovered much new material, were suspected of being spies from Washington tracing the guilt of the Custer affair, saw the first Sundance permitted at Pine Ridge since the Ghost Dance troubles of 1891, and ended by being called the granddaughters of He Dog. . . .
>
> I believe that your readers would be interested. . . .

P.T. Barnum to Harper Brothers, September 18, 1885:

> Gentlemen:
>
> Millions of children and adults (myself included) are mourning the death of *Jumbo.*
>
> Would you like to publish for the holidays *The Life, History, and Death of Jumbo, with Many Incidents & Anecdotes not Heretofore Published,* by P.T. Barnum, profusely illustrated? The title can of course be changed from the above. Probably numerous *cuts* now extant can be used. If properly gotten up, would it not be an interesting Christmas children's book—perhaps on *both* sides of the Atlantic?

Herman Melville to Richard Bentley, June 27, 1850:

My dear Sir,

In the latter part of the coming autumn I shall have ready a new work; and I write you now to propose its publication in England.

The book is a romance of adventure, founded upon certain wild legends in the Southern Sperm Whale Fisheries, and illustrated by the author's own personal experience, of two years and more, as a harpooneer. . . .

Being desirous of early arranging this matter in London—so as to lose no time, when the book has passed through the Harpers' press here—I beg, Mr. Bentley, that you at once write me as to your views concerning it. . . .

Charlotte Brontë to Aylott & Jones, regarding Wuthering Heights by Emily Brontë, The Professor by Charlotte Brontë, and Agnes Grey by Anne Brontë, April 6, 1846:

Gentlemen,

C., E., and A. Bell are now preparing for the press a work of fiction, consisting of three distinct and unconnected tales, which may be published either together, as a work of three volumes, of the ordinary novel size, or separately as single volumes, as shall be deemed most advisable.

It is not their intention to publish these tales on their own account. They direct me to ask you whether you would be disposed to undertake the work, after having, of course, by due inspection of the ms., ascertained that its contents are such as to warrant an expectation of success.

An early answer will oblige, as, in case of your negativing the proposal, inquiry must be made of other publishers.

I am, gentlemen,
Yours truly,
C. Brontë

Leonardo da Vinci to the Duke of Milan, 1482:

Having, most illustrious lord, seen and considered the experiments of all those who pose as masters in the art of inventing instruments of war, and finding that their inventions differ in no way from those in common use, I am emboldened, without prejudice to anyone, to solicit an appointment of acquainting your Excellency with certain of my secrets.

1. I can construct bridges which are very light and strong and very portable, with which to pursue and defeat the enemy; and others more solid, which resist fire or assault, yet are easily removed and placed in position; and I can also burn and destroy those of the enemy.

2. In case of a siege I can cut off water from the trenches and make pontoons and scaling ladders and other similar contrivances.

3. If by reason of the elevation or the strength of its position a place cannot be bombarded, I can demolish every fortress if its foundations have not been set on stone.

4. I can also make a kind of cannon which is light and easy of transport, with which to hurl small stones like hail, and of which the smoke causes great terror to the enemy, so that they suffer heavy loss and confusion.

5. I can noiselessly construct to any prescribed point subterranean passages either straight or winding, passing if necessary underneath trenches or a river.

6. I can make armored wagons carrying artillery, which shall break through the most serried ranks of the enemy, and so open a safe passage for his infantry.

7. If occasion should arise, I can construct cannon and mortar and light ordnance in shape both ornamental and useful and different from those in common use.

8. When it is impossible to use cannon I can supply in their stead catapults, mangonels, *trabocchi,* and other instruments of admirable efficiency. . . .

9. And if the fight should take place upon the sea I can construct many engines most suitable either for attack or defense. . . .

10. In time of peace, I believe that I can give you as complete satisfaction as anyone else in the construction of buildings both public and private, and in conducting water from one place to another. . . .

And if any of the aforesaid things should seem to anyone impossible or impracticable, I offer myself as ready to make trial of them in your park or in whatever place shall please your Excellency, to whom I commend myself with all possible humility.

*T*his note will introduce Mr. Sammy Steward. He is charming. Be gentle with him.

GERTRUDE STEIN, LETTER TO PABLO PICASSO, 1939

Herr Einstein is one of the most original minds that we have ever met. In spite of his youth he already occupies a very honorable position among the foremost savants of his time. What we marvel at him, above all, is the ease with which he adjusts himself to new conceptions and draws all

References, Recommendations, and Introductions

possible deductions from them. He does not cling to classical principles, but sees all conceivable possibilities when he is confronted with a physical problem. In his mind this becomes transformed into an anticipation of new phenomena that may some day be verified in actual experience . . . The future will give more and more proofs of the merits of Herr Einstein, and the University that succeeds in

Although "networking" is a relatively new term, the concept of introducing and recommending our friends to each other undoubtedly goes back to our beginnings. No, there are no letters that old in this chapter; the letter from Cicero to Caesar is the earliest.

In more formal times, letters of introduction were as common as they were socially important. Because they serve the same general purpose as references and recommendations, they are included here. The multiple volumes of Emerson's letters contain many examples of the letter of introduction—he apparently knew and was known to everyone on two sides of the Atlantic.

Abraham Lincoln to Judge Stephen T. Logan, c. 1850:

My dear Judge,

    The bearer of this is a young man who thinks he can be a lawyer. Examine him if you want to. I have done so and am satisfied. He's a good deal smarter than he looks to be.

Sherwood Anderson to Gertrude Stein, December 3, 1921:

Dear Miss Stein:

    I am writing this note to make you acquainted with my friend Ernest Hemingway, who with Mrs. Hemingway is going to Paris to live, and will ask him to drop it in the mails when he arrives there.

    Mr. Hemingway is an American writer instinctively in touch with everything worthwhile going on here, and I know you will find Mr. and Mrs. Hemingway delightful people to know. . . .

Henri Poincaré and Marie Curie, 1911:

    Herr Einstein is one of the most original minds that we have ever met. In spite of his youth he already occupies a very honorable position among the foremost savants of his time. What we marvel at him, above all, is the ease with which he adjusts himself to new conceptions and draws all possible deductions from them. He does not cling to classical principles, but sees all conceivable possibilities when he is confronted with a physical problem. In his mind this becomes transformed into an anticipation of new phenomena that may some day be verified in actual experience. . . . The future will give more and more proofs of the merits of Herr Einstein, and the University that succeeds in attaching him to itself may be certain that it will derive honor from its connection with the young master.

Muhammad Iqbal to Mirza Muhammad Sa'id, October 1926:

My dear Sa'id,

This is to introduce M. Hamid Ahmad Khan, B.A. of Osmania University. I hope you will do all that you can do for him.

Benjamin Franklin, "Model of a Letter of Recommendation of a Person You Are Unacquainted With," c. 1750:

Sir,

The bearer of this, who is going to America, presses me to give him a letter of recommendation, though I know nothing of him, not even his name. This may seem extraordinary, but I assure you it is not uncommon here. Sometimes, indeed, one unknown person brings another equally unknown, to recommend him; and sometimes they recommend one another! As to this gentleman, I must refer you to himself for his character and merits, with which he is certainly better acquainted than I can possibly be. I recommend him, however, to those civilities, which every stranger, of whom one knows no harm, has a right to; and I request you will do him all the good offices, and show him all the favor, that, on further acquaintance, you shall find him to deserve. I have the honor to be, etc.

Cicero to Caesar, 70 B.C.:

I very particularly recommend to your favor the son of our worthy and common friend Praecilius: a youth whose modest and polite behavior, together with his singular attachment to myself, have exceedingly endeared him to me. His father likewise, as experience has now fully convinced me, was always my most sincere well-wisher. For to confess the truth, he was the first and most zealous of those who used both to rally and reproach me for not joining in your cause: especially after you had invited me by so many honorable overtures. . . . You will greatly oblige me by extending to this young man that uncommon generosity which so peculiarly marks your character. . . .

*G*oodman Ace to Groucho Marx, 1953:

Dear Julius:

The magazine on which your daughter now works wrote me for references. And I replied that I had known Miriam Marx for many years, and have always found her to be five feet six and a half inches tall, and that I know her to have the integrity and potential ability of her famous father, Karl. P.S.: She got the job. I haven't heard, but I suppose she's still there. . . .

Love,
Goody

*E*dith Sitwell to Ronald Bottrall, February 25, 1947:

Dylan Thomas and his family (wife and two children) will be going to Italy shortly, for him to write poems. . . .

When he comes, will you be an angel and get him lectures and readings in public to do? It is absolutely essential that he should, as you will understand.

Have you heard him read? It is a *very* great experience—absolutely terrific. I've never heard anything like it.

He is a most enchanting creature—wildly funny and very charming, and she is a darling too. . . . May I tell him to communicate with you when—or before—he arrives?

*C*olette to Jean Fraysse, June 1939:

Dear Jean,

It's still me. The young woman who brings you this letter is Renée Hamon. To explain just who Renée Hamon is would take a long time—I'll leave that to her. She'll know how to be brief. . . . I leave her in your good hands, knowing from experience how effective they can be.

Abraham Lincoln to Major George D. Ramsey, October 17, 1861:

My dear Sir:

The lady bearer of this says she has two sons who want to work. Set them at it if possible. Wanting to work is so rare a want that it should be encouraged.

Ralph Waldo Emerson to the Reverend Robert Collyer, September 25, 1869:

My dear Mr. Collyer,

Mrs. Ann Goddard, a lady long and well known to all of us here, a sister of our Dr. Bartlett, is about to return to Chicago where she has once already resided for a time, and very naturally desires an introduction to you. She is a lady valued among her friends for her social virtues and talents, and has at one time been a successful teacher. Your fold is very large, and I hope there is room for one more lamb.

Franklin Delano Roosevelt to Chiang Kai-shek, August 19, 1944:

My dear Generalissimo:

This will introduce to you my two very good personal friends, General Hurley, former Secretary of War, and now a Major General; and Mr. Donald M. Nelson, the head of the War Production Board. . . .

In the case of both of them, I want you to feel free to talk to them frankly, as they are both literally my personal representatives. . . .

I regret to disoblige you, but I cannot undertake to write eulogies of L'Aiglon for the newspapers. First of all, I am too busy, busy for the University, and, secondly, in all friendliness and frankness, I think the work beneath me.

OSCAR W. FIRKINS, LETTER TO MARIE DIDELOT, 1931

I received your circular for a meeting of the "Protective War-Claim Association" last week, and now I have a new one, which I feel bound to answer.

I go very little to society and club meetings. Some feel more of a call that way, others less; I among the least.

Refusals, Regrets, and Rejections

"To know how to refuse is as important as to know how to consent" (Baltasar Gracián), especially when we need to keep the other person's goodwill. The more well-known people are, the more often they must turn down invitations and requests, obliging some of them (for example, in this chapter, Evelyn Waugh, and Dorothy Canfield Fisher) to fashion multi-purpose form letters of refusal.

Gustave Flaubert to Louise Colet, March 6, 1855:

Madame:

I was told that you took the trouble to come here to see me three times last evening.

I was not in. And, fearing lest persistence expose you to humiliation, I am bound by the rules of politeness to warn you that *I shall never be in.*

Yours,
G.F.

E.B. White to J. Donald Adams, September 28, 1956:

Dear Mr. Adams:

Thanks for your letter inviting me to join the committee of the Arts and Sciences for Eisenhower.

I must decline, for secret reasons.

Sincerely,
E.B. White

W.D. Howells to Lilla C. Perry, March 31, 1913:

Dear Mrs. Perry:

Impossible—impossible! The shattered prose of my being could never rise to the poetry of your most hospitable, most lovable wish to have me your guest! I must stay where I can be shy and glum when I will, or want. . . . But I thank you, I thank you. . . .

Yours Sincerely,
W.D. Howells

Oliver Wendell Holmes, Sr. to the Reverend James Freeman Clarke,
October 24, 1862:

My dear James,

I received your circular for a meeting of the "Protective War-Claim Association" last week, and now I have a new one, which I feel bound to answer.

I go very little to society and club meetings. Some feel more of a call that way, others less; I among the least.

I hate the calling of meetings to order. I hate the nomination of officers, always fearing lest I should be appointed secretary. I hate being placed on committees. They are always having meetings at which half are absent and the rest late. I hate being officially and necessarily in the presence of men most of whom, either from excessive zeal in the good cause or from constitutional obtuseness, are incapable of being *bored*, which state is to me the most exhausting of all conditions, absorbing more of my life than any kind of active exertion I am capable of performing.

I am slow in apprehending parliamentary rules and usages, averse to the business details many persons revel in; and I am not in love with most of the actively stirring people whom one is apt to meet in all associations for doing good.

Some trees grow very tall and straight and large in the forest close to each other, but some must stand by themselves or they won't grow at all. Ever since I used to go to the "Institute of 1770" and hear Rob Rantoul call members to order, and to the "Euphradian," where our poor Loring used to be eloquent about Effie Deans, I have recognized an inaptitude, not to say ineptitude, belonging to me in connection with all such proceedings.

"What if everybody talked in this way?" The Lord arranges his averages in such a way that to every one person like myself there are two or three organizing, contriving, socializing intelligences, and three or four self-sacrificing people, who have forgotten what they like and what they hate by nature, and about a dozen good indifferent folks that will take part in anything they are asked to. . . .

S.J. Perelman to Joseph Bryan III, October 8, 1941:

> Dear Joe,
>
> Neither Roget nor the Pocket Oxford have words to describe how happy we'd be to join your little seminar this weekend. BUT—we have just finished moving our troupe into New York and we're completely disorganized. I'm writing this letter with a mouth full of upholstery nails (you thought I was using a typewriter, didn't you?) and every so often I pluck one out and try to hammer it into the drapes with the heel of an evening slipper. . . .

Ludwig van Beethoven to Franz Anton Hoffmeister, April 8, 1802:

> May the devil ride the whole lot of you, gentlemen—what, suggest to me that I should write a sonata of that sort? At the time of the revolutionary fever—well, at that time it would have been worth considering, but now that everything is trying to get back into the old rut, Bonaparte has made his concordat with the Pope—a sonata of that sort? If at least it were a *Missa pro Sancta Maria a tre voci* or a Vespers, etc.—well, in that case I should immediately take hold of the brush and write down a *Credo in unum* in enormous notes weighing a pound each—but good heavens, a sonata of that sort at the beginning of this new Christian age—ho ho!—count me out of that, for nothing will come of it. . . .

Marc Hamblot, editor at Ollendorf, to Marcel Proust, 1912:

> My dear fellow,
>
> I may perhaps be dead from the neck up, but rack my brains as I may I can't see why a chap should need thirty pages to describe how he turns over in bed before going to sleep.

Diogenes to Aristippus, 4th c. B.C.:

Aristippus:

You send me word that Alexander, King of Macedonia, has a great desire to see me. You did well to give him that title, for whatever the Macedonians may be, you know I am subject to nobody. If that prince has a mind to be acquainted with me, and my manner of life, let him come hither, for I shall always think Athens as far distant from Macedon as Macedon is from Athens. Farewell.

James Thurber to Norman A. Kurland, May 2, 1961:

Dear Mr. Kurland,

I had to give up public appearances when I became a hundred and went blind nearly twenty years ago, and, besides, I am now in Europe and in the Fall expect to be in Jeopardy.

Thanks anyway, and all best wishes,

Ahad Ha-am, editor of Hashiloah, to S.Z., June 13, 1897:

If I undertook to enter into correspondence about articles that I do not accept, life would be too short. What is not accepted is not worth printing, and no explanation is called for.

I am again unable to find space for your contribution, and I advise you to give up writing, as your attempts show no sign of promise. . . .

Søren Kierkegaard to Magnus Eriksson, October 14, 1847:

You yourself request, and I find that quite natural, that I reply "in a few words" to your very lengthy letter. That is to say, you request *without reasons pro or contra that I be brief, a "Yes" or a "No."* Here is my reply: I cannot comply with your request.

Mary E. Wilkins Freeman to Annie Russell Marble, February 15, 1894:

Dear Mrs. Marble,

I thank you most cordially for your very kind invitation to Worcester, and am sorry to have to say in reply, that it is impossible for me to accept. Demands upon my time and strength are such that I have, for a year past, been compelled to refuse nearly all receptions. Trusting that you will accept the apology of a very busy person, and believe me none the less grateful for your courtesy, I am

Very Sincerely,
Mary E. Wilkins

William Faulkner to Dr. Julius S. Bixler, March 8, 1956:

Dear Dr. Bixler:

Your letter of February 20th was at hand when I reached home today.

I thank the Board of Trustees of Colby College very much for the honor proffered me, which I must decline for the following reason. I did not attend school long enough to receive even a certificate of graduation from elementary school. For me to receive an honorary degree from Colby College would be an insult to all those who have gained degrees by means of the long and arduous devotion commensurate with what any degree must be always worth.

Thank you again for the honor proffered me.

Herman Melville to Evert A. Duyckinck, February 12, 1851:

> . . . How shall a man go about refusing a man? Best be round-about, or plumb on the mark? I can not write the thing you want. I am in the humor to lend a hand to a friend, if I can; but I am not in the humor to write the kind of thing you need—and I am not in the humor to write it for Holden's Magazine. If I were to go on to give you all my reasons—you would pronounce me a bore, so I will not do that. You must be content to believe that I *have* reasons, or else I would not refuse so small a thing. . . .

Evelyn Waugh to Diana Cooper, 1951:

> Is this not an ingenious labor-saving device? I answer all correspondence with it—particularly bills and charitable appeals.

> Mr. Evelyn Waugh greatly regrets that he
> cannot do what you so kindly suggest.

Eugene O'Neill to William Lyon Phelps, October 27, 1922:

> My dear Professor Phelps:
> I am very grateful to you for the honor of your invitation but I have never lectured and don't believe I ever will. Frankly, there is a certain prejudice in my mind against it. It seems to me that authors should neither be seen nor heard outside of their work—(not this one, at any rate, for I'm quite certain my plays act better than I ever could—which is faint praise for them indeed!). So, both from the standpoint of personal discretion and of Christian charity toward the audience, I feel bound to decline.
> But again, all gratitude to you for the honor of selecting me. I appreciate that immensely and regret that I cannot accept.

Ernest Hemingway to Thomas Shevlin, April 4, 1939:

Dear Tommy:

It's so hard to write this that I've been trying to do it for five days and haven't been able to.

Listen, kid, I can't come and fish on your team in the tournament. I know that is ratting out and I tell you as soon as possible so that you will be able to get another fisherman.

This is how it is. I went to Cuba intending to write three stories. I wrote the first one and it was good. Then I started on the second one and before I knew it I had fifteen thousand words done and was going better than I have gone since Farewell To Arms and I knew it was a novel. . . .

So there it is. I can't be a sportsman and write a novel at the same time. . . . I've had such stinko luck on fish that it's probably an asset to you not to have me. But I would have loved to fish with you and with Hugo.

Yours always,
Papa

Claude Debussy to Gabriel Fauré, April 29, 1917:

My slowness in replying to your kind letter, cher maître et ami, is due to the simple reason that I can no longer play the piano well enough to risk a performance of the *Etudes*. . . . In public a peculiar phobia takes hold of me: there are too many keys; I haven't enough fingers any more; and suddenly I forget where the pedals are! It's unfortunate and extremely alarming.

I assure you I'm not just being difficult; I should have been particularly happy to do you a favor.

Søren Kierkegaard to his uncle M.A. Kierkegaard, on his refusal to attend his aunt's funeral, May 4, 1855:

Dear Uncle,

Today the undertaker came, did not find me, but left word that a carriage would come at a specified time to pick me up.

It is in this connection that I write you these few lines to tell you what I otherwise would have let you know through the undertaker: that you must excuse me. For many years, I have not attended the funeral service for anyone, not even the service for a close relative, which you, Uncle, know, for I did not attend the service for our Aunt in Gothersgade nor for Nephew Andreas. Therefore I probably would offend others who will be present if I were to make an exception in this case.

For this reason, dear Uncle, please excuse me. And perhaps you will also inform the undertaker, lest there be any misunderstanding and he sends a carriage to pick me up.

Oliver Wendell Holmes, Sr., whose physician was Oliver Wendell Holmes, Jr., to Francis Bartlett, July 29, 1879:

My dear Mr. Bartlett,

My Doctor, O.W.H., M.D., has forbidden my going out evenings for the present, for fear of a return of certain troubles, which I believe I am getting rid of, but for which he is still treating me. I am very sorry that my respect for his opinion, founded on a very long experience with his patient, compels me to deny myself the pleasure of being with you and your guests on Friday evening.

W.D. Howells to Mark Twain, the founder—and at that time the only member—of the Modest Club, May 28, 1880:

My dear Clemens:

The only reason I have for not joining the Modest Club is that I am too modest: that is, I am afraid that I am not modest enough. If I could ever get over this difficulty, I should like to join, for I approve highly of the club and its objects: it is calculated to do a great deal of good, and it ought to be given an annual dinner at the public expense. If *you* think I am not too modest, you may put my name down, and I will try to think the same of you. Mrs. Howells applauded the notion of the Club from the very first. She said that she knew *one* thing: that *she* was modest enough, *anyway*. Her manner of saying it implied that the other persons you had named were not, and created a painful impression in my mind. I have sent your letter and the rules to Hay. But I doubt his modesty; he will think he has a *right* to belong as much as you or I. . . .

Dorothy Canfield Fisher to inquiries, c. 1910:

Mrs. Fisher regrets very much that, for the present, it is impossible for her to make any more engagements for public speaking. She is at present absorbed in a long piece of work, which, added to the usual demands of housekeeping and the care of children, leaves no margin of time or strength for public speaking.

She thanks you for your letter, regrets her inability to write a personal answer, and sends her best greetings.

F. Scott Fitzgerald to Miss Paxton, 1923:

> Dear Miss Paxton:
>
> As I have nothing but respect for Theta Sigma Phi it would be a mean trick for me to agree to make a speech for them. How would you like to have a collapsed novelist wandering wildly over the campus of the University of Illinois? I suggest Mr. Bryant or Mr. Cone as an alternate.
>
> Seriously I'd love to do it but I'm absolutely incapable through constitutional stage fright.

Edna Ferber to William Lyon Phelps, March 25, 1930:

> Dear William Lyon Phelps:
>
> My thanks to you for the letter asking me to become a member of the Town Hall Club. I hope you won't think I am thoroughly mad when I say that I have a sort of horror of joining—I belong to no organization except the Authors' League of America. I don't know any reasonable explanation for this feeling, but there it is. . . .

Groucho Marx to the president of a Hollywood club, c. 1965:

> Please accept my resignation. I don't care to belong to any club that will have me as a member.

Ralph Waldo Emerson to Annie Adams Fields, April 9, 1877:

Dear Mrs. Fields,

    Mr. Fields sends to all of us your kind invitation to come to your house on the evening of the 16th. . . . My wife sends you her thanks but she is an invalid and stays at home; Ellen is not now at home, but I suppose will be on that day; and I myself am grown so old that though I can read from a paper, I am no longer fit for conversation, and dare not make visits. So we send you our thanks, and you shall not expect us.

Charlotte Brontë to the Reverend Henry Nussey, March 5, 1839:

My dear Sir,

    . . . You are aware that I have many reasons to feel grateful to your family, that I have peculiar reasons for affection towards one at least of your sisters, and also that I highly esteem yourself—do not therefore accuse me of wrong motives when I say that my answer to your proposal must be a *decided negative.* In forming this decision, I trust I have listened to the dictates of conscience more than to those of inclination. I have no personal repugnance to the idea of a union with you, but I feel convinced that mine is not the sort of disposition calculated to form the happiness of a man like you. . . . I scorn deceit, and I will never, for the sake of attaining the distinction of matrimony and escaping the stigma of an old maid, take a worthy man whom I am conscious I cannot render happy. . . . It is a pleasure to me to hear that you are so comfortably settled and that your health is so much improved. I trust God will continue His kindness towards you. Let me say also that I admire the good sense and absence of flattery and cant which your letter displayed. Farewell. I shall always be glad to hear from you as a *friend.*

Charles Dickens to George Cattermole, February 1838:

My Dear Cattermole,

Why do you always ask me to dinner on days when I can't come? I have been engaged for next Tuesday a fortnight back, and you pick out that unfortunate day as if there were no other days in the week and no other weeks in the year. I regret this very much, and take it exceedingly ill. . . .

Believe me always,
Most faithfully yours,
Charles Dickens

Chinese Economic Journal to British writer:

We have read your manuscript with boundless delight. If we were to publish your paper, it would be impossible for us to publish any work of a lower standard. And as it is unthinkable that we shall see its equal in the next thousand years, we are, to our regret, compelled to return your divine composition and beg you a thousand times to overlook our short sight and timidity.

*H*ave you got an Egyptian mummy
in your museum that you will sell?
If not, can you tell me where I can buy one?

P.T. BARNUM, LETTER TO MOSES KIMBALL, 1870

I have a great favor to
ask of you, and only a faint
hope that you will hear me.
Perhaps you have heard
something of my arrest, my
trial, and the supreme ratification of the sentence
which was given in the case
concerning me in the year
1849. . . . I was convicted of
the intention (but only the

Requests

intention) of acting against the government. . . . I went to prison—four sad, terrible years. . . . And yet I swear to you that none of those torments was greater than that which I felt when I realized . . . that in banishment I was cut off from my fellow-creatures and unable to serve them with all my powers, desires, and capacities . . . A word from you now can accomplish much with our gracious

If you wonder how Harriet Beecher Stowe wrote so realistically about slavery or how Audubon found the birds he drew or how a talented editor manages to pry a manuscript from a delinquent author, these letters will take you behind the scenes where you will perhaps be surprised to learn one of the uses to which whiskey or rum was once put.

Sometimes, as in the case of the Ursula Nordstrom letters, a request has to be made repeatedly. She could say, with Margaret Halsey, "Bulldogs have been known to fall on their swords when confronted by my superior tenacity." Tenacity, charm, and a hint of humor seem to be requisite for a successful request letter.

E.B. White to Daise Terry, December 14, 1938:

Dear Miss Terry:

Would you have your office order me a copy of "Last Poems" by A.E. Housman? I want to give it to Roger for Christmas. He asked for Housman poems, a bottle of Amontillado, and a top hat. I can only assume that he is going to sit around in the hat, drinking the sherry, reading the poems, and dreaming the long long dreams of youth.

*F*ranklin K. Lane to Samuel G. Blythe, January 6, 1912:

My dear Sam,

. . . Will you support me for Supreme Court Justice? I see that I am mentioned. Between us, I am entirely ineligible, having a sense of humor.

As always yours,
Lane

*V*oltaire to John Ashburnham, first Earl of Ashburnham, June 12, 1718:

My lord,

You are a divinity to whom I usually apply in my tribulations. You will remember you once lent me two horses. I now ask you for half of that favor. Have the charity to confide one of your chargers to the bearer of this letter. I shall have the honor to return it to you in a few days. If you cannot lend me a horse, at least forgive the liberty I take in asking you for it. . . .

Your very humble and obedient servant,
Arouet de Voltaire

Ludwig van Beethoven to Artaria Music Publishers, October 1, 1819:

Excellent *Virtuosi senza Cujoni,*

Whereas we are informing you of this, that and the other, from which you are to draw the most favorable conclusions, we entreat you to send us by way of author's copies six, I say 6, copies of the Sonata in B as well as 6 copies of the Variations on Scottish Songs. . . .

In the hope that you are conducting yourselves in an orderly and lawful manner, I am your, etc.

Devoted B.

Erasmus to Ammonius, 1513:

I have no news for you except that my journey was detestable, and that this place does not agree with me. I have pleaded sickness so far as an excuse for postponing my lectures. Beer does not suit me either, the wine is horrible. If you can send me a barrel of Greek wine, the best which can be had, Erasmus will bless you; only take care it is not sweet. Have no uneasiness about your loan; it will be paid before the date of the bill. Meanwhile I am being killed with thirst. Imagine the rest. . . .

Mark Twain to Charles L. Webster, October 30, 1882:

Dear Charlie,

Give this man the papers he wants, or kill him, I don't care which.

Yours truly,
S.L. Clemens

Fyodor Dostoevsky to General Eduard J. Totleben, March 24, 1856:

Your Excellency Eduard Ivanovitch!

. . . I have a great favor to ask of you, and only a faint hope that you will hear me.

Perhaps you have heard something of my arrest, my trial, and the supreme ratification of the sentence which was given in the case concerning me in the year 1849. . . . I was convicted of the intention (but only the intention) of acting against the government. . . .

I went to prison—four sad, terrible years. . . . And yet I swear to you that none of those torments was greater than that which I felt when I realized . . . that in banishment I was cut off from my fellow-creatures and unable to serve them with all my powers, desires, and capacities. . . . A word from you now can accomplish much with our gracious monarch, who is grateful to you, and loves you. Think of the poor exile, and help him. . . . Some years ago, the public gave me a very hearty and encouraging welcome in the literary sphere. I very much desire permission to publish my works . . . if you can do anything for me, do it, I implore you. . . .

Anna Julia Cooper to W.E.B. DuBois, December 31, 1929:

My dear Doctor Du Bois:

It seems to me that the *Tragic Era* should be answered—ade-quately, fully, ably, finally, and again it seems to me *Thou* art the Man! Take it up seriously through the *Crisis* and let us buy up 10,000 copies to be distributed broadcast through the land.

Will you do it?
Answer.

*R*obert Louis Stevenson, age 16, to his father, March 1866:

Respected Paternal Relative,

I write to make a request of the most moderate nature. Every year I have cost you an enormous—nay, elephantine—sum of money for drugs and physician's fees, and the most expensive time of the twelve months was March.

But this year the biting Oriental blasts, the howling tempests, and the general ailments of the human race have been successfully braved by yours truly.

Does not this deserve remuneration?

I appeal to your charity, I appeal to your generosity, I appeal to your justice, I appeal to your accounts, I appeal, in fine, to your purse.

My sense of generosity forbids the receipt of more—my sense of justice forbids the receipt of less—than half-a-crown. Greetings from, Sir, your most affectionate and needy son,

R.

W.D. Howells to Frederick A. Duneka, January 21, 1915:

Dear Mr. Duneka:

I wish you would let Upton Sinclair use some passages from "A Traveller from Altruria" in an anthology of dangerous thinking which he is making. It will do the book good, and I like to be remembered as a dangerous thinker. . . .

Yours sincerely,
W.D. Howells

John Steinbeck to Felicia Geffen of the Academy of Arts and Letters, February 20, 1951:

Dear Miss Geffen:

I am sick of seeing Marc Connelly parading in regalia to make a peacock squirm while I remain as undecorated as a jaybird. Will you please send to me at the above address, any regalia, buttons, ribbons, small swords, etc., as are befitting to my academic grandeur?

I'll show that upstart Connelly.

Three days later:

Dear Miss Geffen:

Many thanks for your letter and I shall treasure the buttons when they arrive. I must say I am disappointed at the lack of regalia. The French Academy meets dressed in cocked hats, embroidered vests and small swords. The Spanish academicians wear pants made entirely of bird of paradise feathers. Why can't we do something as spectacular and for the same reason—to cover with finery our depressingly small talent? . . .

Two years later:

Dear Miss Geffen:

Will you send me some buttons? My kids pulled mine apart to see how the crinkle got in the ribbon. I deplore it but I always wanted to know too, so I had the double pleasure of finding out and punishing them at the same time. . . .

Franz Schubert to Franz von Schober, one week before his death, November 12, 1828:

Dear Schober,

I am ill. I have had nothing to eat or drink for eleven days now, and can only wander feebly and uncertainly between armchair and bed. Rinna is treating me. If I take any food I cannot retain it at all.

So please be so good as to come to my aid in this desperate condition with something to read. I have read Cooper's "Last of the Mohicans," "The Spy," "The Pilot," and "The Pioneers." If by any chance you have anything else of his, I beg you to leave it for me at the coffee-house with Frau von Bogner. My brother, who is conscientiousness itself, will bring it over to me without fail. . . .

Your friend,
Schubert

Harriet Beecher Stowe to Frederick Douglass, July 9, 1851:

Sir,

You may perhaps have noticed in your editorial readings a series of articles that I am furnishing for the "Era" under the title of "Uncle Tom's Cabin, or Life Among the Lowly."

In the course of my story the scene will fall upon a cotton plantation. I am very desirous, therefore, to gain information from one who has been an actual laborer on one, and it occurred to me that in the circle of your acquaintance there might be one who would be able to communicate to me some such information as I desire. . . . I wish to be able to make a picture that shall be graphic and true to nature in its details. . . . I will subjoin to this letter a list of questions, which in that case you will do me a favor by enclosing to the individual, with the request that he will at earliest convenience answer them. . . .

*U*rsula *N*ordstrom, editor, to Crosby Bonsall, whose manuscript was due:

December 14, 1965
Dear Crosby,
     Where is the book?

December 15, 1965
Dear Crosby,
     Où est le livre?

December 16, 1965
Dear Crosby,
     Donde esta el libre?

December 17, 1965
Dear Crosby,
     Achtung! Wo ist der buch?

December 21, 1965
Dear Crosby,
     Hereway
       isay
         hetay
           oookbay?

*T*heodore Roosevelt to Herbert Putnam, October 6, 1902:

My dear Mr. Putnam:
     As I lead, to put it mildly, a sedentary life for the moment I would greatly like some books that would appeal to my queer taste. I do not suppose there are any histories or any articles upon the early Mediterranean races. That man Lindsay who wrote about prehistoric Greece has not put out a second volume, has he? Has a second volume of Oman's *Art of War* appeared? If so, send me either or both; if not, then a good translation of Niebuhr and Momsen or the best modern history of Mesopotamia. Is there a good history of Poland?

Fanny Burney to Mrs. Locke, April 1789:

My dearest Friends,

I have her Majesty's commands to inquire—whether you have any of a certain breed of poultry?

N.B. *What* breed I do not remember.

And to say she has just received a small group of the same herself.

N.B. The quantity I have forgotten.

And to add, she is assured they are something very rare and scarce, and extraordinary and curious.

N.B. By *whom* she was assured I have not heard.

And to subjoin, that you must send word if you have any of the same sort.

N.B. How you are to find that out, I cannot tell.

And to mention, as a corollary, that, if you have none of them, and should like to have some, she has a cock and a hen she can spare, and will appropriate them to Mr. Locke and my dearest Fredy.

This conclusive stroke so pleased and exhilarated me, that forthwith I said you would both be enchanted, and so forgot all the preceding particulars.

And I said, moreover, that I knew you would rear them, and cheer them, and fondle them like your children.

So now—pray write a very *fair answer* fairly, in fair hand and to fair purpose. . . .

Robert Schumann to Friedrich Wieck, 1839:

Once more I come before you, hand in hand with Clara, to beg your consent to our marriage next Easter. Two years have passed since my first proposal. You doubted if we should remain true to each other; we have done so, nothing can make us waver in our belief in our future happiness. . . . Listen to the voice of nature; do not drive us to extremes! In a few days it will be Clara's twentieth birthday, give peace on that day; say yes. We need rest after so terrible a strife, you owe it to Clara and to me. I look forward with longing to your definite answer.

Raven to Beth Brant, December 10, 1982:

Dear Ms. Brant,

Greetings of peace. I hope my words find you happy and content upon all your paths of living.

As you can see from the above address, I am incarcerated, as a matter of fact I have been sentenced to die. I stand innocent, but there's no justice in white man's courts. I have much knowledge of the law. But I cannot have faith in any courts that sentenced me to death for a crime I never had any part in.

I'm of Cherokee blood, from North Carolina. I also have a little white in me. I've been raised in the white man's world and was forbade more or less to converse with Indian people. . . . Today I am desperate to know my people.

Ms. Brant, I would appreciate anything you can or will do, that will aid me in my need of my people.

Thank you for any and all concern to my words.

I remain

Raven

Robert E. Lee to Jefferson Davis, August 9, 1864:

Mr. President,

The soap ration for this Army has become a serious question. Since leaving Orange C.H. the Commissary Lt. Col. Cole has only been able to make three issues of three days rations each. The great want of cleanliness which is a necessary consequence of these very limited issues is now producing sickness among the men in the trenches, and must affect their self respect & morale. The importance of the subject and the general complaints which have arisen must be my excuse for troubling you with the matter. . . . I hope . . . that contracts will be entered into at once for the future regular and adequate supply of the soap ration to the troops. Their health, comfort & respectability cannot otherwise be secured.

J.J. Audubon to the Reverend John Bachman, October 20, 1835:

My dear Bachman,

I have nearly finished the printing of my third volume. . . . Now the purport of this letter is to give you notice that I am now studying the anatomy of birds, and that in my concluding volume, my intention is to give the anatomical descriptions of at least one bird of each genus—this has never been offered to the scientific world by any author as regards our birds and my anxiety to accomplish this is extreme. . . .

Whenever you shoot birds of *any descriptions* or kind, both of the land or of the waters, place specimens in such jars or other objects as may contain them with a quantity of common whiskey or rum. Have the jars closed and put a memorandum outside of the contents. And keep those until we meet, in as cool a place as possible. . . .

*U*rsula Nordstrom to Edward Gorey, December 23, 1971:

Dear Mr. Gorey:

I wonder if you will remember me? Perhaps my name is vaguely familiar to you? I am the editor at Harper & Row who wanted you to finish your book, *List*, so that we could publish it in the fall of 1972. We wanted to get the book out early so our excellent sales force could spread out across the country and show it to booksellers VERY EARLY, and thus build up a good sale and make you very rich.

Really, Mr. Gorey, I think it would be easier for you to finish the above-mentioned book than to have to receive mournful phone calls from me. And now this letter. Hope is still flickering within my heart—but it is a guttering flame and at any moment may go out.

Won't you start the New Year RIGHT and finish your book in January? We want to give it the best production we possibly can; we don't want to rush the plate-making or the printing. Do, dear Mr. Gorey, try to cooperate a little.

I think you go to movies all the time. Please pull yourself together, and kindly oblige your ever devoted. . . .

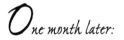ne month later:

Dear Edward:

Thanks for your card telling me you are having a nervous breakdown. Welcome to the club. I think you know that I have His and Her Straitjackets hanging in my office. Come down and slip into one and we can have a good talk.

Honey, I hate to pester you, but we do so want to do beautifully by your book *The Interesting List.* . . .

One year after the first letter:

Dear Mr. E. Gorey:

I withdraw my proposal of marriage. I couldn't be married to a man who refuses to answer his telephone. What if I wanted to phone home to say I was going to dine and spend the night with Spiro Agnew?

However, I do adore the drawings—few though they are—for *An Interesting List.* I think this will be a simple and elegant and classic book, and I beg you to finish it before you start on anything else. Please, Edward. You have a brilliant book started here. Don't put it aside and go to the movies and the ballet, and illustrate books for other publishers.

PLEASE FINISH THIS BOOK. . . .

I wrote Sendak what a joy it was to see you operating at that Showcase jury day. I said you were very strong. He replied saying yes you were indeed a mensche which if you don't know is Yiddish for good person.

But on deadlines you are rotten to the core.

Much love from your ex-fiancee . . .

*T*wo years and one month after first letter:

Dear Edward:

I hope you have opened the envelope and that is why I am writing on the envelope THIS IS NOT ABOUT *THE INTERESTING LIST* but another book.

We loved your jacket for *Freaky Friday* and wonder if you would like to do the jacket for Mary Rodgers' next book?. . .

Now here I am with a lot of space left on this paper and so in spite of my promise on the envelope I will ask you what about your *An Interesting List*. . . . Edward, I see your name as illustrator of books for all other publishers and this doesn't help my inferiority complex one bit. After all, we were at once time engaged and though the engagement was broken by mutual agreement, I am still an admirer of yours and would very much like to get *An Interesting List* on the interesting Harper list before a truck knocks me down and kills me. . . .

Y ou request an autograph and here it is.

ABRAHAM LINCOLN, LETTER TO WILLIAM C. BAKER, 1860

I continue in idleness here
because I cannot carry out
my commission until the general and the assessors are
chosen, and I keep ruminating on how I can sow so
much discord among them
that either here or elsewhere
they may start hitting each
other with their sandals;
and if I do not lose my wits,

Responses

Although many letters can be classified as letters of response, the typical response letter is tightly focused and is more likely to be brief (Lincoln's letters are marvels of the type) than long (Machiavelli is delightfully and characteristically serpentine—he does not appear to have written any brief letters).

Letters of response often begin with some acknowledgment of the other person's letter. In an exercise on the elaboration of ideas, Erasmus lists some 150 different ways to say, "I was glad to receive your letter" (*The Collected Works of Erasmus*, vol. 24). Although you may want to see how many of the 150 you can think of, the basic sentence ("I was glad. . .") is a time-honored way of beginning a letter of response.

Charles Dickens to Charles Smithson, August 1838:

My dear Sir,

It appears to be a mistake—all knowledge of your umbrella is strongly denied, and nobody has seen it—wherefore I plead with legal distinctness—first that we sent it back, secondly that it was an old one when it came, and thirdly that we never had it at all. . . .

Dorothy L. Sayers to David Higham, November 24, 1937:

Dear Mr. Higham,

I really haven't the faintest idea what would be the value of an "original Sayers manuscript," and in any case it feels rather like selling my skin before I am dead. It might be interesting to make inquiries as to price, but my impression is that modern mss. are not likely to fetch very much at the moment, and that it would be more profitable to my heirs as well as more seemly for myself to await my decease.

George Bernard Shaw to Mrs. L. E. Compton, May 7, 1904:

Your letter has just reached me in Rome, where I shall be for some time to come. I am not "one of the Shaws": I am actually THE Shaw, conferring, not deriving, the honor of the name. I know nothing about my ancestry except that they are said to have come to Ireland from Yorkshire in the reign of William III, and to descend from Macduff—the original Shakespearian Thane of Fife. My mother's name was Gurly, a Carlow family of Norman (Gourlay) origin. I cannot guarantee the accuracy of any of the legends; but I can vouch for the family habit of talking about "the Shaws."

Niccolò Machiavelli to Francesco Guicciardini, May 17, 1521:

To his Magnificent Master Francesco Guicciardini, J.U.D., Governor of Mantua and Reggio, most worthy and especially to be honored.

Magnificent Sir, Ruler to be Most Respected:

I was on the privy-seat when your messenger came, and just then I was thinking of the absurdities of this world. . . .

I continue in idleness here because I cannot carry out my commission until the general and the assessors are chosen, and I keep ruminating on how I can sow so much discord among them that either here or elsewhere they may start hitting each other with their sandals; and if I do not lose my wits, I believe I am going to succeed; and I believe that the advice and help of Your Lordship would assist greatly. . . . If you once every day would send me a servant . . . you would make me more esteemed by those in the house, seeing the messages come thick. And I can tell you that on the arrival of this arbalester with the letter, and making a bow down to the earth, and with his saying that he was sent specially and in haste, everybody rose up with so many signs of respect and such a noise that everything was turned upsidedown, and I was asked by several about the news; and I, that its reputation might grow, said that the Emperor was expected at Trent, and that the Swiss had summoned new diets, and that the King of France wanted to go in person to speak with that king, but that his councilors advised him against it; so that they all stood with open mouths and with their caps in their hands; and while I write I have a circle of them around me, and seeing me write at length they are astonished, and look on me as inspired; and I, to make them wonder more, sometimes hold my pen still and swell up, and then they slaver at the mouth; but if they could see what I am writing, they would marvel at it more. . . .

Your faithful Niccolò Machiavelli,
Ambassador to the Minor Friars

Margaret Mitchell to George A. Cornwall, July 25, 1936:

Dear Mr. Cornwall:

Thank you for your letter and all the fine things you said about the book.

I was most interested in the movie cast you selected—especially because you did not pick Clark Gable as "Rhett." All of my friends are determined that he should play this part, as though what anyone thought could influence casting directors! . . .

Thank you for saying you will reread the book. Considering the length, that's the finest compliment you could give me.

George Orwell to Victor Gollancz, January 8, 1940:

Dear Mr. Gollancz,

I cannot *at this moment* lend you *Tropic of Cancer*, because my copy has been seized. While I was writing my last book two detectives suddenly arrived at my house with orders from the public prosecutor to seize all books which I had "received through the post." A letter of mine addressed to the Obelisk Press had been seized and opened in the post. The police were only carrying out orders and were very nice about it, and even the public prosecutor wrote and said that he understood that as a writer I might have a need for books which it was illegal to possess. On these grounds he sent me back certain books, e.g., *Lady Chatterley's Lover*, but it appears that Miller's books have not been in print long enough to have become respectable. . . .

Yours sincerely,
Eric Blair

*M*axwell E. Perkins, February 17, 1942:

We thank you very much indeed for your letter of the 12th speaking so frankly with regard to several of our publications.

As to the two books you name, we should feel that we were disloyal to our profession if we refused to publish the works of distinguished writers because we realized that they would arouse hostility. . . .

But the main point we should like to make is that in a republic people are entitled to express their opinions if those opinions are worth consideration, and it is the duty of a publisher, when it is practically possible, to enable them to do it.

Ever sincerely yours,

H.L. Mencken to Theodore Dreiser, July 10, 1917:

Dear Sir:

Mr. Mencken requests me to inform you that he is quite ignorant of the matters to which you refer. He further instructs me to ask you to kindly refrain from pestering him with a long and vain correspondence. He is engaged at the moment upon patriotic work which takes his whole time and he has no leisure to fool with the bughousery of the literati.

Having no more to say, I will now close.

Very sincerely yours,
Ferdinand Balderdash
Captain, 16th U.S. Secret Service

Charles Darwin to Isaac Anderson-Henry, May 22, 1867:

You are so kind as to offer to lend me Maillet's work, which I have often heard of, but never seen. I should like to have a look at it, and would return it to you in a short time. I am bound to read it, as my former friend and present bitter enemy Owen generally ranks me and Maillet as a pair of equal fools.

Oliver Wendell Holmes, Sr. to James Thomas Fields, about a poem to be written, c. 1850:

$100.00

My dear Sir,

The above is an argument of great weight to all those who, like the late John Rogers, are surrounded by a numerous family.

I will incubate this golden egg two days, and present you with the resulting chicken upon the third.

Yours very truly,
O.W. Holmes

P.S. You will perceive that the last sentence is figurative, and implies that I shall watch and fast over your proposition for forty-eight hours. . . .

J.R.R. Tolkien to Benjamin P. Indick, January 7, 1966:

Dear Mr. Indick,

Thank you very much for your long and interesting letter and comments. They deserve a much fuller answer, but I hope you will forgive me since I am much pressed. Indeed, if I am ever to produce any more of the stories which you ask for, that can only be done by failing to answer letters.

S.J. Perelman to Edmund Wilson, December 24, 1963:

Dear Edmund,

Your Tutankhamen bat enclosure succeeded beyond your most fiendish expectations, inducing a fright just this side of a coronary seizure. . . . It just happens that I was out on the town last night, and as a result of being a bit over-convivial, had a quaking hangover when I opened your letter. As the bat fluttered out at me, I struck out much in the fashion of W.C. Fields in *The Bank Dick* lashing at the small boy with the cowboy pistol when the latter enters the bank with his mother. Since you obviously meant me to perpetrate this horrid trick on others, I thereupon carefully rewound the bat, replaced it in the letter, and when daughter Abby came in, handed it to her. The effect was convulsive. . . .

Well, this was really meant to be merely an acknowledgment of your good wishes (however diabolically transmitted). . . .

Washington Irving to Miss Lydia Minturn Post, March 25, 1859:

Dear Madam,

Your note of March 9th, being directed to Tarrytown instead of Irvington, has been slow in reaching me. You have my full consent to the dedication of your forthcoming "Domestic Annals of the Revolution" to me, if you think it would be of advantage to the work, or a gratification to yourself. I only request that the dedication be extremely simple, and void of compliment.

With great respect, yours, very truly,
Washington Irving

Mark Twain to William T. Stead, when asked for his opinion on a project for world disarmament, January 9, 1899:

No. 1

Dear Mr. Stead,

The Czar is ready to disarm: *I* am ready to disarm. Collect the *others*, it should not be much of a task now.

No. 2

Dear Mr. Stead,

Peace by compulsion. That seems a better idea than the other. Peace by persuasion has a pleasant sound, but I think we should not be able to work it. We should have to tame the human race first, and history seems to show that that cannot be done. Can't we reduce the armaments little by little—on a pro rata basis—by concert of the powers? Can't we get four great powers to agree to reduce their strength 10 per cent a year and thrash the others into doing likewise? For, of course, we cannot expect all of the powers to be in their right minds at one time. It has been tried. We are not going to try to get all of them to go into the scheme peaceably, are we? In that case I must withdraw my influence; because, for business reasons, I must preserve the outward signs of sanity. Four is enough if they can be securely harnessed together. They can compel peace, and peace without compulsion would be against nature and not operative. A sliding scale of reduction of 10 per cent a year has a sort of plausible look, and I am willing to try that if three other powers will join. I feel sure that the armaments are now many times greater than necessary for the requirements of either peace or war. . . .

Perpetual peace we cannot have on any terms, I suppose; but I hope we can gradually reduce the war strength of Europe until we get it down to where it ought to be—20,000 men, properly armed. Then we can have all the peace that is worth while, and when we want a war anybody can afford it.

Ludwig van Beethoven to Archduke Rudolph, 1810:

> I can see that Yr. Imperial Highness wish to try out the effect of my music even on the horses. So be it! I will do my best to make sure that the riders too, turn some skillful somersaults. Well, well, it really makes me laugh to think how Your Imperial Highness consider me even on this occasion; for this, assuredly, my whole life long I shall remain
>
> > Your most obliging servant,
> > Ludwig van Beethoven
>
> N.B. The desired horse music will reach Yr. Imperial Highness at full gallop.

Abraham Lincoln to a woman who had requested "a sentiment" along with his autograph, c. 1863:

> Dear Madam:
> When you ask from a stranger that which is of interest only to yourself, always enclose a stamp. There's your sentiment, and here's your autograph.
>
> > A. Lincoln

*T*he power to console is not within corporeal reach—though its attempt is precious.

EMILY DICKINSON, LETTER TO MRS. HENRY HILLS, 1879

Never saw it or heard about it until your letter came. It is no use: I can't be sympathetic; these things simply make me furious. I want to swear. I do swear. Killed just because people are blasted fools. A chaplain, too, to say nice things about it. It is not his business to say nice things about

Letters of Sympathy and Condolence

T hree years after Abraham Lincoln's beautiful condolence letter to Queen Victoria on the death of her husband, Queen Victoria writes a condolence letter to Mary Todd Lincoln on the death of *her* husband.

W.D. Howells writes his longtime friend Mark Twain on the death of Twain's wife (and in the letter he mentions a letter of condolence he wrote the Twains on the death of their daughter Susy); six years later, he writes Twain's daughter Clara on the death of her father. Among friends, it will always be the case that "There will be a time you bury me / Or I bury you in the garden" (Tomioka Taeko).

George Bernard Shaw to Beatrice Stella Campbell, when her son, Acting Lieutenant-Commander Alan U. Campbell, was killed in action, January 7, 1918:

Never saw it or heard about it until your letter came. It is no use: I can't be sympathetic; these things simply make me furious. I want to swear. I *do* swear. Killed just because people are blasted fools. A chaplain, too, to say nice things about it. It is not his business to say nice things about it, but to shout that the "voice of thy son's blood crieth unto God from the ground."

No, don't show me the letter. But I should very much like to have a nice talk with that dear Chaplain, that sweet sky-pilot, that . . .

No use going on like this, Stella. Wait for a week, and then I shall be very clever and broadminded again and have forgotten all about him. I shall be quite as nice as the Chaplain.

Oh, damn, damn, damn, damn, damn, damn, damn, damn, DAMN.

And oh, dear, dear, dear, dear, dear, dearest!

G.B.S.

Abraham Lincoln to Mrs. Bixby of Boston, November 21, 1864:

Dear Madam,

I have been shown in the files of the War Department a statement of the Adjutant-General of Massachusetts that you are the mother of five sons who have died gloriously on the field of battle. I feel how weak and fruitless must be any words of mine which should attempt to beguile you from the grief of a loss so overwhelming. But I cannot refrain from tendering to you the consolation that may be found in the thanks of the republic they died to save. I pray that our Heavenly Father may assuage the anguish of your bereavement, and leave you only the cherished memory of the loved and lost, and the solemn pride that must be yours to have laid so costly a sacrifice upon the altar of freedom.

Ellen Glasgow to Van Wyck Brooks, November 5, 1942:

Dear Van Wyck:

I am grieved to hear of your loss, yet the end, after a life so well fulfilled, must come as naturally as the closing in of an autumn day. You will miss your stepfather's "keen and delightful mind," but those we mourn for and regret are the unfulfilled—are the lives that are broken off before they have really lived. From what you write, I can imagine no happier fate than that of "an innocent and guileless human being," who dies, at eighty-seven, without pain, in the midst of a war-torn world. Even so, there will be a vacancy in your world, which is not war torn. . . .

May Sarton to S.S. Koteliansky, January 7, 1951:

Dear Kot,

I heard only today, indirectly and with no details, that James Stephens has died. . . .

There is no comfort possible for the loss of such a friend. I know that your whole house is mourning too, and I have just been looking at an old snap of you and James under the pear tree in the garden and I think the garden mourns. For those of us who did not know him well, but loved his poems and him for them, it seems as if one of the few pure voices had gone, as if there were never to be again one special bird, like the thrush. How we shall miss him—thank God the poems are there to go back to. We are all now just a little poorer than we were before he left. . . .

And there you are, and I expect the bulbs in your garden are there all right and there will be a spring. Let us believe so.

I send you my love and many thoughts and much gratefulness for the good days when several times I drank tea at your table with James. Do you remember the wonderful drink you made in the square cut glass bottle? How fine it was to be a little drunk on it and poetry, together.

Yours as ever,
May

Frank Lloyd Wright to Mrs. Darwin D. Martin, December 6, 1935:

My dear Mrs. Martin:

I am terrified by what you say of dear D.D.M. . . .

I should like to see him again—or should I try to see him?

It is good to know that he does not suffer—that all his burden of worry is gone—and that he still haunts the familiar scenes and is a physical presence still although his mind has gone away from him. Perhaps ahead of him, waiting for him!. . .

Evelyn Waugh to Diana Cooper, December 1937:

Dearest Diana,

I was so very sorry to see the news of your mother's death. I am afraid it must have been an anxious and sad Christmas for you. I remember constantly the lyrical days with her and you and *The Miracle.* You must be overwhelmed with letters, but I want you to know that Laura and I are having a mass said for your mother and that you have all our love and sympathy.

Nancy Mitford to Laura Waugh, April 11, 1966:

Oh Laura I am so miserable. I loved Evelyn I really think the best of all my friends, and then such an old friend, such a part of my life. As for you, what *can* one say? If I feel like that about him what must his loss mean to you?

And then the public loss is so great—he was far the best living writer of English without a doubt. . . .

I *absolutely forbid* you to answer—I know you don't like writing letters and you will receive millions—but I had to send you a word.

Much love from
Nancy

Louise Bogan to Rufina McCarthy Helmer, February 27, 1952:

Dear Rufina:

Your telegram came yesterday, and I was grieved to hear of your mother's death, for old time's and old friendship's sake—for I was very fond of her, as you know. The factor of release for her poorly lighted later years we both know and understand. Believing in God, we must think of that side of things as a mercy. . . .

Jenny Lind to Clara Schumann, after the latter had been robbed, April 18, 1871:

Dear Madame Schumann,

It is horrible, it is shameful, that you should be robbed of your keepsakes. It cuts one to the heart. . . . I cannot refrain, dear friend, from begging you to accept the accompanying little brooch with my love, and to wear it on Thursday. The old Queen of Sweden gave it to me, years ago, and as I have a bracelet and several other things as well from her, you need feel no qualms, and it would give me real and great pleasure to know that you had something of mine. One has received so much from you and your husband that it is pardonable to nourish a wish to give you some tiny outward token of love and respect, and to buy anything to give you would not be in accordance with my feelings. I have often worn the brooch. Oh! how sorry I am that you should have been robbed!

> In warm love,
> Your
> Jenny Lind-Goldschmidt

John and Elaine Steinbeck to Mrs. John F. Kennedy, November 24, 1963:

Dear Mrs. Kennedy:

Our sorrow is for you but also for us—for us—

We are in Warsaw as culture mongers at your husband's request which to us was an order. This is Sunday after black Friday. I wish you could see our Embassy here. In the great hall is a photograph and beside it a bust made by a young Pole who asked to bring it in. Since early morning yesterday there has been a long line of people—all kinds but mostly poor people. They move slowly past the picture, place flowers (chrysanthemums are a dollar apiece), and they write their names and feelings in a book. Numbers of volumes have been filled and today the line is longer than ever. It went on all night last night, silent and slow. I have never seen anything like this respect and this reverence. And if we weep, seeing it, it is all right because they are weeping. That's all—our hearts are with you and we love you—all of us.

Muhammad Iqbal to Lady Arnold, July 16, 1930:

My dear Lady Arnold,

It is impossible for me to tell you and Nancy of the terrible shock which came to us all when the news of the untimely death of Sir Thomas Arnold arrived in India. As you know, he was loved by pupils and all those who came into contact with him otherwise. I know words expressive of grief can bring but little consolation to you; but I assure you that your grief is shared by people in England, India and all those countries where his work as a great Orientalist was known. . . . No doubt from our point of view that luminous flame of life is now extinguished, but it is my firm conviction that to those who, like him, devote their life to love and service, death means only "more light."

I earnestly pray that God may grant eternal peace to his loving soul and may give you and Nancy fortitude enough to bear with patience the loss caused by his untimely death.

Eugénie de Guérin to Mademoiselle Antoinette de Boisset, April 11 and 18, 1837:

May God console you, my poor Antoinette; may He sustain, may He succor you! Your sorrow is beyond your strength, beyond all that can be said to you. Accordingly, I say nothing. I can only write tears, and how overwhelmed I am by the loss you have just had. What a thunderbolt!. . .

Your dear sister leaves a blank that you will find greater every day. 'Tis ever so with these dear ones who leave us, and whom nothing can replace. . . . To lose a sister, to see her no more, live with her no more, my poor friend, oh! I can well believe you are desolate.

Abraham Lincoln to the parents of Col. Elmer E. Ellsworth, killed at Alexandria the preceding day, May 25, 1861:

My dear Sir and Madam:

In the untimely loss of your noble son, our affliction here is scarcely less than your own. So much of promised usefulness to one's country and of bright hopes for one's self and friends have rarely been so suddenly dashed, as in his fall. In size, in years, and in youthful appearance, a boy only, his power to command men was surpassingly great. This power, combined with a fine intellect, an indomitable energy, and a taste altogether military, constituted in him, as seemed to me, the best natural talent in that department I ever knew. And yet he was singularly modest and deferential in social intercourse. My acquaintance with him began less than two years ago; yet through the latter half of the intervening period, it was as intimate as the disparity of our ages, and my engrossing engagements, would permit. To me, he appeared to have no indulgences or pastimes; and I never heard him utter a profane or an intemperate word. What was conclusive of his good heart, he never forgot his parents. The honors he labored for so laudably, and, in the sad end, so gallantly gave his life, he meant for them, no less than for himself. . . .

Sincerely your friend in a common affliction,

*A*braham Lincoln to Queen Victoria, on the death of Prince Albert, February 1, 1862:

Great and Good Friend:

By a letter from your son, His Royal Highness, the Prince of Wales, which has just been received, I am informed of the overwhelming affliction which has fallen upon Your Majesty by the untimely death of His Royal Highness the late Prince Consort, Prince Albert of Saxe Coburg.

The offer of condolence in such cases is a customary ceremony, which has its good uses, though it is conventional, and may sometimes be even insincere. But I would fain have Your Majesty apprehend, on this occasion, that real sympathy can exist, as real truthfulness can be practiced, in the intercourse of nations. . . . You are honored on this side of the Atlantic as a friend of the American people. The late Prince Consort was with sufficient evidence regarded as your counselor in the same friendly relation. The American people, therefore, deplore his death and sympathize in Your Majesty's irreparable bereavement with an unaffected sorrow. . . .

*Q*ueen Victoria to Mary Todd Lincoln, April 29, 1865:

Dear Madam,

Though a stranger to you I cannot remain silent when so terrible a calamity has fallen upon you & your country, & must personally express my *deep & heartfelt* sympathy with you under the shocking circumstances of your present dreadful misfortune.

No-one can better appreciate than I can who am myself *utterly broken hearted* by the loss of my own beloved Husband, who was the *light* of my Life—my stay—*my all*,—what your sufferings must be; and I earnestly pray that you may be supported by Him to whom Alone the sorely stricken can look for comfort in the hours of heavy affliction.

With the renewed expression of true sympathy, I remain, dear Madam,

Your sincere friend Victoria

Mari Sandoz to Olivia Pound, July 1, 1958:

Dear Olivia,

You will know with what degree of sorrow all of us who were privileged to know you and your sister Louise heard of her death.

Those of us who were fortunate enough to have had Miss Pound as our teacher will never think of her as gone. The good teacher is immortal and if that is true, what can one say for the great teacher?

Louise Imogen Guiney to Mary Winefride Day, December 14, 1910:

My dear poor Mary,

I am so sorry I wrote yesterday, inquiring after little Dart, for the letter must have given you an extra pang. This morning I have a card from Preston, which sadly mentions your loss. So I must send you my love at once, and ever so loving a sympathy. . . . There should be one comfort for you besides, that Dart's little span was all sunshine, and of your own giving. Dear Mary, I am ever so sorry for you.

L.I.G.

Oscar W. Firkins to Walter Speakman, November 27, 1929:

My Dear Walter:

I was told a few weeks ago that you were out of work in New York City. I was sorry to hear this. . . . I ought to have known that in a calling like yours success may both succeed and precede adversity. Please write to me within a day or two after receiving this, and let me know how things stand with you. . . .

I hope that rumor has exaggerated your distress, or at worst that time has lessened it.

John O'Hara to Kate Bramwell, whose son had Hodgkin's disease and committed suicide, January 3, 1966:

Dear Kate:

If trouble could get us used to trouble, you would be used to it now, but it doesn't work out that way. How do your friends lessen your sorrow? They don't, except by wishing they could.

Many years ago I made a study of suicide for my first novel, and I have never stopped studying it. Of one thing I am convinced: from Julian English to Jim Forrestal, from Louie Macy Gates to young Jerry Bramwell, no one who committed suicide could have done anything else. There is an inevitability to it that has a logic of its own, so powerful as to prevail over self-preservation, therefore more powerful than the most fundamental of our instincts.

We are sorry for the sadness to you and Jerry and the girls, but who can argue with the power of the inevitable?

Margaret Oliphant to Bessie and Emma Blackwood, November 10, 1881:

Dear Bessie and Emma,

I feel so startled and overwhelmed by the sad announcement I have just seen in the papers, that I have no words to say to you how I feel for you and how deeply I grieve in your grief. I feel more thankful than I can say that I saw so much of your dear mother this autumn, and so entirely renewed the affectionate regard which I had always felt for her. How kind she was! how thoughtful and good to everybody! I wish I were near enough to go to you and cry with you, dear girls. God bless you. I cannot say any more.

Yours in deep sympathy and affection,

Ayn Rand to Mary Shannon, March 23, 1946:

Dear Mary:

No, we didn't know or suspect that you and Rollie were going to break up. And your letter was quite a shock to both of us.

You say you want to hear my reaction. . . .

I am terribly sorry that it had to happen, and I feel sad for both you and Rollie, simply because I thought you were happy together. But if you weren't happy and knew you couldn't be—then it was better to end it now, rather than live your whole life as a pretense. Sacrifice never works, it only destroys both people involved. No marriage can be preserved as a matter of mere duty. Every person's first duty is to find his real and honest happiness.

That's my reaction—with the advice that no reaction, neither mine or anybody else's, is of any importance in such a question. Nothing is important, except your own best judgment.

So, of course, we're still friends—if that's what you questioned by implication in your letter. . . .

Edith Wharton to Charles Eliot Norton, June 30, 1908:

Dear Mr. Norton,

When Teddy and I heard yesterday from Lily of Taffy's sad taking-off we both really felt a personal regret in addition to our profound sympathy for his master.

His artless but engaging ways, his candid enjoyment of his dinner, his judicious habit of exercising by means of those daily rushes up and down the road, had for so many years interested and attracted us that he occupies a very special place in our crowded dog-memories. . . .

Somebody says "Hope is the most faithful of lovers"—but I really think it should be put in the plural and applied to dogs. Staunch and faithful little lovers that they are, they give back a hundredfold every sign of love one ever gives them—and it mitigates the pang of losing them to know how very happy a little affection has made them.

Teddy joins me in condolences, and we both send our love to Sally.

Ruth Draper to Malvina Hoffman, April 19, 1922:

My heart is very full, my dearest Mallie—of your pain, of the dumb acceptance of the great mystery, and of the almost joyful consciousness that you must feel, in the knowledge that her beautiful brave soul is free at last. . . .

In my life I have not seen nor do I expect to see, more heroic or more lovely human qualities than your Mother possessed, and I am proud to count back the many years that I have known her, and to think of the loyal devoted affection between her and my mother.

The way you have borne the strain of these months, has left me silent with admiration and sympathy. . . .

My dear friend, I know the agony, the baffling sense of loss, but I know that your head is high, and that the consciousness that all is well with her, outweighs the human sorrow.

But we are human, and my hand is in yours, and my heart aching for the pain that has been in your heart for so long, and that still must be, though of another kind.

Ivan Turgenev to George Eliot, December 3, 1878:

My dear Mrs. Lewes,

An hour ago I received from your daughter a letter telling me of the very dangerous illness of her father, and just now I read in the newspapers a telegramme relating the fatal termination of this illness! I don't dare to trouble the very deep grief you must feel; I only ask the permission to send you the expression of my heartfelt and sincere sympathy. May you find in your own great mind the necessary fortitude to sustain such a loss! All your friends, all learned Europe mourn with you. Believe me, my dear Mrs. Lewes,

Yours very truly,
Iv. Tourgueneff

W.D. Howells to Samuel L. Clemens (Mark Twain), on the death of his wife who had kept in her worn old bible a letter Howells wrote her when the Clemens' daughter Susy died, June 4, 1904:

My dear old Friend,

I had written to you as soon as I knew of the fact, just to let you know that I was with you in that insurpassable sorrow of yours; but you must have known it already. Pilla and I tried to read your letter aloud; we couldn't. It wrings my heart to think about you. . . .

My love to your dear girls; Pilla has written already.

I cannot speak of your wife's having kept that letter of mine, where she did. You know how it must humiliate a man in his unworthiness to have anything of his so consecrated. She hallowed what she touched, far beyond priests.

Yours affectionately,

W.D. Howells to Clara Clemens, daughter of Mark Twain, April 22, 1910:

My dear Clara,

I found Mr. Paine's telegram when I came in late last night; and suddenly your father was set apart from all other men in a strange majesty. Death had touched his familiar image into historic grandeur.

You have lost a father. Shall I dare tell you of the desolation of an old man who has lost a friend, and finds himself alone in the great world which has now wholly perished around?

We all join in sending you our helpless love.

*H*earty thanks for the pretty box of
bon-bons—exquisite in taste both
inside and out. It is very pleasant, I find, to have
friends who think of one and tell one so in bon-bons.
The style is faultless.

GEORGE ELIOT, LETTER TO GEORGE SMITH, 1867

The typewriter came
Wednesday night, and is
already beginning to have
its effect on me. Of course it
doesn't work: if I can persuade some of the letters to
get up against the ribbon
they won't get down again
without digital assistance.
The treadle refuses to have
any part or parcel in the

performance, and I don't
know how to get the roller
to turn with the paper.
Nevertheless, I have begun
several letters to My d ar
... refers to spell
your respected name, and I
don't despair yet of sending
you something in its beautiful handwriting—after
I've had a man out from
the agent's to put it in order.
It's fascinating in the
meantime, and it wastes my
time like an old friend. . . .

Thank-You Letters

The best thank-you letters are specific and descriptive. They don't need to be long (Hilaire Belloc once rhymed to Maurice Baring a simple "Of all the gifts of God by far / The best is Russian Caviare") although some letterwriters, once launched, make a return gift of their enthusiastic and lengthy thanks. One letter in this chapter (W.D. Howells to Mark Twain) is only barely discernible as a thank-you letter; it might as easily have been a letter of complaint.

Thank-you letters may be catching: Thomas Bailey Aldrich writes one to W.D. Howells; Howells writes one to Mark Twain; Twain writes one to his brother.

Henry Wadsworth Longfellow to his sister, Anne Longfellow, March 13, 1840:

My dearly beloved Annie,

Permit me to thank you once more for those cotton articles (without a name). They are just right; and very seasonable. The only change I have to suggest is to put two or three small buttons down in front. They will then be perfect.

Most truly yours,
H.W.L.

John Steinbeck to Princess Grace of Monaco, November 6, 1962:

Her Serene Highness
Princess Grace of Monaco
Palace of Monaco
Principality of Monaco

Dear Grace honey:

It was very kind of you to wire congratulations on the Nobel award. We liked that. And I remembered what you said one night at dinner soon after you had an Oscar. Judy Garland, I believe, was your runner up. You said, "I felt so sorry she didn't win but I felt very glad that I did." That was a statement of truth. And I feel the same. Maybe I don't deserve it, but I'm glad I got it.

Thanks again for your telegram.

Yours,
John Steinbeck

George Eliot to Mr. and Mrs. Albert Druce, January 1, 1875:

Dear Friends,

 Let me tell you of our delight in the beautiful flowers which came an hour ago and in the friendship which sent them. Thanks seem to me somehow rather clumsy coarse things on such an occasion. I want you chiefly to know that your impulse in sending us that remembrance has been just as sweetly beneficent as you wished it to be. . . .

Indira Gandhi to Dorothy Norman, December 22, 1956:

Dorothy darling,

 Just a line to say how wonderful it has been to be with you and to say thank you for all the trouble you took to make my stay just perfect. One has got into the habit of saying thank you for so many small things—the opening of a car door and other such normal attentions that when one really means something much deeper and more keenly felt, there just aren't the right words to say it in and one realizes the inadequacy of language.

        Love and good wishes for 1957,

Grover Cleveland to Don M. Dickinson, March 19, 1896:

 I was made very happy yesterday by the receipt of the painting you sent me of the duck hunter. It is a very *relieving* picture to look at, and every time my eye falls on it in these dreadfully dark and trying days I say to myself, "I wish I was in that old fellow's place.". . .

W.D. Howells to Mark Twain, who promised his old typewriter to Howells, but instead traded it for a saddle with his publisher—when Howells complained, Twain assured him Mr. Bliss would soon tire of the typewriter, which he did, November 5, 1875:

My dear Clemens:

The typewriter came Wednesday night, and is already beginning to have its effect on me. Of course it doesn't work: if I can persuade some of the letters to get up against the ribbon they won't get down again without digital assistance. The treadle refuses to have any part or parcel in the performance, and *I* don't know how to get the roller to turn with the paper. Nevertheless, I have begun several letters to *My d ar lemans*, as it prefers to spell your respected name, and I don't despair yet of sending you something in its beautiful handwriting—after I've had a man out from the agent's to put it in order. It's fascinating, in the meantime, and it wastes my time like an old friend. . . .

Edna St. Vincent Millay to Edmund Wilson, March 4, 1926:

Dear Bunny:

This is just a snowball at your window—I *can't* write letters. But I did think you a darling to give me the champagne, both bottles too. . . . How did you guess that a lacquer serpent with a ruby eye was just what I had written Santa Claus please to bring me? I didn't have a single lacquer serpent to my name, Bunny, let alone one with a ruby eye. . . .

Albert Schweitzer to Prince Rainier III of Monaco, February 26, 1957:

. . . I often think about Your Highness when the diesel motor hums and illuminates the operating room, which has been provided with the most modern furniture and equipment thanks to your generosity. . . .

Theodore Roosevelt to Booker T. Washington, April 2, 1908:

My dear Mr. Washington:

. . . I was delighted that we were able to appoint Williams. Yes, I recall that we now have got in office all the men whom you and I discussed when I first came into the Presidency; and I wish to thank you now, not so much on my own account as on behalf of the people of this country, and especially the colored people, for the high character of the men whom you have suggested. . . .

Langston Hughes to Arna Bontemps, March 11, 1963:

Arna—

After its lying around unread for a week (we're all so BUSY it seems) I've just opened the February "Crisis" and find your charming review of "Fight for Freedom." It's FINE! Thanks a lot! I'll almost forgive you for not getting your Dodd Mead book done since I realize it's such "little" things that always keep one from major writing. (Well, to my woe, do I know!) So *double* thanks for such a nice review.

Lang

Louise Imogen Guiney to Florence A. Crocker, March 18, 1908:

My Zoul! WhatEVER! Bless your dear old heart for a maker of Christmas in the middle of Lent. I didn't even know you could create such beauties, and am so lost in admiration of 'em that Thank You comes last, instead of first. The colors are a delight. I don't like to tread on them, and have been speculating on the question of wearing one shoe on either ear, while the chilly weather lasts, outdoors!. . . I am as pleased as ever I can be, and immensely grateful. But—my zoul! How could you?. . .

Thomas Bailey Aldrich to W.D. Howells, December 13, 1875:

Dear Howells,

We had so charming a visit at your house that I have about made up my mind to reside with you permanently.

I am tired of writing. I would like to settle down in just such a comfortable home as yours, with a man who can work regularly four or five hours a day, thereby relieving one of all painful apprehensions in respect to clothes and pocket-money.

I am easy to get along with. I have few unreasonable wants and never complain when they are constantly supplied. I think I could depend on you.

Ever yours,
T.B.A.

Sylvia Townsend Warner to Alyse Gregory, December 23, 1946:

Dearest Alyse,

Usually one begins a thank-letter by some graceless comparison, by saying, I have never been given such a very scarlet muffler, or, This is the largest horse I have ever been sent for Christmas. But your matchbox is a nonpareil, for never in my life have I been given a matchbox. Stamps, yes, drawing-pins, yes, balls of string, yes, yes, menacingly too often; but never a matchbox. Now that it has happened I ask myself why it has never happened before. They are such charming things, neat as wrens, and what a deal of ingenuity and human artfulness has gone into their construction; for if they were like the ordinary box with a lid they would not be one half so convenient. This one though is especially neat, charming, and ingenious, and the tray slides in and out as though Chippendale had made it. . . .

*S*ylvia Plath to Aurelia Schober Plath, October 27, 1950:

Dear Mum,

I couldn't wait another minute before writing you how touched I was to get my birthday package, which just came. . . . The Viyella maroon blouse is a dream (no wonder you are bankrupt) and the socks are warm and fit just right. I think I'll share the cake with the freshmen in the house tomorrow . . . the bureau scarf just *makes* the room. This is my first birthday away from home, so I was rather overwhelmed by the packages. . . .

Love,
Sivvy

*F*ranklin K. Lane to John H. Wigmore, November 14, 1898:

My dear Wigmore,

This is a formal note of acknowledgment of the service rendered me in the campaign, which has just closed successfully. There were only three Democrats elected on the general ticket, the Mayor, Assessor, and myself. I ran 4,500 votes ahead of my ticket. It was a splendid tribute to worth! I never before realized how discriminating the American public is. A man who scoffs at Democratic institutions must be a tyrant at heart, or a defeated candidate. I tell you the people know a good man when they see one. . . .

*G*eorge Washington to Benjamin Goodhue, October 15, 1797:

Dear Sir,

The fish you had the goodness to send me arrived very safe and are excellent. For your recollection of that request of mine, and the trouble you were at to obtain the best kind, I pray you to accept my grateful thanks. . . .

Margaret Mitchell to Kenneth A. Fowler, on his review of her books, July 26, 1936:

My dear Mr. Fowler:

. . . When you write me that your review is "inadequate" I feel like taking an oath from Gerald and shouting "God's nightgown!" For if your review is inadequate then I will never get a good review this side of paradise. I thought it perfectly marvelous and I've about read it to pieces. How can I say "thank you" in enough different ways to show you my real appreciation? . . .

How grand of you to say the book might probably become a "classic of American literature"! I wish I could honestly believe that. . . .

Vincent van Gogh to Theodore Van Gogh, November 1889:

My dear Theo,

I have to thank you very much for a parcel of paints, which was accompanied also by an excellent woolen jacket.

How kind you are to me, and how I wish I could do something good, so as to prove to you that I would like to be less ungrateful. The paints reached me at the right moment, because those I had brought back from Arles were almost exhausted.

. . . Thank you again for the paints, and the woolen jacket, and a good handshake in thought.

Abraham Lincoln to Mrs. Esther Stockton, July 8, 1864:

Madam,

Learning that you who have passed the eighty-fourth year of life, have given to the soldiers some three hundred pairs of stockings, knitted by yourself, I wish to offer you my thanks. Will you also convey my thanks to those young ladies who have done so much in feeding our soldiers while passing through your city?

Mary Devlin Booth to Josephine Graham, November 1, 1861:

My dear Mrs. Graham,

What shall I say in praise of the "wee blanket" wrought by your hands—and which was safely delivered to me yesterday morning?

I was prepared for the receipt of it by Mr. Graham's letter—and your kind thought for the "little stranger" I hope soon to welcome touched me deeply. The beauty of the precious little covering I prize dearly *now*—and its utility shall be proven hereafter. . . .

May Sarton to Margaret Foote Hawley, January 12, 1949:

Margaret darling,

Just a word to thank you for the vermilion cigarette case—what a color, the color of elation I think. And with my initials on it too. You are a dear to remember and to always keep me in cases and this is such a beauty. I wonder how things are going with you. It is wretched that we are so far apart and I can't run in and find out now and then and sit down for innumerable cups of tea and talk. I miss you here or wherever I am where you are not. Often I need your wisdom and your saving laughter. . . . .

I must get to work—but it is good to know you are there and that however awful I may be, you still manage to love me, dear Margaret, as I love you.

> Your old
> May

In the carrying out of this enterprise of the Indies, neither reason nor mathematics nor maps were any use to me.

Christopher Columbus, letter to King Ferdinand and Queen Isabella of Spain, 1502

Up to the period of my reaching these shores I experienced most excellent weather, but the night of my arrival came on with a dreadful tempest. . . . Eighty-eight days did this fearful tempest continue, during which I was at sea, and saw neither sun nor stars; my ships lay exposed, *with sails torn, and anchors, rigging, cables, boats and a great quantity of provisions lost; my people were very weak and humbled in spirit, ... promising to lead a religious life. . . . This is the account I have to give of my voyage. The men who accompanied me were a hundred and fifty in number, among whom were many calculated for pilots and good sailors, but none of them can explain whither I*

Letters About Travel

Although Peg Bracken believed that one's travel life is as incommunicable as one's sex life, people continue to write letters about their travels. Vita Sackville-West agreed: "Travel is the most private of pleasures. There is no greater bore than the travel bore. We do not in the least want to hear what he has seen in Hong-Kong." In 1894 Gertrude Bell wrote, "All the earth is seamed with roads, and all the sea is furrowed with the tracks of ships, and over all the roads and all the waters a continuous stream of people passes up and down. . . . What is it, I wonder, that they go out to see?" The letters in this chapter tell what they went out to see and show that, in the hands of a deft writer, we *do* want to hear what they have seen in Hong-Kong.

Agnes de Mille to Anna George de Mille, August 2, 1934:

> Dearest Mum,
>   Tomorrow at dawn, or literally very early, we motor north. The
> address will be
>   BRYNHFRYD
>   PONTFADOG
>   WREXHAM
>   DENBIGHSHIRE
>   This is not a cable code. It is a Welsh address recognized by the
> Royal Automobile Club and the post office. . . .

*Lillian Carter, Peace Corps Volunteer in Godrej Colony-Vikhroli, Bombay, to her
daughter Gloria Carter Spann, January 16, 1967:*

>   I have had four days of complete inertia caused by homesick-
> ness and no mail . . . nobody loves me, I am forgotten, I hate Mabel's
> guts, they push me too hard here, no clothes, no food, no nothing, I
> wish I were dead!
>   I ran home to lunch, and sat down to cry when I heard foot-
> steps on the stairs—God! The mailman! Letters from home!
>   I'm pepped up, everybody loves me, I don't have enough to
> do, Mabel is real sweet, food is even better than I expected, and life is
> wonderful!

Hart Crane, postcard from Paris to Samuel Loveman, January 23, 1929:

>   Dinners, soirées, poets, erratic millionaires, painters, transla-
> tions, lobsters, absinthe, music, promenades, oysters, sherry, aspirin,
> pictures, Sapphic heiresses, editors, books, sailors. *And How!*

Christopher Columbus to King Ferdinand and Queen Isabella of Spain, from Jamaica, July 7, 1503:

> . . . Up to the period of my reaching these shores I experienced most excellent weather, but the night of my arrival came on with a dreadful tempest. . . . Eighty-eight days did this fearful tempest continue, during which I was at sea, and saw neither sun nor stars; my ships lay exposed, with sails torn, and anchors, rigging, cables, boats and a great quantity of provisions lost; my people were very weak and humbled in spirit, many of them promising to lead a religious life. . . .
>
> This is the account I have to give of my voyage. The men who accompanied me were a hundred and fifty in number, among whom were many calculated for pilots and good sailors, but none of them can explain whither I went nor whence I came; the reason is very simple: I started from a point above the port of Brazil, and while I was in Española, the storm prevented me from following my intended route, for I was obliged to go wherever the wind drove me. . . .

Mark Twain to W.D. Howells, Rome, November 1878:

> . . . I wish I *could* give those sharp satires on European life which you mention, but of course a man can't write successful satire except he be in a calm, judicial good-humor; whereas I *hate* travel, and I *hate* hotels, and I *hate* the opera, and I *hate* the old masters. In truth, I don't ever seem to be in a good-enough humor with anything to satirize it. No, I want to stand up before it and curse it and foam at the mouth, or take a club and pound it to rags and pulp. I have got in two or three chapters about Wagner's operas, and managed to do it without showing temper, but the strain of another such effort would burst me!. . .

Joanne Sandstrom to friends during a four-year sailing cruise around the world taken by her, her husband, and their two sons:

January 4, 1976

Dear Friends,

Except for the inevitable problems involved in having Cain and Abel aboard and except for living in close proximity to a teenager, we are doing fine. The times of four captains and no crew have decreased, though the "old" man and the "incipient" man often clash. Reminds me of the bull seals in that Disney movie, though there's been no bloodshed. At such stressful times Erik, of course, becomes the model child. "See how much nicer I am than my brother." The joys of parenthood! Remember, these boys may be rented on a long- or short-term lease. . . .

December 22, 1976

Dear Friends,

Because of the postal strike in Lima, this letter is coming to you from Sioux City, Iowa. A prize will be given for the most original explanation of how this came about. To be considered, each entry must be received. . . .

June 17, 1977

Dear Friends,

. . . The joys of cruising, item # ???. Donald and I just figured out that we haven't enjoyed a night of uninterrupted sleep for two months. And our last hot shower was on March 12. It's a good thing we're godly (?), because we sure aren't cleanly.

We've been beating for so long that Donald is convinced that the trade winds are a myth—probably found only along the Mythythyppi. (You see what being cooped up is doing to us.)

*H*annah Whitall Smith to her friends, June 6, 1888:

> On my crossing from America, Mrs. Brooks completely saddled herself on me. She had her chair put beside mine on deck and considered herself to be "under my wing," as she expressed it. I am afraid she found it a wing of marble. I could not gush with her worth a cent. . . .
>
> Mary's daughter, Ray, my first grandchild, is the sweetest little thing that ever was. She sleeps all night like a softly breathing seraph, and when I wake I hear her little rustlings like a tiny bird in its nest. My spectacles charmed her at once, and in a few minutes after we first met we were intimate friends, and in an incredibly short space of time we assumed our proper positions of mistress and slave. When I tell you that she sucks my watch and uses my spectacles as a hammer, you will understand which one of us is mistress, and which the slave! She is in short a perfectly delicious baby, and I am a perfectly idiotic grandmother!

*W*illiam Faulkner to his mother, October 15, 1925:

> Dear Moms,
>
> England was too dear for me. I walked some, saw quite a bit of the loveliest, quietest country under the sun, and have spent the last two days on a Breton fishing boat—a tub of a thing that rocks and rolls in a dead calm. We made a good haul, though, including two three-foot sharks which they killed with boat hooks. These people eat anything though: I don't doubt but what I've eaten shark without knowing it, and liked it. A French cook can take an old shoe and make it taste good. . . .
>
> Billy

Isabel Arundell Burton to her mother, 1865:

> . . . It was fortunate that I had the foresight to take iron bed-steads along, as already at Lisbon three-inch cockroaches seethed about the floor of our room. I jumped onto a chair and Burton growled, "I suppose you think you look very pretty standing on that chair and howling at those innocent creatures." My reaction was to stop scream-ing and reflect that he was right; if I had to live in a country full of such creatures, and worse, I had better pull myself together. I got down among them, and started lashing out with a slipper. In two hours I had a bag full of ninety-seven, and had conquered my queasiness. . . .

Anton Chekhov to his brother Alexandr, June 5, 1890:

My European Brother,

It is, of course, unpleasant to live in Siberia; but better to live in Siberia and feel oneself a man of moral worth, than to live in Peters-burg with the reputation of a drunkard and a scoundrel. No reference to present company. . . .

Siberia is a cold and long country. I drive on and on and see no end to it. I see little that is new or of interest, but I feel and experi-ence a great deal. I have contended with flooded rivers, with cold, with impassable mud, hunger and sleepiness: such sensations as you could not get for a million in Moscow! You ought to come to Siberia. Ask the authorities to exile you. . . .

I bless you with both hands.
Your Asiatic brother,

Fredrika Bremer to Her Majesty, Carolina Amalia, Queen Dowager of Denmark, April 1851:

Your Majesty,

"Write to me from America!" were Your Majesty's last kind words to me at parting. . . .

Have I not, more than once, heard Your Majesty express the wish and the hope for "a community on earth in which all the members should have equal opportunity for the attainment of virtue, knowledge, a life of activity and prosperity—a community in which goodness and capacity should constitute the highest aristocracy, and in which the highest rank should depend upon the highest human worth"? However far the United States of America may be from having attained this ideal of social life, still it cannot be denied that they are aiming at this, that they are daily more and more advancing toward this ideal—more, perhaps, than any other nation on the earth. . . .

Henry Miller to Anaïs Nin, Grand Canyon, May 3, 1941:

Anaïs—

Just got your letter—gets here quicker than the mail from across the canyon, ten miles distant. That takes four days, going through four states!! No birds fly across it, no animals cross it either. Strange phenomenon. Well, it's one of the places on earth I dearly wanted to see. It's no letdown. The rocks are so cut as to resemble the façades of Hindu or Siamese temples. Some of the rocks which jut up alone and isolate are named after ancient temples. It is a tremendous drama of geology. . . . At night, when you can see nothing it is awesome. You *feel* this big hole—a mile deep. I haven't been down it yet—afraid to walk it because I might not get up—it's like climbing up five Empire State Buildings. . . .

John Muir to Louie Muir and their daughters Wanda and Helen, June 14, 1899:

Dear Louie and Bairns,

We are just entering Sitka Harbor after a delightful sail down Peril Straits, and a perfectly glorious time in Glacier Bay—five days of the most splendid weather I ever saw in Alaska. . . . Great changes have taken place. The Pacific Glacier has melted back four miles and changed into three separate glaciers, each discharging bergs in grand style. One of them, unnamed and unexplored, I named last evening, in a lecture they made me give in the social hall, the Harriman Glacier, which was received with hearty cheers. After the lecture Mr. Harriman came to me and thanked me for the great honor I had done him. It is a very beautiful glacier, the front discharging bergs like the Muir—about three quarters of a mile wide on the sea wall. . . .

Susan Hale to Lucretia P. Hale, October 1, 1872:

Dear Lucretia,

. . . Westminster Abbey interesting, but rather in the Louvre line; a delicious guide, in a black gown, as if he were a minister, who showed everything in the richest cockney, which I shall imitate for a Brain Club. Don't tell, but all abbeys are just alike (I have seen two). . . . But I should like to take these things on full gallop, instead of dawdling along gaping at them. I get fearfully tired, and a very little abbey goes a long way with me. . . .

Eugénie de Guérin to Louise de Bayne, October 15, 1838:

My dear friend,

We have traversed Paris in every direction, have taken daily walks of three and four hours, and that without my feeling any fatigue, without even remembering that I was walking. One has no body, one has only a soul to see and admire. What marvels to be sure!

Gertrude Bell to her stepmother, Lady Florence Bell, Anavarza, Turkey, April 21, 1905:

. . . Remembering the heat of yesterday I got up at dawn and at 6 o'clock started out to grapple with my churches. The whole plain, my tents included, lay under a thick white mist, but the sun was shining on the earth rock and as I climbed up I saw the great white peaks of Taurus all glittering. . . . I took my soldier with me and taught him to hold the measuring tape. He soon understood what I wanted and measured away at doors and windows like one to the manner born. After five hours' very hard work I found I had arrived at results more interesting than I had expected. In a word, the churches here are not of the Syrian type which they ought by rights to be, but of the Central Asia Minor type—and I think they will surprise Strzygowski not a little. One very delightful thing happened. One of the biggest of the churches is razed to the ground—nothing but the traces of the foundations remain. I looked round about for any scraps of carving that might give an indica-tion of the style of decoration and found, after much search, one and one only—and it was dated! . . . "The year 511." I don't know if they used the Christian era here, but it must be pretty close to it anyway, for that's about the date one would have expected. Wasn't it a great piece of luck! Two things I dislike in Anavarza. The mosquitoes and the snakes; the mosquitoes have been the most hostile of the two: the snakes always bustle away in a great hurry. . . .

After tea I rode round the rocks on the eastern side and met a shepherd boy. So we tied my horse to a stone and the shepherd and I climbed together up the only path which leads to the castle keep. It was rocky enough in all conscience and it wound cheerfully in and out of precipices and led us at last to a little hole in the wall through which we climbed to the highest tower. Like all ruined castles it was more beautiful from without than from within; but the position is glorious and worth climbing for; the walls built on the edge of a straight drop of a couple of hundred feet or more, the great plain all round and the ring of snows beyond. We dislodged the vultures who were sitting in rows on the castle top—they left a horrid smell behind them—and in a small deep window I found a nest with two evil-looking brown eggs in it. It is not often that one finds vultures' nests. . . .

*Paula Modersohn-Becker to her parents, Otto and Helen Modersohn,
January 17, 1900:*

. . . Paris is wonderful, but one needs nerves, nerves, and more
nerves—strong, fresh, and receptive nerves. To keep them under control
in the face of these overpowering impressions here is not easy. . . .

The Louvre! The Louvre has me in its clutches. Every time I'm
there rich blessings rain down upon me. I am coming to understand
Titian more and more and learning to love him. And then there is Bot-
ticelli's sweet Madonna, with red roses behind her, standing against a
blue-green sky. And Fiesole with his poignant little biblical stories, so
simply told, often so glorious in their colors. I feel so well in this society of saints—and then the Corots, Rousseaus, Millets that you told me
about. . . .

And the street life! Every moment there is something new
to see. . . .

S. J. Perelman to Anne Gregg, April 13, 1975:

. . . When I arrived here last Tuesday I bundled up my frillies
needful of washing and bore them to a laverie on the outskirts of
Souillac—the only one, apparently, available for miles. As I entered its
portals veiled with steam, I realized I'd forgotten to mark "NO
STARCH" in French for my chemises, but had clean forgotten the word
for starch though I knew it ended in "on." Determined to brazen it
through somehow, I handed over the bundle to the young man in
charge and with a series of sliding, uphill thrusts, said I didn't want
any "dindon" in the chemises. "Dindon? Dindon?" he repeated help-
lessly. Then, genius that he was, he realized what this insane foreigner
was driving at. "Ah, oui! Pas de amidon!" It wasn't till I got back to
my pocket lexicon that I realized I'd been begging him not to put
turkey in my shirts. . . .

Meriwether Lewis to President Thomas Jefferson, St. Louis, September 23, 1806:

Sir,

It is with pleasure that I announce to you the safe arrival of myself and party at 12:00 today at this place with our papers and baggage. In obedience to your orders we have penetrated the continent of North America to the Pacific Ocean, and sufficiently explored the interior of the country to affirm with confidence that we have discovered the most practicable route which does exist across the continent by means of the navigable branches of the Missouri and Columbia Rivers. . . .

I am very anxious to learn the state of my friends in Albemarle particularly whether my mother is yet living. I am, with every sentiment of esteem Your Obt. and very Humble servant,

There was a day when I liked writing letters—it has gone. Unfortunately the passion for getting them remains.

VIRGINIA WOOLF, LETTER TO KATHERINE ARNOLD-FORSTER, 1923

All letters, methinks, should be free and easy as one's discourse, not studied, as an oration, nor made up of hard words like a charm; 'tis an admirable thing to see how some people will labor to find out terms that may obscure a plain sense, like a gentleman I knew, who would never say "the weath-

er grew cold," but that "winter begins to salute us." I have no patience for such coxcombs and cannot blame an old uncle of mine that threw the candle at his man's head because he wrote a letter for him where instead of saying (as his master bid him) that he would have written himself but that he had the gout in his hand, he said that the gout in his hand would not permit him to put pen to

Letters About Letters

Ardent letterwriters often indulge in epistolary musing about their activities. They wonder why they write letters, what makes a good letter, and why there are always too many letters and not enough time.

Agnes Repplier says letterwriter extraordinaire Lady Mary Wortley Montagu "wrote more letters, with fewer punctuation marks, than any Englishwoman of her day; and her nephew, the fourth Baron Rokeby, nearly blinded himself in deciphering the two volumes of undated correspondence which were printed in 1810. Two more followed in 1813, after which the gallant Baron either died at his post or was smitten with despair; for sixty-eight cases of letters lay undisturbed."

John Henry Newman to his sister, Mrs. John Mozley, May 18, 1863:

> . . . It has ever been a hobby of mine, though perhaps it is a truism, not a hobby, that the true life of a man is in his letters. . . . Not only for the interest of a biography, but for arriving at the inside of things, the publication of letters is the true method. Biographers varnish, they assign motives, they conjecture feelings, they interpret Lord Burleigh's nods; but contemporary letters are facts.

Anne Sexton to Brother Dennis Farrell, March 28, 1963:

> . . . In a letter (no matter how quickly it is written or honestly or freely or lovingly) it is more possible to be loving and lovable, more possible to reach out and to take in. . . . I feel I have somehow deceived you into thinking this is really a human relationship. It is a letter relationship between humans. . . .

Thomas Bailey Aldrich to Edward Sylvester Morse, c. 1875:

> It was very pleasant to me to get a letter from you the other day. Perhaps I should have found it pleasanter if I had been able to decipher it. I don't think that I mastered anything beyond the date (which I knew) and the signature (which I guessed at). There's a singular and a perpetual charm in a letter of yours; it never grows old, it never loses its novelty. . . . Other letters are read and thrown away and forgotten, but yours are kept forever—unread. One of them will last a reasonable man a lifetime.

James Russell Lowell to Mrs. Francis G. Shaw, c. 1870:

> . . . I do not like shuttle-cock correspondence. What is the use of our loving people if they can't let us owe them a letter? They can't be sure we keep on loving them if we don't keep sending an acknowledgment under our hands and seals once a month? As if there were a statute of limitations for affection! . . . I have been waiting for sunshine before I wrote—I mean for one of those moods that would make a letter worth sending; and such a mood is not dependent on mere cheerfulness, but almost altogether on having nothing to do, so that one can have time to hatch one's thoughts fairly out as one goes along.

William Cowper to Lady Hesketh, April 24, 1786:

> Your letters are so much my comfort, that I often tremble, lest by any accident I should be disappointed. . . . It is well for me that you write faster than anybody, and more in an hour than other people in two, else I know not what would become of me. When I read your letters, I hear you talk; and I love talking letters dearly, especially from you.

Geraldine Jewsbury to Jane Welsh Carlyle, June 15, 1841:

> . . . I wish there were some photographic process by which one's mind could be struck off and transferred to that of the friend we wish to know it, without the medium of this confounded letterwriting!

Edward Fitzgerald to Frederic Tennyson, October 10, 1844:

> My dear Frederic,
>
>   . . . I wrote half a letter to you three months ago; and mislaid it; spent some time in looking for it, always hoping; and then some more time despairing; and we all know how time goes when we have got a thing to do which we are rather lazy about doing. As for instance, getting up in the morning. Not that writing a letter to you is so bad as getting up, but it is not easy for mortal man who has heard, seen, done, and thought, nothing since he last wrote, to fill one of these big foreign sheets full as a foreign letter ought to be. . . .

Hilaire Belloc to Mrs. Raymond Asquith, November 22, 1927:

>   I have just got your letter with immense joy. I at once, as is my custom, when I had read it, wrote an answer in my head. It was some thirty-two pages long and one brilliant cataract of verbal jewels: and so full of a playful wisdom, an underlying sincerity, an ambient affection, a profound vision, an actual seizure of reality, a diamond concision as would have moved to tears the most advanced emulary of Petronius.
>
>   But reduced to writing it will never be. . . .

Duchess of Somerset to Lady Luxborough, February 25, 1754:

> Dear Madam,
>
>   Pray never think excuse can be necessary to me about exactness in answering my letters; I am always glad to hear from you when it is agreeable to you to write. . . .

Dorothy Osborne to William Temple, September 1653:

Sir,

. . . All letters, methinks, should be free and easy as one's discourse, not studied, as an oration, nor made up of hard words like a charm; 'tis an admirable thing to see how some people will labor to find out terms that may obscure a plain sense, like a gentleman I knew, who would never say "the weather grew cold," but that "winter begins to salute us." I have no patience for such coxcombs and cannot blame an old uncle of mine that threw the pen stand at his man's head because he wrote a letter for him where instead of saying (as his master bid him) that he would have written himself but that he had the gout in his hand; he said that the gout in his hand would not permit him to put pen to paper; the fellow thought . . . that putting pen to paper was much better than plain writing. . . .

I am yours,

Alexander Pope to Jonathan Swift, June 18, 1714:

. . . A letter is a very useful as well as an amusing thing: if you are too busied in state-affairs to read it, yet you may find entertainment in folding it into divers figures, either doubling it into a pyramidical, or twisting it into a serpentine form: or if your disposition should not be so mathematical, in taking it with you to that place where men of studious minds are apt to sit longer than ordinary; where, after an abrupt division of the paper, it may not be unpleasant to try to fit and rejoin the broken lines together. . . .

I am, with the truest of affection, yours, etc.

Washington Irving to Antoinette Bolviller, May 28, 1828:

    . . . Oh! this continually accumulating debt of correspondence!
It grows while we sleep, and recurs as fast as we can pay it off. Would
that I had the turn and taste for letter-writing of our friend the prince,
to whom it seems a perfect delight; who, like an industrious spider, can
sit in that little dark room and spin out a web of pleasant fancies from
his own brain; or rather, to make a more gracious comparison, like a
honey-bee goes humming about the world, and when he has visited
every flower, returns buzz—buzz—buzz to his little hive, and works all
that he has collected into a perfect honeycomb of a letter. For my part I
know no greater delight than to receive letters; but the replying to them
is a grievous tax upon my negligent nature. I sometimes think one of
the greatest blessings we shall enjoy in heaven will be to receive letters
by every post and never be obliged to reply to them. . . .
    With the greatest regard, your friend,
                            Washington Irving

Susan Hale to Charlotte A. Hedge, June 8, 1909:

    . . . I am reading for the millionth time the "Correspondence
of Samuel Richardson," edited by Mrs. Barbauld. Delicious. Those people of the eighteenth century (Queen Anne's) knew much better what
they were about than we do. They had time for things, wrote drooling
long letters, had some knowledge of each other's characters, and what
books they had, they read. They had a thing called "Leisure" which we
don't possess, although, to be sure, they, even then, regarded themselves as being in a hurry, and spent much time and paper in explaining why they didn't write oftener; the facts being they had nothing to
communicate, and as a general thing, wrote much too frequently for
comfort either to themselves or their correspondents. . . .

Samuel Johnson to Mrs. Thrale, October 27, 1777:

Dearest Madam,

You talk of writing and writing, as if you had all the writing to yourself. If our correspondence were printed, I am sure posterity, for posterity is always the author's favorite, would say that I am a good writer too. . . . To sit down so often with nothing to say: to say something so often, almost without consciousness of saying, and without any remembrance of having said, is a power of which I will not violate my modesty by boasting, but I do not believe that everybody has it.

Some, when they write to their friends, are all affection; some are wise and sententious; some strain their powers for efforts of gaiety: some write news, and some write secrets; but to make a letter without affection, without wisdom, without gaiety, without news, and without a secret, is, doubtless, the great epistolic art.

In a man's letters, you know, Madam, his soul lies naked. His letters are only the mirror of his breast; whatever passes within him is shown undisguised. . . . Is not my soul laid open before you in these veracious pages? Do you not see me reduced to my first principles? This is the pleasure of corresponding with a friend, where doubt and distrust have no place, and everything is said as it is thought. . . . These are the letters by which souls are united, and by which minds naturally in unison move each other as they are moved themselves. . . .

Acknowledgments and Sources

The editor and publisher are grateful to those who granted permission to reprint copyrighted material in this anthology. Every effort was made to trace and contact copyright holders prior to publication and to give full and correct acknowledgment for reprinting. However, in some instances this has proved impossible. If any errors or omissions have occurred, please contact the publisher so that they can be corrected in subsequent editions. The acknowledgments and sources below are listed alphabetically by the names of the letterwriters.

ABIGAIL ADAMS: Charles Francis Adams, ed., *Familiar Letters of John Adams and His Wife Abigail Adams, During the Revolution* (New York: Hurd and Houghton, 1876).

LOUISA MAY ALCOTT: Ednah D. Cheney, ed., *Louisa May Alcott: Life, Letters, and Journals* (Boston: Roberts Brothers, 1892).

THOMAS BAILEY ALDRICH: H. Jack Lang, ed., *Dear Wit* (New York: Prentice Hall, 1990).

PRINCESS ALICE: Curtis Gentry, *Fifty Famous Letters of History* (New York: Thomas Y. Crowell, 1930).

FRED ALLEN: Joe McCarthy, ed., *Fred Allen's Letters* (New York: Doubleday, 1965), reprinted by permission of the William Morris Agency.

SHERWOOD ANDERSON: Howard Mumford Jones, ed., *Letters of Sherwood Anderson* (New York: Little Brown, 1953), reprinted by permission of the publisher; *Letters to Bab: Sherwood Anderson to Marietta D. Finley, 1916–33,* © 1985 by Eleanor C. Anderson and William A. Sutton, used with permission of the University of Illinois Press.

ANONYMOUS WOMAN: Duke of Argyll, ed., *Intimate Society Letters of the Eighteenth Century,* vol. 1 (London: Stanley Paul, 1910).

SUSAN B. ANTHONY: Lynn Sherr, ed., *Failure Is Impossible: Susan B. Anthony in Her Own Words* (New York: Random House, 1995), © 1995 by Lynn Sherr, reprinted by permission of the publisher.

ISAAC ASIMOV: Stanley Asimov, ed., *Yours, Isaac Asimov: A Lifetime of Letters,* © 1995 by Estate of Isaac Asimov, used by permission of Doubleday, a division of Random House, Inc.

J.J. AUDUBON: Howard Corning, ed., *Letters of John James Audubon* (Kraus Reprint, 1930).

JANE AUSTEN: R.W. Chapman, ed., *Jane Austen's Letters to Her Sister Cassandra and Others* (New York: Oxford University Press, 1969).

CLAUDE A. BARNETT AND ETTA M. BARNETT: Paula L. Woods and Felix H. Liddell, eds., *I Hear a Symphony: African Americans Celebrate Love* (New York: Doubleday, 1994); Claude A. Barnett Papers, Chicago Historical Society. Reprinted by permission of The Chicago Historical Society and of Mrs. Etta M. Barnett.

P.T. BARNUM: A.H. Saxon, ed., *Selected Letters of P.T. Barnum* (New York: Columbia University Press, 1983).

LUDWIG VAN BEETHOVEN: Michael Hamburger, ed., *Beethoven: Letters, Journals and Conversations* (New York: Pantheon Books, 1952), reprinted by permission of the publisher; Hans Gal, ed., *The Musician's World: Letters of the Great Composers* (New York: Thames & Hudson, 1965), reprinted by permission of the publisher.

GERTRUDE BELL: Lady Bell, ed., *The Letters of Gertrude Bell*, vol. 1 (London: Boni and Liveright, 1927).

HILAIRE BELLOC: Robert Speaight, ed., *Letters From Hilaire Belloc* (London: Hollis & Carter, 1958).

AMBROSE BIERCE: Bertha Clark Pope, ed., *The Letters of Ambrose Bierce* (San Francisco: Book Club of California, 1922).

KAREN BLIXEN: Frans Lasson, ed., *Isak Dinesen: Letters From Africa 1914–1931*, Anne Born, trans. (Chicago: University of Chicago Press, 1981), © 1978 by The Rungstedlund Foundation, © 1981 by The University of Chicago Press, reprinted by permission of the publisher and of Florence Feiler.

LOUISE BOGAN: Ruth Limmer, ed., *What the Woman Lived: Selected Letters of Louise Bogan 1920–1970* (San Diego: Harcourt Brace Jovanovich, 1973), reprinted by permission of Ruth Limmer.

DIETRICH BONHOEFFER: Reprinted with the permission of SCM Press and Simon & Schuster, Inc., from *Letters and Papers From Prison*, revised, enlarged edition by Dietrich Bonhoeffer, translated by Reginald Fuller, Frank Clark et al. Copyright © 1953, 1967, 1971 by SCM Press, London.

ARNA BONTEMPS: Charles H. Nichols, ed., *Arna Bontemps–Langston Hughes Letters 1925–1967* (New York: Dodd Mead, 1980).

MARY DEVLIN BOOTH: L. Terry Oggel, ed., *The Letters and Notebooks of Mary Devlin Booth* (Westport, CT: Greenwood Press, 1987).

FREDRIKA BREMER: Adolph B. Benson, ed., *America of the Fifties: Letters of Fredrika Bremer* (New York: American-Scandinavian Foundation, 1924).

CHARLOTTE BRONTË: Muriel Spark, ed., *The Letters of The Brontës: A Selection* (Norman: University of Oklahoma Press, 1954).

ELIZABETH BARRETT BROWNING AND ROBERT BROWNING: *The Letters of Robert Browning and Elizabeth Barrett Browning 1845–1846*, vol. 1 (New York: Harper & Brothers, 1898).

BEAU BRUMMELL: Lewis Melville, *Beau Brummell: His Life and Letters* (London: Hutchinson, 1924).

MRS. C. BURGOYNE: Duke of Argyll, ed., *Intimate Society Letters of the Eighteenth Century*, vol. 1 (London: Stanley Paul, 1910).

FANNY BURNEY: Charlotte Barrett, ed., *Diary and Letters of Madame d'Arblay*, vol. 3 (London: Bickers and Son, 1842).

ISABEL ARUNDELL BURTON: Olga Kenyon, ed., *800 Years of Women's Letters* (London: Faber & Faber, Ltd., 1993).

GEORGE GORDON, LORD BYRON: Stella Stewart Center, ed., *Selected Letters* (New York: Charles E. Merrill, 1915).

MOTHER FRANCES CABRINI: Giovanni Serpentelli, ed., *The Travels of Mother Frances Xavier Cabrini As Related in Several of Her Letters* (Exeter, England: Stretham Hall, 1925).

BEATRICE STELLA CAMPBELL: Alan Dent, ed., *Bernard Shaw and Mrs. Patrick Campbell: Their Correspondence* (New York: Alfred A. Knopf, 1952).

LEWIS CARROLL: Morton N. Cohen, ed., *The Letters of Lewis Carroll* (New York: Oxford University Press, 1979), reprinted by permission of A.P. Watt Ltd. on behalf of The Trustees of the C.L. Dodgson Estate, Morton N. Cohen, and Roger Lancelyn Green, and by permission of Oxford University Press, Inc.

RACHEL CARSON: Martha Freeman, ed., *Always, Rachel: The Letters of Rachel Carson and Dorothy Freeman, 1951–1964* (Boston: Beacon Press, 1995), © 1995 by Roger Allen Christie, reprinted by permission of Beacon Press, Boston.

LILLIAN CARTER: Lillian Carter and Gloria Carter Spann, *Away From Home: Letters to My Family* (New York: Simon & Schuster, 1977), reprinted by permission of the publisher.

WILLA CATHER: L. Brent Bohlke, ed., *Willa Cather in Person* (Lincoln: University of Nebraska Press, 1986), reprinted by permission of the publisher.

CATHERINE THE GREAT: A. Lentin, ed., *Voltaire and Catherine the Great: Selected Correspondence* (Oriental Research Partners, 1974).

MARGARET CAVENDISH: Margaret Cavendish, *Sociable Letters, Written by the Thrice Noble, Illustrious, and Excellent Princess, the Lady Marchioness of Newcastle* (1664).

PAUL CELAN: Barbara Wiedemann, ed., *Paul Celan, Nelly Sachs: Correspondence*, Christopher Clark, trans. (Riverdale-on-Hudson, NY: Sheep Meadow Press, 1995).

PAUL CÉZANNE: John Rewald, ed., *Paul Cézanne: Letters*, Marguerite Kay, trans. (London: Bruno Cassirer, 1941).

RAYMOND CHANDLER: Frank MacShane, ed., *Selected Letters of Raymond Chandler* (New York: Columbia University Press, 1981), reprinted by permission of Ed Victor Ltd.

ANTON CHEKHOV: Constance Garnett, trans., *Letters of Anton Tchehov to His Family and Friends* (London: Chatto & Windus, 1920), reprinted by permission of A.P. Watt Ltd. on behalf of The Executors of the Estate of Constance Garnett.

LYDIA MARIA CHILD: Lydia Maria Child, *Letters of Lydia Maria Child* (Boston: Houghton Mifflin, 1883).

CHINESE ECONOMIC JOURNAL: quoted in *The Letter Exchange*, Fall 1987.

FREDERIC CHOPIN: Henryk Opienski, ed., *Chopin's Letters* (New York: Alfred A. Knopf, 1931); Hans Gal, ed., *The Musician's World: Letters of the Great Composers* (London: Thames & Hudson, 1965).

QUEEN CHRISTINA OF SWEDEN: Helene Scheu-Riesz, ed., *Will You Marry Me? Proposal Letters of Seven Centuries* (American Book-Stratford Press, 1940).

CLEMENTINE AND WINSTON CHURCHILL: Mary Soames, *Clementine Churchill: The Biography of a Marriage* (London: Cassell, 1979), reprinted by permission of Curtis Brown on behalf of The Lady Mary Soames DBE, copyright © Mary Soames, and by permission of Curtis Brown on behalf of The Estate of Sir Winston S. Churchill, copyright © Winston S. Churchill.

CICERO: Vicesimus Knox, ed., *Elegant Epistles*, vol. 1 (London: J. Mawman, 1814).

GROVER CLEVELAND: Allan Nevins, ed,. *Letters of Grover Cleveland* (Boston: Houghton Mifflin, 1933), reprinted by permission of the publisher.

COLETTE: Robert Phelps, trans., *Letters From Colette* (New York: Farrar Straus Giroux, 1980), reprinted by permission of Farrar, Straus and Giroux, LLC; translation copyright © 1980 by Farrar, Straus and Giroux, LLC; introduction, compilation, and editing copyright © 1980 by Robert Phelps.

CHRISTOPHER COLUMBUS: R.H. Major, ed., trans., *Christopher Columbus: Four Voyages to the New World: Letters and Selected Documents* (New York: Corinth Books, 1961).

JOSEPH CONRAD: John A. Gee and Paul J. Sturm, eds., *Letters of Joseph Conrad to Marguerite Poradowska 1890–1920* (New Haven: Yale University Press, 1940), reprinted by permission of the publisher.

ANNA JULIA COOPER: Charles Lemert and Esme Bhan, eds., *The Voice of Anna Julia Cooper* (Lanham, MD: Rowman & Littlefield Publishers, Inc., 1998).

WILLIAM COWPER: Vicesimus Knox, ed., *Elegant Epistles*, vol. 2 (London: J. Mawman, 1814); Rev. Hedley V. Taylor, ed., *Letters of Great Writers* (London: Blackie and Son, 1912).

HART CRANE: Langdon Hammer and Brom Weber, eds., *O My Land, My Friends: The Selected Letters of Hart Crane* (New York/London: Four Walls Eight Windows, 1997), reprinted by permission of the publisher; Brom Weber, ed., *The Letters of Hart Crane* (Berkeley: University of California Press, 1965).

E.E. CUMMINGS: F.W. Dupee and George Stade, eds., *Selected Letters of E.E. Cummings* (San Diego: Harcourt Brace, 1969), copyright © 1969 by the Trustees for the E.E. Cummings Trust, reprinted by permission of Harcourt, Inc., and by permission of Liveright Publishing Corporation.

ELIZABETH CUSTER AND GEORGE ARMSTRONG CUSTER: Marguerite Merington, ed., *The Custer Story: The Life and Intimate Letters of General Custer and His Wife Elizabeth* (New York: Devin-Adair, 1950).

CHARLES DARWIN: Francis Darwin and A.C. Seward, eds., *More Letters of Charles Darwin*, vol. 1 (New York: Appleton, 1903).

ALEXANDRA DAVID-NEEL: Sarah August Taintor and Kate M. Monro, eds., *The Book of Modern Letters* (New York: Macmillan, 1933).

LEONARDO DA VINCI: M. Lincoln Schuster, ed., *A Treasury of the World's Great Letters* (New York: Simon & Schuster, 1940).

SIMONE DE BEAUVOIR: Quintin Hoare, ed., trans., *Letters to Sartre*, © 1990 by Editions Gallimard, © 1991 Quintin Hoare (English translation), by permission of Little, Brown and Company (Inc.) and of Random House Century Group.

CLAUDE DEBUSSY: François Lesure and Roger Nichols, eds., *Debussy Letters* (Cambridge: Harvard University Press, 1987), reprinted by permission of Henri Thieullent on behalf of Madame Dolly Tinan.

EUGÉNIE DE GUÉRIN: Guillaume S. Trébutien, ed., *Letters of Eugénie de Guérin* (Christian Press Association, 1865).

MARY GRANVILLE PENDARES DELANY: Ada M. Ingpen, ed., *Women As Letter-Writers* (London: Hutchinson, 1909).

AGNES DE MILLE: Agnes de Mille, *Speak to Me, Dance With Me* (New York: Atlantic Monthly Press, 1973).

MADAME DE STAËL: James F. Marshall, ed., *De Staël–Du Pont Letters* (Madison: University of Wisconsin Press, 1968).

CHARLES DICKENS: Mamie Dickens and Georgina Hogarth, eds., *The Letters of Charles Dickens*, vol. 1 (New York: Scribner's, 1879); J.W. Cross, ed., *George Eliot's Life as Related in Her Letters and Journals*, vol. 2 (New York: Crowell, 1885); Madeline House and Graham Storey, eds., *The Letters of Charles Dickens*, vol. 1 (London: Clarendon, 1965), reprinted by permission of Oxford University Press; Bill Adler, ed., *Funny Letters from Famous People* (Pittsburgh: Four Winds Press, 1969); Kathleen Tillotson, ed., *The Letters of Charles Dickens*, vol. 4 (Oxford: Clarendon, 1977), reprinted by permission of Oxford University Press.

EMILY DICKINSON: Reprinted by permission of the publishers from *The Letters of Emily Dickinson*, edited by Thomas H. Johnson, Cambridge, Mass.: The Belknap Press of Harvard University Press, copyright © 1958, 1986 by the President and Fellows of Harvard College; Martha Dickinson Bianchi, ed., *The Life and Letters of Emily Dickinson* (Boston: Houghton Mifflin, 1924).

BASSETT DIGBY: Gregory, Kenneth, ed,. *Your Obedient Servant: A Selection of the Most Witty, Amusing and Memorable Letters to The Times of London 1900–1975* (New York: Methuen, 1976).

DIOGENES: Curtis Gentry, ed., *Fifty Famous Letters of History* (New York: Thomas Y. Crowell, 1930).

DOROTHEA DIX: Charles M. Snyder, ed., *The Lady and the President: The Letters of Dorothea Dix and Millard Fillmore* (Lexington: University Press of Kentucky, 1975).

FYODOR DOSTOEVSKY: Ethel Colburn Mayne, trans., *Letters of Fyodor Michailovitch Dostoevsky to His Family and Friends* (London: Chatto & Windus, 1914).

RUTH DRAPER: Neilla Warren, ed., *The Letters of Ruth Draper* (New York: Scribner's, 1979), reprinted by permission of the publisher.

CHARLES R. DREW: Paula L. Woods and Felix H. Liddell, eds., *I Hear a Symphony: African Americans Celebrate Love* (New York: Doubleday, 1994); letter from the Charles

Drew Papers, Moorland Spingarn Research Center, Howard University. Reprinted by permission of Moorland Spingarn Research Center, Howard University.

PAUL LAURENCE DUNBAR: Jay Martin and Gossie H. Hudson, eds., *The Paul Laurence Dunbar Reader* (New York: Dodd Mead, 1975); Mildred Howells, ed., *Life in Letters of William Dean Howells* (New York: Doubleday Doran, 1928), reprinted by permission of Polly Howells Werthman.

AMELIA EARHART: George Palmer Putnam, *Soaring Wings: A Biography of Amelia Earhart* (San Diego: Harcourt Brace, 1939); Jean L. Backus, *Letters From Amelia: 1901–1937* (Boston: Beacon Press, 1982), reprinted by permission of the publisher.

MARIA EDGEWORTH: Augustus J.C. Hare, *The Life and Letters of Maria Edgeworth*, vol. 1 (Boston: Houghton Mifflin, 1895).

GEORGE ELIOT: J.W. Cross, ed., *George Eliot's Life as Related in Her Letters and Journals*, vols. 1–3 (New York: Crowell, 1885); Gordon S. Haight, ed., *The George Eliot Letters*, vols. 1–9 (New Haven: Yale University Press, 1954–1978), reprinted by permission of Yale University Press, and by permission of collections holding some of the letters: The National Library of Scotland; Princeton University; The British Library.

ELIZABETH I: G.B. Harrison, *The Letters of Queen Elizabeth I* (New York: Funk & Wagnalls, 1935).

RALPH WALDO EMERSON: Ralph L. Rusk, ed., *The Letters of Ralph Waldo Emerson* (New York: Columbia University Press, 1939), reprinted by permission of the Ralph Waldo Emerson Memorial Association.

ERASMUS: J.A. Froude, ed., *Life and Letters of Erasmus* (New York: Scribner's, 1895).

WILLIAM FAULKNER: Joseph Blotner, ed., *Selected Letters of William Faulkner* (New York: Vintage, 1977), © 1977 by Jill Faulkner Summers, reprinted by permission of Random House, Inc.

EDNA FERBER: William Lyon Phelps, *Autobiography With Letters* (New York: Oxford University Press, 1939).

OSCAR W. FIRKINS: Ina Ten Eyck Firkins, ed., *Memoirs and Letters of Oscar W. Firkins* (Minneapolis: University of Minnesota Press, 1934), reprinted by permission of the publisher.

DOROTHY CANFIELD FISHER: Elizabeth Yates, *Pebble in a Pool* (New York: Dutton, 1958).

M.F.K. FISHER: Norah K. Barr et al., eds., *M.F.K. Fisher: A Life in Letters* (Washington, D.C.: Counterpoint, 1997).

EDWARD FITZGERALD: Stella Stewart Center, ed., *Selected Letters* (New York: Charles E. Merrill, 1915).

F. SCOTT FITZGERALD: Andrew Turnbull, ed., *The Letters of F. Scott Fitzgerald* (New York: Scribner's, 1963), reprinted by permission of Harold Ober Associates; Matthew J. Bruccoli, ed., *F. Scott Fitzgerald: A Life in Letters* (New York: Scribner's, 1994), excerpted with permission of Scribner, a Division of Simon & Schuster, Inc. Copyright © 1994 by The Trustees under Agreement Dated July 3, 1975, Created by Frances Scott Fitzgerald Smith. Reprinted by permission of the publisher.

ZELDA SAYRE FITZGERALD: Nancy Milford, *Zelda* (New York: Harper, 1970), reprinted by permission of Brandt & Brandt.

GUSTAVE FLAUBERT: Francis Steegmuller, ed., *The Letters of Gustave Flaubert 1830–1857* (Cambridge: Belknap Press of Harvard University Press, 1980); Barbara Beaumont, ed., *Flaubert and Turgenev: A Friendship in Letters* (New York: Fromm International, 1987).

MARJORIE FLEMING: Lachlan MacBean, *Marjorie Fleming's Book: The Story of Pet Marjorie Together With Her Journals and Letters* (London: Boni and Liveright, 1903).

FELIX FRANKFURTER: Ephraim London, ed., *The World of Law: The Law as Literature*, vol. 2 (New York: Simon & Schuster, 1960), reprinted by permission of the publisher.

BENJAMIN FRANKLIN: Stella Stewart Center, ed., *Selected Letters* (New York: Charles E. Merrill, 1915); Mary Owens Crowther, ed., *The Book of Letters* (New York: Nelson Doubleday, 1923).

EMPRESS FREDERICK: Sir Frederick Ponsonby, ed., *The Letters of the Empress Frederick* (London: Macmillan Publishers Ltd., 1929).

MARY E. WILKINS FREEMAN: Brent L. Kendrick, ed., *The Infant Sphinx: Collected Letters of Mary E. Wilkins Freeman* (Lanham, MD: Scarecrow, 1985).

PHILIP FRENEAU: *Letters on Various Interesting and Important Subjects* (Scholars' Facsimiles and Reprints, 1943).

SIGMUND FREUD: Jeffrey Moussaieff Masson, ed., *The Complete Letters of Sigmund Freud to Wilhelm Fliess 1887–1904* (Cambridge: Belknap Press of Harvard University Press, 1985).

INDIRA GANDHI: Dorothy Norman, ed., *Indira Gandhi: Letters to An American Friend 1950–1984* (San Diego: Harcourt Brace Jovanovich, 1985), copyright © 1985 by Dorothy Norman, reprinted by permission of Harcourt, Inc., and by permission of Ray Pierre Corsini for the Dorothy Norman Estate.

FEDERICO GARCÍA LORCA: Federico García Lorca, *Selected Letters* (New York: New Directions, 1954), reprinted by permission of the publisher.

ELIZABETH CLEGHORN GASKELL: J.A.V. Chapple and Arthur Pollard, eds., *The Letters of Mrs. Gaskell* (Manchester, England: Manchester University Press, 1966), reprinted by permission of the publisher and Harvard University Press.

ELLEN GLASGOW: Blair Rouse, ed., *Letters of Ellen Glasgow* (San Diego: Harcourt Brace, 1958), © copyright 1958 by Irita Van Doren and Frank Vigor Morley for the Estate of Ellen Glasgow and renewed 1986 by Fanchon R. Rouse, Janet Rouse Schwartz, and James Blair Rouse, reprinted by permission of Harcourt, Inc.

OLIVER GOLDSMITH: Stella Stewart Center, ed., *Selected Letters* (New York: Charles E. Merrill, 1915).

LOUISE IMOGEN GUINEY: Grace Guiney, ed., *Letters of Louise Imogen Guiney* (New York: Harper, 1926).

AHAD HA-AM: Leon Simon, ed., *Ahad Ha-am: Essays, Letters, Memoirs* (London: East and West Library/Phaidon, 1946).

SUSAN HALE: Caroline P. Atkinson, *Letters of Susan Hale* (Boston: Marshall Jones, 1918).

MARC HAMBLOT: André Bernard, *Rotten Rejections* (Pushcart Press, 1990), and H. Jack Lang, *Dear Wit: Letters From the World's Wits* (Prentice Hall, 1991).

KATHARINE HATHAWAY: Katharine Butler Hathaway, *The Journals & Letters of The Little Locksmith* (New York: Coward-McCann, 1946), reprinted by permission of F. Anthony Butler.

VÁCLAV HAVEL: Paul Wilson, trans., *Letters to Olga: June 1979–September 1982* (New York: Henry Holt and Company, Inc., 1983). Translation copyright © 1988 by Paul Wilson. Reprinted by permission of Alfred A. Knopf, a division of Random House, Inc., and Rowhalt Taschenbuch Verlag.

BESSIE HEAD: Randolph Vigne, ed., *A Gesture of Belonging: Letters From Bessie Head, 1965–1979* (Portsmouth, NH: Heinemann Educational Books, 1991).

ERNEST HEMINGWAY: Carlos Baker, ed., *Ernest Hemingway Selected Letters 1917–1961* (New York: Scribner's, 1981), reprinted with permission of Scribner, a Division of Simon & Schuster, Inc., copyright © 1981 The Ernest Hemingway Foundation, Inc., and with permission of The Ernest Hemingway Foreign Rights Trust.

HENRY VIII: Frederick E.S. Birkenhead, ed., *The Five Hundred Best English Letters* (London: Cassell, 1931); M. St. Clare Byrne, ed., *The Letters of King Henry VIII* (New York: Funk & Wagnalls, 1936).

OLIVER WENDELL HOLMES, SR.: John T. Morse, Jr., *Life and Letters of Oliver Wendell Holmes* (Boston: Houghton Mifflin, 1896).

W.D. HOWELLS: Mildred Howells, ed., *Life in Letters of William Dean Howells* (New York: Doubleday Doran, 1928), reprinted by permission of Polly Howells Werthman; Clara Clemens, *My Father, Mark Twain* (New York: Harper, 1931), copyright © 1931 by Clara Clemens Gabrilowitsch, renewed © 1958 by Clara Clemens Samossoud. Reprinted by permission of HarperCollins Publishers, Inc.

LANGSTON HUGHES: Charles H. Nichols, ed., *Arna Bontemps–Langston Hughes Letters 1925–1967* (New York: Dodd Mead, 1980).

ZORA NEALE HURSTON: Alice Walker, ed., *I Love Myself When I Am Laughing . . . And Then Again When I Am Looking Mean and Impressive: A Zora Neale Hurston Reader* (New York: Feminist Press, 1979).

MUHAMMAD IQBAL: Bashir Ahmad Dar, ed., *Letters of Iqbal* (Lahore, Pakistan: Iqbal Academy, 1978).

WASHINGTON IRVING: Pierre M. Irving, ed., *The Life and Letters of Washington Irving* (London: Richard Bentley, 1862).

HELEN HUNT JACKSON: Valerie Sherer Mathes, ed., *The Indian Reform Letters of Helen Hunt Jackson* (Norman: University of Oklahoma Press, 1998); March 29, 1885, letter reprinted by permission of Special Collections and Archives, Charles Leaming Tutt Library, Colorado College; August 8, 1885, letter in the collection at Princeton University Library.

GERALDINE JEWSBURY: Mrs. Alexander Ireland, ed., *Selections From the Letters of Geraldine Endsor Jewsbury to Jane Welsh Carlyle* (London: Longmans Green, 1892).

SAMUEL JOHNSON: James Boswell, *The Life of Samuel Johnson* (1791); George Birkbeck Hill, ed., *Letters of Samuel Johnson*, vol. 1 (New York: Harper & Brothers, 1892).

EMPRESS JOSEPHINE: Imbert de Saint-Amand, *The Court of the Empress Josephine* (New York: Scribner's, 1891).

FRANZ KAFKA: N.N. Glatzer, ed., *Letters to Ottla and the Family*, Richard and Clara Winston, trans. (New York: Schocken, 1982).

FRIDA KAHLO: Martha Zamora, ed., *The Letters of Frida Kahlo: Cartas Apasionadas* (San Francisco: Chronicle Books, 1995), reprinted by permission of Banco de Mexico, Fiduciario en el Fideicomiso relativo a los Museos Diego Rivera y Frida Kahlo.

HELEN KELLER: Karen Payne, ed., *Between Ourselves: Letters Between Mothers & Daughters* (Boston: Houghton Mifflin, 1983), reprinted by permission of Michael Joseph Ltd.

SØREN KIERKEGAARD: Henrik Rosenmeier, trans., *Kierkegaard: Letters and Documents.* Copyright © 1978 by Princeton University Press. Reprinted by permission of Princeton University Press.

THE REVEREND MARTIN LUTHER KING, JR.: Alex Ayres, ed., *The Wisdom of Martin Luther King, Jr.* (New York: Penguin Books, 1993).

RUDYARD KIPLING: Elliot L. Gilbert, ed., *"O Beloved Kids": Rudyard Kipling's Letters to His Children* (San Diego: Harcourt Brace Jovanovich, 1984), reprinted by permission of A.P. Watt Ltd. on behalf of The National Trust for Places of Historic Interest or Natural Beauty and Elliot Gilbert.

OSKAR KOKOSCHKA: Olda Kokoschka and Alfred Marnau, eds., *Oskar Kokoschka Letters 1905–1976* (New York: Thames and Hudson, 1992), reprinted by permission of the publisher.

LESLIE LAND: Leslie Land and Roger Phillips, *The 3,000 Mile Garden: An Exchange of Letters on Gardening, Food, and the Good Life* (New York: Viking Penguin, 1996), reprinted by permission of the publisher.

FRANKLIN K. LANE: Anne Wintermute Lane and Louise Herrick Wall, eds., *The Letters of Franklin K. Lane: Personal and Political* (Boston: Houghton Mifflin, 1922).

J.B. LEE: Letter courtesy of and copyright by the Honorable Ed Foreman, reprinted with permission.

ROBERT E. LEE: Douglas Southall Freeman, ed., *Lee's Dispatches: Unpublished Letters of General Robert E. Lee, C.S.A. to Jefferson Davis and the War Department of The Confederate States of America 1862–1865* (New York: G.P. Putnam's Sons, 1915).

MERIWETHER LEWIS: Donald Jackson, ed., *Letters of the Lewis and Clark Expedition* (Champaign: University of Illinois Press, 1962), © 1990 by Cathy Jackson, reprinted by permission of the publisher; letter to his mother reprinted by permission of the Missouri Historical Society.

ABRAHAM LINCOLN: John G. Nicolay and John Hay, eds., *Complete Works of Abraham Lincoln*, vols. 1–12 (Francis D. Tandy, 1905); Gilbert A. Tracy, ed., *Uncollected Letters of Abraham Lincoln* (Boston: Houghton Mifflin, 1917); Carl Sandburg, *Abraham Lincoln: The Prairie Years*, vol. 2 (San Diego: Harcourt Brace, 1926); Emanuel Hertz, ed., *Abraham Lincoln: A New Portrait* (London: Horace Liveright, 1931); H. Jack Lang, ed., *The Wit and Wisdom of Abraham Lincoln as Reflected in His Briefer Letters and Speeches* (Cleveland: World Publishing Company, 1941); Roy P. Basler et al., eds., *The Collected Works of Abraham Lincoln*, vol. 5 (Piscataway, NJ: Rutgers University Press, 1953), reprinted by permission of the Abraham Lincoln Association.

MARY TODD LINCOLN: *Mary Todd Lincoln: Her Life and Letters* by Justin G. Turner and Linda Levitt Turner, copyright © 1972 by Justin G. Turner and Linda Levitt Turner, reprinted by permission of Alfred A. Knopf, Inc.

JENNY LIND: Berthold Litzmann, *Clara Schumann: An Artist's Life, Based on Material Found in Diaries and Letters*, Grace E. Hadow, trans., vols. 1, 2 (London: Macmillan, 1913).

ANNE MORROW LINDBERGH AND CHARLES A. LINDBERGH: Anne Morrow Lindbergh, *War Within and Without: Diaries and Letters of Anne Morrow Lindbergh 1938–1944* (San Diego: Harcourt Brace Jovanovich, 1980), copyright © 1980 by Anne Morrow Lindbergh, reprinted by permission of Harcourt, Inc.

FANNY LONGFELLOW: Edward Wagenknecht, ed., *Mrs. Longfellow: Selected Letters and Journals of Fanny Appleton Longfellow* (London: Longmans Green, 1956).

HENRY WADSWORTH LONGFELLOW: Andrew Hilen, ed., *The Letters of Henry Wadsworth Longfellow*, vol. 2 (Cambridge: Belknap Press of Harvard University Press, 1966).

JAMES RUSSELL LOWELL: Stella Stewart Center, ed., *Selected Letters* (New York: Charles E. Merrill, 1915).

NICCOLÒ MACHIAVELLI: Allan Gilbert, ed., *The Letters of Machiavelli* (Chicago: University of Chicago Press, 1961), reprinted by permission of the publisher.

ARCHIBALD MACLEISH: R.H. Winnick, ed., *The Letters of Archibald MacLeish 1907–1982*. Copyright © 1983 by the Estate of Archibald MacLeish and by R.H. Winnick. Reprinted by permission of Houghton Mifflin Company. All rights reserved.

DOLLY MADISON: Dorothy P. Madison, ed., *Memoirs and Letters of Dolly Madison* (Boston: Houghton Mifflin, 1886).

GUSTAV MAHLER: Donald Mitchell, ed., *Gustav Mahler: Memories and Letters*, Basil Creighton, trans. (London: John Murray Ltd., 1946), reprinted by permission of the publisher; Hans Gal, ed., *The Musician's World: Letters of the Great Composers* (New York: Thames & Hudson, 1965).

KATHERINE MANSFIELD: J. Middleton Murry, ed., *The Letters of Katherine Mansfield* (New York: Alfred A. Knopf, 1936), reprinted by permission of The Society of Authors as the literary representative of the Estate of Katherine Mansfield.

HARRIET MARTINEAU: Valerie Sanders, ed., *Harriet Martineau: Selected Letters* (Oxford: Clarendon, 1990).

GROUCHO MARX: Groucho Marx, *The Groucho Letters* (New York: Simon & Schuster, 1967), reprinted with permission of Simon & Schuster, Inc. Copyright © 1967 by Groucho Marx. Copyright renewed © 1995 by Miriam Marx, Arthur Marx, and Melinda Marx.

MARSHALL MCLUHAN: Matie Molinaro et al., eds., *Letters of Marshall McLuhan* (New York: Oxford University Press, 1988); copyright © 1988 by Matie Molinaro and Corinne McLuhan; used by permission of Oxford University Press, Inc.

HERMAN MELVILLE: Merrell R. Davis and William H. Gilman, eds., *The Letters of Herman Melville* (New Haven: Yale University Press, 1960), reprinted by permission of Yale University Press.

H.L. MENCKEN: Guy J. Forgue, ed., *Letters of H.L. Mencken.* Copyright © 1961 by Alfred A. Knopf, Inc. Reprinted by permission of Alfred A. Knopf, Inc., and by permission of the Enoch Pratt Free Library in accordance with the terms of the will of H.L. Mencken.

FELIX MENDELSSOHN: Rudolf Elvers, ed., *Felix Mendelssohn: A Life in Letters* (New York: Fromm International, 1986), reprinted by permission of the publisher.

YEHUDI MENUHIN: Brenda Niall and John Thompson, eds., *The Oxford Book of Australian Letters* (New York: Oxford University Press, 1998), reprinted by permission of Clara Menuhin-Hauser.

EDNA ST. VINCENT MILLAY: Allan Ross Macdougall, ed., *Letters of Edna St. Vincent Millay* (New York: Harper, 1952), excerpts from Letters 69, 83, 138, and entire Letter 147. Copyright 1952, 1980 by Norma Millay Ellis. All rights reserved. Reprinted by permission of Elizabeth Barnett, literary executor.

HENRY MILLER: Gunther Stuhlmann, ed., *Henry Miller: Letters to Anaïs Nin* (New York: G.P. Putnam's, 1965), reprinted by permission of Valentine Miller and Tony Miller on behalf of the Estate of Henry Miller.

MARGARET MITCHELL: Richard Harwell, ed., *Margaret Mitchell's Gone With the Wind Letters 1936–1949* (New York: Macmillan Books, 1976), reprinted by permission of the William Morris Agency.

NANCY MITFORD: Charlotte Mosley, ed., *The Letters of Nancy Mitford* (Boston: Houghton Mifflin, 1993). Compilation copyright © 1993 by Charlotte Mosley. Letters of Nancy Mitford copyright © 1993 by the Estate of Nancy Mitford. Reprinted by permission of Houghton Mifflin Company. All rights reserved.

PAULA MODERSOHN-BECKER: Günter Busch and Liselotte von Reinken, eds., *Paula Modersohn-Becker: The Letters and Journals*, Arthur S. Wensinger and Carole Clew Hoey, eds., trans. (Evanston: Northwestern University Press, 1990), © 1979 S. Fischer Verlag and © 1983 Taplinger Publishing Co., reprinted by permission of Northwestern University Press.

LADY MARY WORTLEY MONTAGU: Vicesimus Knox, ed., *Elegant Epistles*, vol. 2 (London: J. Mawman, 1814); Dorothy Van Doren, ed., *The Lost Art* (New York: Coward-McCann, 1929); Robert Halsband, ed., *The Selected Letters of Lady Mary Wortley Montagu* (New York: St. Martin's Press, 1971).

WOLFGANG AMADEUS MOZART: Hans Mersmann, ed., *Letters of Wolfgang Amadeus Mozart*, M.M. Boxman, trans. (London: J.M. Dent, 1928); Hans Gal, ed., *The Musician's World: Letters of the Great Composers* (New York: Thames & Hudson, 1965).

JOHN MUIR: William Frederick Bade, *The Life and Letters of John Muir* (Boston: Houghton Mifflin Company, 1924).

LEWIS MUMFORD: Robert E. Spiller, ed., *The Van Wyck Brooks–Lewis Mumford Letters: The Record of a Literary Friendship, 1921–1963* (New York: E.P. Dutton, 1970), reprinted by permission of the Lewis Mumford Estate.

NAPOLEON: J.M. Thompson, ed., *Napoleon's Letters* (New York: E.P. Dutton, 1934).

OGDEN NASH: Linell Nash Smith, ed., *Loving Letters From Ogden Nash* (New York: Little Brown, 1990), reprinted by permission of the publisher and of Curtis Brown Ltd.

JOHN HENRY NEWMAN: Anne Mozley, ed., *Letters and Correspondence of John Henry Newman* (London: Longmans Green, 1891).

FRIEDRICH NIETZSCHE: Christopher Middleton, ed., trans., *Selected Letters of Friedrich Nietzsche* (Cambridge, MA: Hackett Publishing Co. Ltd., 1996), © 1969 by the University of Chicago Press, reprinted 1996 by Hackett Publishing Company, used by permission of Hackett Publishing Company, all rights reserved.

URSULA NORDSTROM: Leonard S. Marcus, ed., *Dear Genius: The Letters of Ursula Nordstrom* (New York: HarperCollins, 1998), copyright © 1998 by Leonard Marcus. Used by permission of HarperCollins Publishers.

FLANNERY O'CONNOR: Sally Fitzgerald, ed., *The Habit of Being* (New York: Farrar Straus Giroux, 1979), reprinted by permission of Farrar, Straus and Giroux, LLC, and by Harold Matson Co., Inc.; copyright © 1979 by Regina O'Connor.

JOHN O'HARA: Matthew J. Bruccoli, ed., *Selected Letters of John O'Hara* (New York: Random House, 1978), reprinted by permission of United States Trust of New York as Trustee under the will of John O'Hara.

GEORGIA O'KEEFFE: Jack Cowart, Juan Hamilton, and Sarah Greenough, eds., *Art and Letters*, National Gallery of Art, Washington, in association with New York Graphic Society Books (New York: Little Brown, 1987).

MARGARET OLIPHANT: Mrs. Harry Coghill, ed., *The Autobiography and Letters of Mrs. M.O.W. Oliphant* (New York: Dodd Mead, 1899).

EUGENE O'NEILL: William Lyon Phelps, *Autobiography With Letters* (New York: Oxford University Press, 1939); copyright © 1939 by William Lyon Phelps; used by permission of Oxford University Press, Inc., and of Yale University.

GEORGE ORWELL: Sonia Orwell and Ian Angus, eds., *The Collected Essays, Journalism and Letters of George Orwell: An Age Like This 1920–1940*, vol. 1 (San Diego: Harcourt Brace, 1968), reprinted by permission of Harcourt, Inc., and A.M. Heath, Inc.

DOROTHY OSBORNE: G.C. Moore Smith, ed., *The Letters of Dorothy Osborne to William Temple* (New York: Oxford University Press, 1928), reprinted by permission of the publisher.

DOROTHY PARKER: Alexander Woollcott, "Our Mrs. Parker," *While Rome Burns* (New York: Viking, 1934).

BLAISE PASCAL: O.W. Wight, ed., *The Thoughts, Letters, and Opuscules of Blaise Pascal* (1859).

S.J. PERELMAN: Prudence Crowther, ed., *Don't Tread on Me: The Selected Letters of S.J. Perelman* (New York: Viking, 1987). Copyright © 1987 by Abby Perelman and Adam Perelman. Preface and introduction copyright © 1987 by Prudence Crowther. Used by permission of Viking Penguin, a division of Penguin Putnam Inc.

MAXWELL E. PERKINS: John Hall Wheelock, ed., *Editor to Author: The Letters of Maxwell E. Perkins* (New York: Scribner's, 1979). Excerpted with permission of Scribner, a Division of Simon & Schuster, Inc. Copyright © 1950 by Charles Scribner's Sons. Copyright renewed © 1978 by John Hall Wheelock.

SYLVIA PLATH: Aurelia Schober Plath, ed., *Letters Home* (New York: Harper & Row, 1973), reprinted by permission of the publisher and by Faber & Faber, Ltd.

PLINY: Vicesimus Knox, ed., *Elegant Epistles*, vol. 1 (London: J. Mawman, 1814).

EDGAR ALLAN POE: John Ward Ostrum, ed., *The Letters of Edgar Allan Poe*, vol. 1 (Staten Island, NY: Gordian Press, 1966).

HENRI POINCARÉ AND MARIE CURIE: M. Lincoln Schuster, *The World's Great Letters* (New York: Simon & Schuster, 1940).

ALEXANDER POPE: Vicesimus Knox, ed., *Elegant Epistles*, vol. 1 (London: J. Mawman, 1814).

KATHERINE ANNE PORTER: Isabel Bayley, ed., *Letters of Katherine Anne Porter* (New York: Atlantic Monthly Press, 1990), reprinted by permission of the publisher.

SERGEI PROKOFIEV: Gertrude Norman and Miriam Lubell Shrifte, eds., *Letters of Composers: An Anthology 1603–1945* (New York: Alfred A. Knopf, 1946), reprinted by permission of The Serge Prokofiev Archive, London.

BARBARA PYM: Hazel Holt and Hilary Pym, eds., *A Very Private Eye: An Autobiography in Diaries and Letters* (New York: E.P. Dutton, 1984), reprinted by permission of the publisher.

AYN RAND: Michael S. Berliner, ed., *Letters of Ayn Rand* (New York: Penguin/Dutton, 1995), reprinted by permission of the publisher.

RAVEN: Beth Brant, ed., *A Gathering of Spirit: A Collection by North American Indian Women* (Ithaca, NY: Firebrand Books), © 1988 by Beth Brant, reprinted by permission of the publisher.

MARJORIE KINNAN RAWLINGS: Gordon E. Bigelow and Laura V. Monti, eds., *Selected Letters of Marjorie Kinnan Rawlings* (Gainesville: University Press of Florida, 1983).

JEAN RHYS: Francis Wyndham and Diana Melly, eds., *The Letters of Jean Rhys* (New York: Viking, 1984), reprinted by permission of the publisher.

FRANKLIN DELANO ROOSEVELT: Elliott Roosevelt, ed., *F.D.R.: His Personal Letters 1928–1945*, vol. 2 (New York: Duell, Sloan and Pearce, 1950).

THEODORE ROOSEVELT: Elting E. Morison, ed., *The Letters of Theodore Roosevelt*. Copyright © 1951, 1952, 1954 by the President and Fellows of Harvard College, © 1979, 1980, 1982 by Elting E. Morison. Reprinted by permission of Harvard University Press.

CHRISTINA G. ROSSETTI: Anthony H. Harrison, ed., *The Letters of Christina Rossetti*, vol. 1 (Charlottesville: University Press of Virginia, 1997). Reprinted by permission of the University Press of Virginia.

IGNATIUS SANCHO: Vincent Carretta, ed., *Letters of the Late Ignatius Sancho, An African* (New York: Penguin, 1998), reprinted by permission of the publisher.

GEORGE SAND: Veronica Lucas, ed., *Letters of George Sand* (Boston: Houghton Mifflin, 1930).

MARI SANDOZ: *Letters of Mari Sandoz*, edited and with an introduction by Helen Winter Stauffer, reprinted by permission of the University of Nebraska Press, © 1992 by the University of Nebraska Press.

JOANNE SANDSTROM: Joanne Sandstrom, *There and Back Again* (Oakland, CA: Earendil Press, 1983), reprinted by permission of the author.

MAY SARTON: Susan Sherman, ed., *May Sarton: Selected Letters 1916–1954* (New York: W.W. Norton, 1997), reprinted by permission of the Berg Collection of English and American Literature, The New York Public Library, Astor, Lenox and Tilden Foundations.

DOROTHY L. SAYERS: Barbara Reynolds, ed., *The Letters of Dorothy L. Sayers*, vol. 2 (New York: St. Martin's Press, 1997), reprinted by permission of David Higham Associates, Ltd.

ARNOLD SCHOENBERG: Erwin Stein, ed., *Arnold Schoenberg Letters* (New York: St. Martin's Press, 1965), reprinted by permission of Lawrence A. Schoenberg.

FRANZ SCHUBERT: Otto Erich Deutsch, ed., *Franz Schubert's Letters and Other Writings*, Venetia Savile, trans. (New York: Faber & Gwyer, 1928), reprinted by permission of the publisher.

ROBERT SCHUMANN: Berthold Litzmann, *Clara Schumann: An Artist's Life, Based on Material Found in Diaries and Letters*, Grace E. Hadow, trans., vol. 1 (London: Macmillan, 1913); Hans Gal, ed., *The Musician's World: Letters of the Great Composers* (New York: Thames & Hudson, 1965).

ALBERT SCHWEITZER: Hans Walter Bähr, ed., *Albert Schweitzer: Letters 1905–1965*, Joachim Neugroschel, trans. (New York: Macmillan Books, 1992), reprinted by permission of Simon & Schuster, Inc. Translation Copyright © 1992 by Joachim Neugroschel.

ANNE SEXTON: Linda Gray Sexton and Lois Ames, eds., *Anne Sexton: A Self-Portrait in Letters* (Boston: Houghton Mifflin, 1977).

GEORGE BERNARD SHAW: Dan H. Laurence, ed., *Bernard Shaw: Collected Letters 1898–1910* (New York: Dodd Mead, 1972), reprinted by permission of The Society of Authors on behalf of the Bernard Shaw Estate; Mrs. Patrick Campbell, *My Life and Some Letters* (London: Hutchinson, 1921).

SILLA-LABBUM AND ELANI: A. Leo Oppenheim, trans., *Letters From Mesopotamia* (Chicago: University of Chicago Press, 1967), reprinted by permission of the University of Chicago Press.

EDITH SITWELL: John Lehmann and Derek Parker, eds., *Selected Letters* (New York: Vanguard, 1970).

HANNAH WHITALL SMITH: Logan Pearsall Smith, ed., *A Religious Rebel: The Letters of "H.W.S."* (Hitchin, Hertfordshire: Nisbet, 1949), reprinted by permission of the publisher.

LILLIAN SMITH: Margaret Rose Gladney, ed., *How Am I to Be Heard? Letters of Lillian Smith* (Chapel Hill: University of North Carolina Press, 1993), reprinted by permission of the publisher.

DUCHESS OF SOMERSET: Vicesimus Knox, ed., *Elegant Epistles*, vol. 1 (London: J. Mawman, 1814).

LADY HESTER STANHOPE: Duchess of Cleveland, *The Life and Letters of Lady Hester Stanhope* (London: John Murray Ltd., 1914).

ELIZABETH CADY STANTON: Carol DuBois, ed., *Elizabeth Cady Stanton–Susan B. Anthony: Correspondence, Writings, Speeches* (New York: Schocken Books, 1981).

CHRISTINA STEAD: R.G. Geering, ed., *Talking Into the Typewriter: Selected Letters (1973–1983): Christina Stead* (Sydney: ETT Imprint, 1995), reprinted by permission of Editions Tom Thompson.

SIR RICHARD STEELE: Rev. Hedley V. Taylor, ed., *Letters of Great Writers* (London: Blackie and Son, 1912).

GERTRUDE STEIN: Edward M. Burns et al., eds., *The Letters of Gertrude Stein and Thornton Wilder* (New Haven: Yale University Press, 1996), reprinted by permission of the Estate of Gertrude Stein.

JOHN STEINBECK AND ELAINE STEINBECK: Elaine Steinbeck and Robert Wallsten, eds., *Steinbeck: A Life in Letters* (New York: Viking, 1975), reprinted by permission of McIntosh & Otis, Inc.

ROBERT LOUIS STEVENSON: Bradford A. Booth and Ernest Mehew, eds., *The Letters of Robert Louis Stevenson*, vol. 1 (New Haven: Yale University Press, 1994), Beinecke Rare Book and Manuscript Library, Yale University.

HARRIET BEECHER STOWE: Annie Fields, ed., *Life and Letters of Harriet Beecher Stowe* (Boston: Houghton Mifflin, 1898).

TERESA OF AVILA: E. Allison Peers, ed., *The Letters of Saint Teresa of Jesus* (London: Sheed & Ward, 1980), reprinted by permission of the publisher.

CELIA THAXTER: A.F. and R.L., eds., *Letters of Celia Thaxter* (Boston: Houghton Mifflin, 1895).

DYLAN THOMAS: Constantine Fitzgibbon, ed., *Selected Letters of Dylan Thomas* (New York: New Directions, 1966), reprinted by permission of Harold Ober Associates for the Estate of Dylan Thomas.

HENRY D. THOREAU: Walter Harding and Carl Bode, eds,. *The Correspondence of Henry David Thoreau* (New York: New York University Press, 1958).

JAMES THURBER: Helen Thurber and Edward Weeks, eds., *Selected Letters of James Thurber* (New York: Atlantic Monthly Press, 1981).

J.R.R. TOLKIEN: Humphrey Carpenter, ed., *The Letters of J.R.R. Tolkien* (Boston: Houghton Mifflin, 1981). Copyright © 1981 by George Allen & Unwin (Publishers), Ltd. Reprinted by permission of Houghton Mifflin Company. All rights reserved.

HENRI DE TOULOUSE-LAUTREC: Lucien Goldschmidt and Herbert Schimmel, eds., *Unpublished Correspondence of Henri de Toulouse-Lautrec* (London: Phaidon, 1969).

HARRY TRUMAN: Robert H. Ferrell, *Dear Bess: The Letters From Harry to Bess Truman, 1910–1959* (New York: W.W. Norton, 1983), reprinted by permission of the University of Missouri Press; Ira R.T. Smith, "*Dear Mr. President . . . ,*" (New York: Julian Messner, 1949).

IVAN TURGENEV: Gordon S. Haight, ed., *The George Eliot Letters*, vol. 9 (New Haven: Yale University Press, 1978), reprinted by permission of Yale University Press and Balliol College, Oxford.

MARK TWAIN: Albert Bigelow Paine, ed., *Mark Twain's Letters* (New York: Harper, 1917); Bernard DeVoto, ed., *The Portable Mark Twain* (New York: Viking, 1946); Samuel Charles Webster, ed., *Mark Twain, Business Man* (New York: Atlantic Monthly Press, 1946); Henry Nash Smith and William M. Gibson, eds., *Mark Twain–Howells Letters*, vol. 2 (Cambridge: Belknap Press of Harvard University Press, 1960); Lewis Leary, ed., *Mark Twain's Letters to Mary* (New York: Columbia University Press, 1961); Hamlin Hill, ed., *Mark Twain's Letters to His Publishers 1867–1894* (Berkeley: University of California Press, 1967), © 1967 The Mark Twain Company, reprinted by permission of the publisher; Lewis Leary, ed., *Mark Twain's Correspondence With Henry Huttleston Rogers 1893–1909* (Berkeley: University of California Press, 1969).

VINCENT VAN GOGH: Mark Roskill, ed., *The Letters of Vincent van Gogh* (New York: Atheneum, 1963), reprinted by permission of the publisher.

QUEEN VICTORIA: Richard Hough, ed., *Advice to My Granddaughter* (New York: Simon & Schuster, 1975); Justin G. Turner and Linda Levitt Turner, *Mary Todd Lincoln: Her Life and Letters* (New York: Alfred A. Knopf, 1972).

VOLTAIRE: Theodore Besterman, ed., *Select Letters of Voltaire* (Nashville, TN: Thomas Nelson, 1963).

HEINRICH VON KLEIST: C.H. Charles, ed., *Love Letters of Great Men and Women* (London: Stanley Paul, 1924).

SYLVIA TOWNSEND WARNER: William Maxwell, ed., *Letters: Sylvia Townsend Warner* (New York: Viking, 1982), reprinted by permission of Susanna Pinney and Chatto & Windus.

GEORGE WASHINGTON: *Letters & Recollections of George Washington* (New York: Doubleday Doran, 1932).

JAMES L. WATSON: Paula L. Woods and Felix H. Liddell, eds., *I Hear a Symphony: African Americans Celebrate Love* (New York: Doubleday, 1994); James L. Watson Papers, Manuscripts, Archives, and Rare Books Division, Schomburg Center for Research in Black Culture, The New York Public Library, Astor, Lenox and Tilden Foundations. Printed by permission of Judge James L. Watson.

EVELYN WAUGH: Artemis Cooper, ed., *The Letters of Evelyn Waugh and Diana Cooper* (New York: Ticknor & Fields, 1992). Evelyn Waugh letters copyright © 1991 by the Estate of Laura Waugh. Reprinted by permission of Houghton Mifflin Company. All rights reserved.

EDITH WHARTON: R.W.B. Lewis and Nancy Lewis, eds., *The Letters of Edith Wharton* (New York: Scribner's, 1989), reprinted by permission of the Estate of Edith Wharton and the Watkins/Loomis Agency.

JAMES MCNEILL WHISTLER: Rupert Hart-Davis, ed., *Selected Letters of Oscar Wilde* (New York: Oxford University Press, 1976).

E.B. WHITE: Dorothy Lobrano Guth, ed., *Letters of E.B. White* (New York: Harper & Row, 1976), copyright © 1976 by E.B. White. Reprinted by permission of HarperCollins Publishers, Inc.

PATRICK WHITE: Brenda Niall and John Thompson, eds., *The Oxford Book of Australian Letters* (New York: Oxford University Press, 1998), reprinted by permission of Barbara Mobbs for Patrick White.

OSCAR WILDE: Rupert Hart-Davis, ed., *Selected Letters of Oscar Wilde* (New York: Oxford University Press, 1962), reprinted by permission of Fourth Estate Ltd. from *The Letters of Oscar Wilde* by Merlin Holland and Sir Rupert Hart-Davis. Copyright Letters © the Estate of Oscar Wilde 1962, 1985, 2000. Editorial matter © Sir Rupert Hart-Davis 1962, 1985, 2000, Merlin Holland 2000. Letters © 1962 by Vyvyan Holland, reprinted by permission of Henry Holt and Company, LLC.

THORNTON WILDER: Edward M. Burns et al., eds., *The Letters of Gertrude Stein and Thornton Wilder* (New Haven: Yale University Press, 1996), reprinted by permission of Yale University Press and the Barbara Hogenson Agency.

EDMUND WILSON: Elena Wilson, ed., *Edmund Wilson: Letters on Literature and Politics* (New York: Farrar Straus Giroux, 1957), reprinted by permission of Farrar, Straus and Giroux, LLC; copyright © 1977 by Elena Wilson.

P.G. WODEHOUSE: P.G. Wodehouse, *Author! Author!* (New York: Simon & Schuster, 1962), reprinted by permission of A.P. Watt Ltd. on behalf of The Trustees of the Wodehouse Estate.

ALEXANDER WOOLLCOTT: Beatrice Kaufman and Joseph Hennessey, eds., *The Letters of Alexander Woollcott.* Copyright © 1944 by The Viking Press, Inc. Used by permission of Viking Penguin, a division of Penguin Putnam Inc.

FRANK LLOYD WRIGHT: Frank Lloyd Wright, *Letters to Clients* (Fresno: The Press at California State University, 1986), reprinted by permission of The Frank Lloyd Wright Foundation. Copyright © 1986 Frank Lloyd Wright Foundation, Scotsdale, AZ.

WILBUR AND ORVILLE WRIGHT: Fred C. Kelly, ed., *Miracle at Kitty Hawk: The Letters of Wilbur and Orville Wright* (New York: Farrar Straus and Young, 1951), reprinted by permission of Farrar, Straus and Giroux, LLC; copyright © 1951 by Fred C. Kelly, copyright renewed © 1978 by Brian Kelly and Jean Kelly.

W.B. YEATS: Mrs. Patrick Campbell, *My Life and Some Letters* (London: Hutchinson, 1921).

Index of Letterwriters